Exploring with
BYRD

RICHARD E. BYRD, REAR ADMIRAL, U. S. N. (RET.)

Exploring with BYRD

EPISODES OF AN ADVENTUROUS LIFE

RICHARD EVELYN BYRD

ROWMAN & LITTLEFIELD
Lanham • Boulder • New York • London

Published by Rowman & Littlefield
A wholly owned subsidiary of The Rowman & Littlefield Publishing Group, Inc.
4501 Forbes Boulevard, Suite 200, Lanham, Maryland 20706
www.rowman.com

Unit A, Whitacre Mews, 26-34 Stannary Street, London SE11 4AB

Distributed by NATIONAL BOOK NETWORK

Copyright © 1937 by Richard E. Byrd
Cloth edition originally published by G. P. Putnam's Sons in 1937
Cloth edition by the Easton Press 1990
First Rowman & Littlefield paperback edition © 2015

All rights reserved. No part of this book may be reproduced in any form or by
any electronic or mechanical means, including information storage and retrieval
systems, without written permission from the publisher, except by a reviewer who
may quote passages in a review.

British Library Cataloguing in Publication Information Available

Library of Congress Cataloging-in-Publication Data Available

Paperback: 978-1-4422-4168-8
E-book: 978-1-4422-4169-5

♾™ The paper used in this publication meets the minimum requirements of
American National Standard for Information Sciences—Permanence of Paper for
Printed Library Materials, ANSI/NISO Z39.48-1992.

Printed in the United States of America

CONTENTS

ILLUSTRATIONS

EXPLORING WITH BYRD

Chapter I

~~~~~~

EDUCATION OF A PILOT

ONE of my first and most striking impressions of aviation came the day a man rushed into my stateroom aboard the battleship waving a newspaper that had just been brought us by the pilot.

"For God's sake, listen to this!" he exclaimed. "Jack Towers has fallen fifteen hundred feet in an airplane and lived to tell the tale."

I couldn't believe it.

"He was thrown out of his seat." (In those days the flyer sat right out in the open on a little bench.) "But he caught by a brace and dangled in mid-air. On the way down he kicked at the control wheel. Apparently he righted the plane just before it hit. *Think of the nerve of the man!*"

I did think of his nerve; and many times since I've admired the courage of those early pilots who flew thousands of feet in the air with defective machines about which they knew almost nothing. And it's good to feel that my friend, Captain John W. Towers, U.S.N., the hero of the incident, is alive today and still a flyer of note.

The horror people felt fifteen years ago in reading about Towers' escape is still felt when newspapers print tragic details of some aeronautical accident without regard for technical reasons behind the accident. As a result many citizens still look on flying as one of the most attractive forms of suicide.

If I had a son twenty years old today and he should come to me with the question: "Is it all right for me to fly?" I'd answer: "Go to it. And I hope you get your pilot's license soon because I want you to do a lot of flying before you're through."

8

He might break his neck. But also he might be run over by a taxi, burn up, catch pneumonia, or be struck by lightning. Those things happen to people every day.

My first aerial adventure was in the Annapolis gymnasium. I was captain of the Navy Gym Team, which was out to win the intercollegiate championship of the year. In line with this ambition I devised a hair-raising stunt on the flying rings. My plan was to get a terrific swing, high enough to be able to count on an appreciable pause at the end of it.

I figured I could at this moment do what was called "dislocate," which meant swing completely head over heels without changing grip, with arms at full length—unbending and forcing my shoulders through a quick jerk, that made it look as if they were put out of joint. In addition, I was going to make another complete turn, legs outside, letting go with my hands as my ankles passed my forearms, and catching again as I fell.

The day before the meet the gym was crowded with people watching practice. I hoped that my stunt would give us the points needed to win. Never before had I reached the altitude I reached that afternoon when my last turn came on the rings. I was conscious of the dead silence as I swooped through the air for my final effort.

With a quick whirl I "dislocated." It felt all right. The next second I was spinning into the second turn. I let go; caught—but only with one hand. For an instant I strained wildly to catch the other ring. But it had gone. People afterwards told me that a queer sharp sigh went up from the crowd at this moment.

I fell. It was a long way down even for a flyer. I came down more or less feet foremost. The crash when I struck echoed from the steel girders far above me, and there was a loud noise of something snapping. I tried to rise, but fell back stunned. The effort told me though, that I was far from dead. I noted there was no feeling in my right leg. I glanced down as willing hands came to lift me and saw that my ankle and foot were badly crumpled; the same foot I had broken playing football against Princeton.

That was December, 1911. I was to graduate in June. I missed the semi-annual examination and was absent from the class room for months while I wrestled with nature on one hand and with the specter of academic failure on the other. The Navy made no allowances for me and wanted me to go back a class. I don't believe I could have pulled through but for my great desire to go out into the fleet with my classmates. When I returned to the Academy, the bones in my foot and leg had all knit but one. The bony knot on the outer side of my right ankle was still in two pieces. It clicked when I walked. Some one told me if I walked a lot I would grate the fragments together and induce flow of osseous fluid. I did this for weeks. It hurt; but it apparently worked. I had to take my semi-annual examinations and my final examinations at the same time. After a great struggle I managed to graduate.

The struggle I had made to graduate taught me a great lesson—that it is by struggle that we progress. I learned concentration during that time I never thought I possessed.

My time in the battleship fleet was a great experience. One day I fell down a gangway and did something to that bum leg of mine. The surgeons decided to nail the bone together.

Several years passed, and my leg did not get entirely well. The Navy Regulations would not allow my promotion on account of it. Finally I was retired on three-quarters pay; ordered home for good. Career ended. Not enough income to live on; no chance of coming back; trained for a seafaring profession and temperamentally disinclined for business.

War did a lot of things for a lot of men. In a sense it saved me. For a willing near-cripple suddenly became as valuable as a whole man who might be unwilling. Washington used me to mobilize the Rhode Island State Militia. Thence I was promoted to a "swivel chair" job in the Navy Department. I transferred enlisted men from station to station, and official papers from basket to basket.

For several years I had known my one chance of escape from a life of inaction was to learn to fly. But the doctors said, "No, not with that leg." To which I wanted to burst out angrily, "But you don't fly with your legs!" Only I didn't; I'd been schooled never to do any bursting out.

I lost twenty-five pounds worrying over the uselessness of what I had become—just a high-class clerk—when I had been trained to go out and fight—fight wind and seas and the country's enemy. And here I was, lost behind a big desk, deep baskets, reams of official papers. I went up again before the medical board. "You'll have to take leave, Byrd," they said. "You're in terrible condition."

Truly I was on the verge of a breakdown. Yet that short half hour in the Board Room was the turning point of my life.

"Give me a chance," I begged them. "I want to fly. Give me a month of it; and, if I don't improve to suit you, I'll do anything you say."

They were sports, those surgeons. They decided to give me one short month of my heart's desire. I was sent to Pensacola. Fresh air, the deep joy of flying compounded a tonic that strengthened me at once. When the time came, I passed all tests with flying colors, was pronounced in perfect health. This was the winter of 1917. Congress had declared war. Our first destroyers had gone over to join the British Grand Fleet.

I'll never forget my first day at Pensacola. Glistening Florida sunshine brought all the details of the station out in sharp relief. Men in whites and in khaki were hurrying to and fro. Big open hangars gaped like reptiles that had disgorged the birds they had swallowed and found indigestible. The birds themselves—Navy seaplanes—were drawn up along the sea ramp; some were in the water; some roared overhead. Men were hauling them up and down, starting engines, taking off and landing. A hive of activity, typical of the thousand military hives buzzing throughout the country.

Something attracted my attention; a shout, or an uplifted hand. I glanced to a training plane in the azure sky above me. It wobbled as I looked. It hesitated, dipped, then dove straight down. It came leisurely enough at first. I didn't realize its seeming lack of speed was due to its great height. Soon it was dropping like a plummet. Tail skyward, it plunged into the Bay. Across the still water came a terrific crash. I stood rooted to the spot, horrorstruck.

A speedboat dashed out toward the wrecked plane. On its deck, ready for their gruesome task, I saw stretcher bearers, surgeons and divers.

The tail of the wrecked plane and a part of one wing protruded from the surface of the water. Pilot and student were caught in the wreckage below, dead. The crash boat drew alongside. Divers splashed overboard with pliers and wrenches. In twenty seconds one emerged dragging a limp form after him. I think I must have held my breath while the rescue party struggled for the other flyer. Finally the boat shoved off. Some one near me said in a low voice, "The wrecking barge'll have to get it."

"It." So that's what you were after a crash! Just a body. *It!*

After a while I walked away. Perhaps I'd get used to it. Suddenly I was grabbed from behind.

"Hello, Dick Byrd!"

It was my old friend and classmate, Nathan Chase. I suppose my face revealed more than I wanted it to. "Don't mind that," he said and nodded toward the wrecking barge.

"Have 'em often?" I asked him.

"Oh, every day," he said. "Sometimes two or three times a day." Then in the next breath: "Want to go up, old man?"

I'm frank to say that was not the moment I would have selected to go up. I hadn't lost my nerve. Nor had I changed my mind about becoming an aviator. I was just temporarily nonplused. I've since learned what the feeling means. And I've found that the best antidote for it is prompt and vigorous action.

Chance had given me the action I needed. Still in a bit of a fog, I presently found myself wearing helmet and goggles. A plane stood nearby with its engine turning over. Before we climbed in Nat handed me some cotton.

"Stuff it in your ears," he shouted. "You'll be deaf if you don't."

Mechanically I did as I was told. We were in line with the barge grappling for the wrecked plane just ahead of us.

The plane was exactly like a land one, except that its wheels had been replaced by a pontoon, which now rested on a truck. When we had taken our seats, mechanics pushed the truck down a concrete ramp into the water. As our pontoon floated, Chase gave her the gas. We skidded thunderously away and swerved into the wind for a take-off. I felt the whole body rear back, and spray flew high all around us. Gradually we assumed an even keel, the spray lessened, waves began to slap bumpily against the bottom of the float. We were in the air.

My pilot pointed to an instrument in front that read in hundreds of feet. I gathered this told our altitude. When the pointer read 4,000 feet he turned and smiled at me. I suppose Chase knew how I was feeling about the fatal crash. The medicine he chose was to go through all the stunts he knew. We dived and rolled and slipped. We did a tail spin until I could almost see the rescue boat on its way out to us. There weren't even names then for some of the things Chase did. For minutes I couldn't tell which was sea and which was sky.

Suddenly we came out of a spin. He nudged me with a nod towards the stick. The next instant I realized I had control of the plane. That was Nathan's idea of a joke. The responsibility cleared my brain. It was perfectly idiotic for me to try to fly. I knew that. But this was no time to argue. I managed to keep our course straight ahead; nothing but common sense. But soon we were headed downward, judging from the roar of the engine and the wind singing through the wires. I glanced at the altimeter; it showed a loss of a thousand feet. Chase took her back and brought us safely to earth.

My training now began in earnest, groundwork as well as flying. I remember taking apart my first airplane engine. The vast number of cams, valves, rods, screws, bolts, and other pieces fascinated me. They all seemed so dead, so unrelated when spread around on the greasy canvas at my feet.

I made my first solo flight after about six hours' flying with an instructor. The solo alone is probably the greatest event in an aviator's life. Never again does he feel the same thrill, the same triumph, as when he first eases back the controls and lifts his airplane clear of all natural support.

"Twenty minutes' flying is enough," warned my instructor, Ensign Gardiner. This was the usual warning given on account of the strain of the first solo hop. As my plane was shoved into the water, I glanced back. The poor fellow could not hide his anxiety. I knew he felt that if I lost my life it would be as much his fault as mine.

As the machine bobbed up, I shot my throttle wide and pulled the controls back to ride high on the waves. When I had some speed I shoved the controls forward again to make the float coast. A minute or so later I figured I could lift. With a fine elation I took off.

For what seemed a long time I flew straight ahead. It was too good to be true. I was flying at last. I glanced down at the water. It looked dark and sparkling in the fresh sea breeze just picking up. The station seemed very *hard* and *dead* by comparison. Quickly I glanced back at my instruments. Nothing was wrong yet.

I began to think what I'd do next. I concluded that I should try some landings. After all, if I could land safely, I might then call myself a flyer. Anyone could get a plane up into the air. I nosed down gradually. But when I leveled off, I was going too fast. As it had been drummed into my head not to lose flying speed, I was taking no chances. I struck the surface with a big splash and porpoised—that is, leaped out—some distance beyond where I hit. But I didn't smash anything, which was a comfort. I tried three more landings in quick succession. In all I kept at it for an hour and twenty minutes on that first flight. When I finally taxied up to the landing, I felt a confidence that was the pleasantest sensation I had ever known.

As I came alongside the mechanic in charge of my plane called out to me: "How'd she go?"

"Couldn't have been sweeter."

Instantly his rugged face melted. And right away he began to nuzzle his engine like a mother cat who's just taken her own brood back. I knew at last how he felt. I had flown; had come down safe; I had him to thank for an engine that kept on running.

After I had made the grade with single pontoon planes, I took instruction in the twin pontoon type and in the big flying boats. Crashes in these machines were the worst because their engines were above and behind the pilot, smashing down on him when the plane made a bad landing.

When the Navy Department, through the Commandant, handed me my pilot's wings and a clean bill of health, I was sitting on the top of the world.

Being one of the few regular officers on the Pensacola Air Station in 1917 I was detailed to the "Crash Board." This was really a sort of "Coroner's Jury." Officially, we had to "sit" on the ghastly evidence that came out of each tragedy. Also I had to go out with the rescue boat and help haul the mangled bodies of my friends out of the water. It wasn't exactly what you might call stimulating work; certainly not for the beginner.

I remember my first case came while I was still a student. A plane nose-dived into the Bay a few hundred yards from the landing. Though rescue boat and divers reached the wreckage in a few moments, both victims were dead before we arrived. We examined the wreckage carefully as soon as it could be hoisted to the wrecking barge. We found control wires were in good shape, and enough of the body and wings intact to indicate that the equipment was still all right when the plane took her fatal dive.

Next day the Senior Member of the Crash Board looked around the table after all evidence was in.

"The only things that really help," he said, "are that a student was aboard and that the plane was up only about six hundred feet when she went into a spin."

The rest of us sat there like dummies. As we were all flyers, we would have given our bottom dollar to know what had killed our friends. The same fate might be ours before the day was out. Moreover, solution of the mystery could possibly save a score of lives that week, taking the whole country into consideration.

"Probably the student was at the controls," went on the Senior Member, but without conviction, "and made a bad turn. The plane side slipped and then went into a spin. Before the instructor could get her out she was down."

Pretty vague; altogether unsatisfying. But the best we could do in those days.

Three days later I was standing on the beach waiting for my engine to be warmed up. Suddenly the siren sounded. Another crash.

I ran to the rescue boat, boarding her just as she shoved off. Along the ramp and landing were gathering silent men. Out of the quarters hurried wives and mothers, children, even servants. "Who now?" was the question every man and woman wanted to ask.

When we rounded up to the plane's wreck, only one wing was visible above the water. We dove in; our diver followed. As I came to the surface, I saw the surgeon preparing his kit, frantic to help, but useless until the diver brought up something.

He finally came up—empty-handed. A gunner's mate said: "Only one man down there. He's gone. Not a chance to get him out here. Got to lift the whole mess."

We looked for the other body. It was never found. When the wrecked plane came up at the end of the crane tackle, we saw snarled up in it the student. Both hands had a death-grip on the driving wheel. The student had lost his nerve in the air and grabbed the thing nearest him as a drowning man grabs his rescuer, throwing the plane into a spin.

When these disasters happened, little was said about them in quarters. No one felt inclined to discuss details of a tragedy that could strike anywhere among us. Sometimes it seemed to me our mess was a little gayer after a crash—probably a subconscious effort to throw off the depression such things brought.

Among my best friends I numbered the Morgan Drapers. This ensign and his lovely young wife had come to the station filled with enthusiasm for flying and brimming with excitement over the prospect of getting to Europe for active service in the air. Night after night I dined with the happy pair.

Morgan Draper was a splendid flyer with plenty of nerve. Stunt flying had a peculiar fascination for him. I believe he would have made a great combat pilot had he lived to reach the western front.

One afternoon he took up a new plane which I had just tested. It was in perfect working order and one of the best machines on the station. Its engine was hot, and the controls had stood full test. I doubt if anyone could have gone up under safer circumstances.

As the friend he had with him climbed into the front seat, Draper winked at me. I gathered this meant he was going to do some of the trick flying at which he had become so skilled. I didn't worry. I had no cause to. But the very fact I knew he was in the air risking his life in a dozen wild ways made it impossible for me to get him out of my mind.

Five hours passed and no word from the plane. In those days people didn't fly five hours without advertising the flight in advance, and making more preparations than we make today for a trans-Atlantic flight. We knew the plane must be down.

A messenger came up and saluted: "Telephone call from Pensacola, sir. Clerk in a clothing store says he saw a plane hit the water in a straight nose dive and that the spray went a hundred feet into the air!"

"When did he see this?"

"About two hours ago, sir."

Two hours! And men drown in two minutes. It was Morgan Draper, I knew.

Frantically boats were sent about the harbor of Pensacola in search of the wreck. We got the wrecking barges underway and used their searchlights when night fell. There was always a chance an injured man might be clinging to a wing or broken fuselage.

Meanwhile another complication bobbed up. Lieutenant Hoyt had been flying near the area in which Morgan Draper had crashed. Reports now reached us that Hoyt's plane had been sighted empty, drifting. Some one suggested that he and his men might have sighted the wreckage of Draper's plane, and tried diving for the bodies.

"Or stalled on the water, tried to swim ashore and drowned," was another theory. As it turned out, both notions were partially true. For Hoyt and his companion, after sighting the wreckage, had set about diving; first thing they knew a puff of wind carried their own plane out of reach faster than they could pursue it. They were picked up by a passing boat, nearly drowned.

Meanwhile in the glare of searchlights we hoisted out the pitiful mess of what had been Morgan Draper's machine. Had the plane struck a concrete surface, I doubt if it could have been worse shattered. It must have struck, as we had thought, with engine full on, and diving straight without a spiral. Few people realize that water is hard as ice when it is hit going fast. Poor old Morgan had, I felt almost certain, tried the stunt he had long been talking about—changing seats with his co-pilot while flying.

In the center of the wreckage we found the torn body of Draper's friend. Of Morgan himself there was no sign. Brave Mrs. Draper would not believe Morgan had been killed. Not until his body was washed up by the tide a fortnight later would she give up hope.

The high point in my Pensacola training period came when I rammed another plane going sixty miles an hour. I had just got off the water and was intent on gaining speed so I could zoom upward. The first thing I knew I saw almost directly ahead of me a plane plunging down on the water out of the sky. Its pilot was a beginner. He had been intent, I think, on gauging his distance from the water in order to make as perfect a landing as possible.

The crash was deafening. We were just enough out of line to make our wings lock. As a result both planes flung around with violent centrifugal force that was the result of our 120 miles per hour of aggregate speed.

Both planes were demolished. I fell dazed and bruised into the water. A few minutes later the rescue party hauled us into the speed boat, safe and sound, but crestfallen at the damage we had done to our planes.

It may seem as if we got hardened to all this sort of thing. In a way we did. But there was none of the emotional stimulus of battle. And we were so far from the scene of action that killing young pilots somehow seemed unnecessary. However, as I have said, it was the inevitable price for the education of a pilot.

∿∿∿∿∿∿∿∿∿∿∿∿∿∿∿∿∿∿∿∿∿∿∿∿∿

FLIGHT TO THE NORTH POLE

THERE is one thing, at least, which I can truly say of my career: it is that from the moment I became a full-fledged Navy pilot my ambition was to make a career in aviation. Not merely in the sense of routine flying, but rather in the pioneering sense. At the time I was learning to fly, the airplane was just on the verge of becoming a tool which mankind could fit to its hand. My ambition was to test the tool to the utmost and, through a series of long-range flights, help to show the way, if I could, toward improving technologies. That was a common ambition among pilots of my day, I must confess; for once you have tasted the heady satisfactions of flight, you never lose the love of them, nor the desire to make them known to others.

I found myself transferred to Nova Scotia, where I was given command of two air stations, one at North Sydney and the other at Dartmouth. My job was scouting for submarines in the northwest Atlantic. All the while I hammered at the Bureau of Aeronautics in the Navy Department for permission to fly the Atlantic in one of the long-range flying boats which the Navy was building. That came to nothing. But my research work in air navigation landed me the job of navigation officer of the NC flying boats that were to attempt a crossing of the Atlantic. I accompanied the planes for the first two legs of the flight as navigator.

For several years I was marooned in Washington as the Navy's liaison with Congress. Important and even instructive as this work was, it failed to appease my appetite for aviation. From this vacuum I received reprieve in the shape of an order to report to England for duty aboard the dirigible ZR-3, which was to be flown to the United States. But a few days after I reached England, that ship, while on a test cruise, exploded over the Humber River, killing forty-five men. I missed being aboard that day by what seemed to me to be a miracle. Instead of flying the Atlantic, I had the sad duty of recovering the bodies of my shipmates.

These disappointments convinced me that my naval career was headed toward futility. On my return from England, I found that along with the rest of my class at Annapolis I was to be demoted back to lieutenant from the war-time rank of lieutenant commander. Whereupon, I asked to be transferred to the inactive list, believing that I could better hasten my career in aviation outside the Service.

Now I turned toward the polar regions, which had drawn my interest from boyhood. With my great friend, Captain Bob Bartlett, I organized in 1925 an expedition for aerial exploration in North Greenland. At the request of the Navy Department, whose planes were to be used, we subsequently combined forces with Commander Donald B. MacMillan, who was preparing to lead a similar expedition into approximately the same region. That expedition, my first to the polar regions, was as exciting a trip as I ever made. It gave me my initiation into polar flying. It introduced to me Floyd Bennett, assigned to me by the Navy as a pilot-mechanic, as noble a character as I have ever found among men. Altogether Bennett and I flew some 2,500 miles over the Greenland Ice Cap and the pack-strewn waters to the westward. As polar flights are reckoned today, this may not seem impressive; but the kind of plane we flew twelve years ago was at best a doubtful and dangerous vehicle; and, considering the severity of conditions around Greenland—the lack of landing places, the sudden squalls and snowstorms—we were lucky to do as much as we did without accident. More, we learned enough, Bennett and I, during the Greenland initiation, to become convinced that, with the new improvements being built into airplanes, a flight to the North Pole was no longer a crazy notion but a reasonable and practicable project.

This time, however, we resolved to base at Spitzbergen, near the northern tip of Norway. It had many advantages over other likely hopping-off places, foremost among which were the facts: (1) that it was only 720 miles from the Pole and (2) the Gulf Stream thereabouts starts wafting the pack ice away from the coast as early as April, which meant we could get into Kings Bay at a seasonable time with a supply ship. True, we realized the hazardous nature of the flight. Experienced polar travelers told us we were fools. The fog which lies over the Arctic Ocean would add to the already great risks; and, if we came a cropper, it would take us, they said, at least two years to walk back to land, if we ever made land at all. Nevertheless, these were risks we were prepared to take.

Neither Bennett nor I was able to begin serious work of preparation as easily as we had hoped. Official duties engaged us both until the middle of January, 1926. Then Secretary of the Navy Wilbur and my Chief Admiral Moffett allowed us leave. We were going this time on our own hook. We didn't ask the Navy to send us, as we felt the hazardous nature of the undertaking would make it unfair to do so. From then on came a crescendo of toil which culminated when we finally sailed.

After carefully weighing our own experience at Etah, as well as the opinion of aeronautical experts, we selected for our flight a Fokker, three-engine monoplane.

One was available that had already flown 20,000 miles. It had 200 horse-power, Wright, air-cooled motors, any two of which would keep it up in the air (provided the load was not too heavy) if the third failed. That, of course, added to our chances of success.

The plane was 42 feet 9 inches long in body, with a wing spread of 63 feet 3 inches. Two 100-gallon gasoline tanks were set in each wing; and two others, each holding 110 gallons, were carried in the fuselage. Whatever additional gasoline we might need could be carried in five-gallon cans in the fuselage.

We named the plane *Josephine Ford* in honor of the daughter of my friend Edsel Ford. Careful tests of the plane were made before we sailed. Its fuel consumption at cruising speed was twenty-seven or twenty-eight gallons per hour—lower than was anticipated, and therefore most encouraging. It was capable of a speed as high as 120 miles an hour.

Through the generosity of the Shipping Board I was able to secure the steamer *Chantier*. She was of about 3,500 tons displacement and had ample space for our flying gear.

There were half a hundred members of the expedition, nearly all volunteers, all young and adventurous. I selected some from the list of men in the Naval Reserve who had had sixteen and twenty years' service in the Navy. We obtained the others by culling out the best of the thousands of volunteers.

After months of toil, we left New York on April 5th, 1926, with half a hundred men and six months' food supply aboard. I suspect to this day that Captain Brennan and his three mates from the Merchant Marine had many misgivings in starting out on a 10,000 mile cruise with a ship's company made up mostly of landlubbers.

We arrived at Kings Bay, Spitzbergen, at 4 P.M. April 29th and found the Amundsen-Ellsworth-Nobile Expedition members making preparations to receive the great Italian dirigible *Norge* soon to leave Italy for a flight to the Pole.

Fate lost no time in placing serious obstacles in our path. The little harbor of Kings Bay was choked with ice, but skillful work by Captain Brennan brought the *Chantier* to anchor within 900 yards of the shore.

To my dismay, I found that there were no facilities for landing my heavy plane. I had counted on the dock at the coaling station. Previous inquiry told me the water there was deep enough for our ship; and permission was only a matter of asking the local manager.

Now we found tied up to this sole landing a small Norwegian gunboat, the *Heimdahl*, taking on coal. Of course, I went ashore immediately and asked if we could have the dock for a few hours, at least.

"Sorry but our ship was nearly lost a few days ago," I was informed. "Drifting ice caught her and carried her helplessly toward the land." I knew the danger from the drifting ice, and could see it was no use to argue.

The only thing to do was to anchor as close as possible to the shore and send our plane through the drift ice on some kind of raft. When the Norwegians heard about the plan, they urged us to desist. "You know nothing about ice," was the gist of their warning, "or you would not attempt such a thing. The ice is almost certain to start moving before you can get ashore."

By laying heavy planks across the gunwales of our four whaleboats the crew constructed a big raft. Of course that left the *Chantier* without boats, which I did not like on account of the constant threat from drifting ice. It began to snow; and the air was cold and raw as all hands worked at top speed.

In the midst of a snow squall, the First Mate, de Lucca, hoisted the fuselage of the *Josephine Ford* from the ship's hold, and lowered it safely and skillfully on the raft. A change in tide began to close the lane we had opened among the heavy cakes of ice blocking the way to the shore. Yet, by tireless work and unswerving determination our men managed to prop the awkward body of the plane on its frail support.

We were taking a tremendous chance in doing this; for, had a wind sprung up, the raft might have been crushed by ice or blown out to sea. It was either get our personnel and equipment ashore this way or come back to the States as ignominious failures. We preferred to risk the first rather than weakly accept the alternative.

Just as we finished the raft, the very thing we dreaded happened. The ice started moving with great force, and we had quite a struggle saving the raft and even the steamer itself.

An iceberg came whooping down on the tide. Drifting snow concealed it, and we did not see the danger until the berg was almost upon us. It threatened the ship's rudder, and we had to land dynamite on a corner of the oncoming monster and blow it into pieces small enough to be fended off or swept clear by the current.

My relief was great when we at last reached the ice foot protruding from the beach. Luck was with us—we must admit that.

No one knew how efficiently a big plane like the *Josephine Ford* would perform on skis. We had much to learn.

The edge of the landing field was about a mile from the ice foot. If it was a big undertaking for the men to get the plane ashore it was an equally difficult job for them to get the plane and equipment up to the top of the long incline through the deep snow in a temperature 15 degrees below zero.

Not having a level stretch smooth enough for a take-off with a heavy load, we were forced to try another new stunt—to take off going down hill. Smoothing the surface of the take-off runway was the biggest job of all. The men had to work eighteen hours a day, but I never heard a single complaint.

The plane's first attempt to get off on a trial flight ended in a snowdrift. A ski was broken to bits and the landing gear bent and broken.

Things then looked black, but the men refused to lose heart. Then twice again we tried to get off, and each time a ski collapsed in pretty much the same way. If this was the best we could do with the plane lightly loaded, how could we expect to lift the polar load of 10,000 pounds?

Noville, Mulroy and "Chips" Gould, the carpenter, worked two days and two nights making new skis. No other hard wood being available in all Kings Bay, they reinforced the skis with wood from the oars of the *Chantier's* life boats. Profiting from our first experience, we treated the bottom of the skis with a mixture of rosin and tar. The runway was fairly smooth for the second attempt, and the plane was lightly loaded. We held our breaths.

This time the airplane moved forward rapidly, then rose gracefully into the air. With Lieutenant Noville and Lieutenant Parker aboard, in addition to Bennett, she made a trial flight of more than two hours and showed a remarkably low gas consumption. The cold-weather cowling on the engines came up to our highest expectations. Our worst fears were at an end.

Final preparations were completed on May 8. Meteorologist Haines told us that the weather was right.

We warmed the motors; heated the oil; put the last bit of fuel and food aboard; examined our instruments with care. Bennett and I climbed in, and we were off. Off, but alas, not up. Our load proved too great, the snow too "bumpy," the friction of the skis too strong a drag. The plane simply would not get into the air. We over-ran the runway at a terrific speed, jolting over snow hummocks and landing in a snowdrift; the plane just missed turning over on her back.

A dozen men came up, weary, heartsick and speechless. They had worked almost to the limit of their endurance to give us our chance. I waded through the deep snow to the port landing gear. Great! Both it and the ski were O.K. Then I stumbled to the other side and found that they also had withstood the terrible pounding.

My apprehension turned to joy, for I knew that if the landing gear would stand that strain we could eventually take off for the Pole with enough fuel to get there and back.

We dug the plane out of the snowdrift and taxied up the hill to try again. We held another council, and concluded to work through the night lengthening and smoothing the runway. Meanwhile, with the idea of reducing the load, we jettisoned some emergency equipment and a little reserve fuel.

The weather still held good. We decided to try to get off as near midnight as possible, when the cold of night would harden the snow and give a better run to the skis. Finally, at a half hour past midnight (Greenwich time), all was in readiness. Bennett and I had had almost no sleep for thirty-six hours, but that did not bother us.

We carefully iced the runway in front of the skis (so that we could make a faster start), while Bennett and Kinkaid made their motor preparations.

Bennett came up for a last talk, and we decided to stake all on getting away—to give the *Josephine Ford* full power and full speed—and get off or crash at the end of the runway in the jagged ice.

With a total load of nearly 10,000 pounds we raced down the runway, dangerously close to the broken ice at the end. Just when it seemed we must crash into it as we had done before, Bennett, with a mighty pull on the wheel, lifted the plane cleanly into the air, and we were clear at last.

For months previous to this hour, utmost attention had been paid to every detail that would assure safety in case of accident. We had a short-wave radio set operated by a hand dynamo for use in the event of a forced landing. A handmade sledge, presented by Amundsen, was stowed in the fuselage, on which to carry food and clothing should we be compelled to walk to Greenland. We had food for ten weeks.

The first stage of the flight carried us past the well-known landmarks in the vicinity of Kings Bay. We climbed to 2,000 feet to get a good view of the coast and the magnificent snow-covered mountains inland. Within an hour of taking the air we crossed the edge of the polar ice pack. It was much nearer the land than we had expected.

Ahead, the sea ice shone in the rays of the midnight sun—a fascinating scene whose lure had drawn men into its clutches, never to return. It was with a feeling of exhilaration that we felt that for the first time two men, aloof in a plane, could gaze upon its charms, and discover its secrets, out of reach of those sharp claws.

Though it was important to hit the Pole from the standpoint

of achievement, it was more important to do so from that of our lives, so that we could get back to Spitzbergen, a target none too big. We could not fly back to land from an unknown position. We must put every possible second of time and our best concentration on the job of navigating and of flying a straight course—our lives depended on it.

We could see mountains astern gleaming in the sun at least a hundred miles behind us. That was our last link with civilization. The unknown lay ahead.

Bennett and I took turns piloting. At first, and for some unaccountable reason, the plane veered time and time again, to the right. Bennett could glance back to where I was working, through a door leading to the two pilots' seats. Every minute or two he would look at me, to be checked if necessary, on the course by the sun compass. If he happened to be off the course, I would wave him to the right or left until he got on it again. Once every three minutes while I was navigating, I checked the wind drift and ground speed, so that in case of a change in wind I could detect it immediately and allow for it.

We had three sets of gloves which I constantly changed to fit the job in hand, and sometimes removed entirely for short periods to write or figure on the chart. I froze my face and one of my hands in taking sights with the instruments from the trapdoors. But I noticed these frostbites at once and was more careful thereafter in the future. Ordinarily a frostbite need not be dangerous if detected in time and if the blood is rubbed back immediately into the affected parts. We also carried leather helmets that would cover the whole face when necessary to use them.

Finally, when certain of our course, I turned my attention to the ice pack, which I had wondered about ever since I was a youngster. We were flying at about 2,000 feet, and I could see at about 50 miles in every direction. There was no sign of land. The pack was crisscrossed with pressure ridges, but here and there were stretches that appeared long and smooth enough to land on. However, from 2,000 feet pack ice is extraordinarily deceptive.

I now turned my mind to wind conditions, for I knew they were a matter of interest to all those contemplating the feasibility of a polar airway. We found them smooth. This was as we had anticipated, for the flatness of the ice and the Arctic temperature are not conducive to air currents, such as are sometimes found over land. Had we struck an Arctic gale, I cannot say what the results would have been as far as air roughness is concerned. Of course, we still had the advantage of spring and 24-hour daylight.

It was time now to relieve Bennett again at the wheel, not only that he might stretch his legs, but so that he could pour gasoline into the tanks from the five-gallon tins stowed all over the cabin. Empty cans were thrown overboard to get rid of the weight, small though it was.

On one occasion, as I turned to look over the side, my arm struck some object in my left breast pocket. It was filled with good-luck pieces!

I am not superstitious, I believe. No explorer, however, can go off without such articles. Among my trinkets was a religious medal put there by a friend. It belonged to his fiancée, and he firmly believed it would get me through. There was also a tiny horseshoe made by a famous blacksmith. Attached to the pocket was a little coin carried by Peary, pinned to his shirt, on his trip to the North Pole.

We were now getting into areas never before viewed by mortal eye. The feelings of an explorer superseded the aviator's. I became conscious of that extraordinary exhilaration which comes from looking into virgin territory. At that moment I felt repaid for all our toil.

At the end of this unknown area lay our goal, somewhere beyond the shimmering horizon. We were opening unexplored regions at the rate of nearly 10,000 square miles an hour, and were experiencing the incomparable satisfaction of searching

PENSACOLA 1918

A training plane "on the step"; *i.e.,* just about to leave the water

A HAZARDOUS UNDERTAKING

Admiral Byrd's airplane being ferried across the ice-strewn waters of Kings Bay, Spitzbergen

(© Pathé)

for new land. Once, for a moment, I mistook a distant, vague, low-lying cloud formation for the white peaks of a far-away land.

To the right, somewhere, the rays of the midnight sun shone down on the scenes of Nansen's heroic struggles to reach the goal that we were approaching at the rate of nearly 100 miles an hour. To our left, lay Peary's trail.

When our calculations showed us to be about an hour from the Pole, I noticed through the cabin window a bad leak in the oil tank of the starboard motor. Bennett wrote on a note: "That motor will stop."

Bennett then suggested that we try a landing to fix the leak. But I thought that more dangerous still. We decided to keep on for the Pole. We would be in no worse fix should we come down near the Pole than we would be if we had a forced landing where we were.

When I took to the wheel again, I kept my eyes glued on that oil leak and the oil-pressure indicator. Should the pressure drop, we would lose the motor immediately. It fascinated me. There was no doubt in my mind that the oil pressure would drop any moment. But the prize was actually in sight. We could not turn back.

At 9:02 A.M., May 9th, 1926, Greenwich civil time, our calculations showed us to be at the Pole! The dream of a lifetime had at last been realized.

We headed to the right to take two confirming sights of the sun, then turned and took two more.

After that we made some moving and still pictures, then went on for several miles in the direction we had come, and made another larger circle to be sure to take in the Pole. Thus we made a non-stop flight around the world in a very few minutes. In doing that we lost a whole day in time; and, of course, when we completed the circle, we gained that day back again.

Two great questions confronted us now: Were we **exactly**

where we thought we were? If not—and could we be absolutely certain?—we should miss Spitzbergen. And, even if we were on a straight course, would that engine stop?

As we flew there at the top of the world, we saluted the gallant, indomitable spirit of Peary and verified his report in every detail.

At 9:15 A.M. we headed for Spitzbergen, abandoning the plan to return via Cape Morris Jesup on account of the oil leak.

The reaction coming from the realization that we had accomplished our mission, together with the narcotic effect of the motors, made us drowsy when we were steering. I dozed off at the wheel and in turn had to relieve Bennett several times because of his sleepiness.

I quote from my impressions cabled to the United States on our return to Kings Bay:

"The wind began to freshen and change direction soon after we left the Pole, and soon we were making over 100 miles an hour.

"The elements were surely smiling that day on us, two insignificant specks of mortality flying over that great, vast white area in a small plane with only one companion, speechless and deaf from the motors, just a dot in the center of 10,000 square miles of visible desolation.

"We felt no larger than a pinpoint and as lonely as the tomb; as remote and detached as a star.

"Here, in another world, far from the herds of people, the smallnesses of life fell from our shoulders. What wonder that we felt no great emotion of achievement or fear of death that lay stretched beneath us, but instead, impersonal, disembodied. On, on we went. It seemed forever onward.

"Our great speed had the effect of quickening our mental processes, so that a minute appeared as many minutes, and I realized fully then that time is only a relative thing. An instant can be an age, an age an instant."

We were aiming for Grey Point, Spitzbergen, and finally when we saw it dead ahead, we knew that we had been able to keep on our course! That we were exactly where we had thought we were!

But, to our astonishment, a miracle was happening. That motor was still running. It is a hundred to one shot that a leaky engine such as ours means a motor stoppage. It is generally an oil lead that breaks. We afterward found out the leak was caused by a rivet jarring out of its hole; and when the oil got down to the level of the hole it stopped leaking. Flight Engineer Noville had put an extra amount of oil in an extra tank.

It was a wonderful relief not to have to navigate any more. We came into Kings Bay flying at about 4,000 feet. The tiny village was a welcome sight, but not so much so as the good old *Chantier*, which looked so small beneath. I could see the steam from her welcoming and, I know, joyous whistle.

On my return to New York I sent a radio asking that an officer-messenger come for my charts and records. The Navy Department complied. Through the Secretary of the Navy I submitted everything to the National Geographic Society. The papers were referred to a special committee of the Society, consisting of its President, Dr. Gilbert Grosvenor, the Chairman of its Research Committee, Dr. Frederick Coville, and Colonel E. Lester Jones, a member of the Board of Trustees, who was also Director of the United States Coast and Geodetic Survey.

This committee appointed a sub-committee of expert mathematicians and calculators. The final report was submitted to the Secretary of the Navy and read in part as follows:

"We have the honor of submitting the following report of our examination of Lieutenant Commander Richard Evelyn Byrd's 'Navigation Report of Flight to Pole.' We have carefully examined Commander Byrd's original records of his observations en route to and from the North Pole. . . . We have verified all his computations. We have also made a satisfactory examination of the sextant and sun compass used by Commander Byrd.

"It is the opinion of your committee that at very close to 9 hours 3 minutes, Greenwich civil time, May 9, 1926, Lieutenant Commander Richard Evelyn Byrd was at the North Pole, insofar as an observer in an airplane, using the most accurate instruments and methods available for determining his position, could ascertain."

Chapter III

~~~~~~

FOG OVER PARIS

IN SPITE of my preoccupation with polar matters, I had never lost sight of my original plan to fly the Atlantic Ocean. When we hoisted anchor at Spitzbergen after the North Pole flight, I turned to Bennett and said:

"Now we can fly the Atlantic."

To which he replied: "I hope you take me with you."

"We go together," I said, not foreseeing the cruel circumstances that would prevent my ever carrying out the promise.

Bennett and I discussed types of planes at great length. We wanted to be scientific, to point the way for the trans-Atlantic plane of the future, to the practical way of crossing the Atlantic commercially. I knew, from past conversations on the subject, that many aeronautical men at home would favor our using a single-engined plane. We had a number of single-engined planes that could cross the Atlantic; and engines were already reliable enough for the flyer to put considerable trust in them. We felt that, if we could fly to Europe in a ship that would be a precursor of the practical trans-Atlantic airplane of the future, we would possibly be contributing more to the progress of ocean flying. Extra power and the advantage of being able to maintain flight (under certain conditions of load) on two engines if one went out were our main reasons for thinking that a multi-engined plane would be the machine of the future, especially for passenger flying.

We knew that we had an extremely tough job ahead of us because no one knew how far a three-engined plane would fly and it was going to be very difficult to find out. It would be considerably less than a single-engined plane because it is

more efficient to have the power in a single unit and one engine
has less resistance through the air than three.

I knew that it had long been the desire of Rodman Wanamaker to send an airplane to Paris. He felt deeply, as I did
also, the value of such a flight to international good will. I had
no difficulty in gaining his approval and backing for our plans
for a New York to Paris flight. Mr. Wanamaker was one of
the finest men I have ever known. It was his wish that we
build an entirely new plane at his expense. But I foresaw the
chance of hitting on a design that would not be practicable on
first production. There are always many kinks to get out of an
entirely new design. So I stuck to the type—a Fokker—which
had successfully carried Bennett and me over the Pole; this
time, however, we wanted a bigger plane.

In the winter of 1926 the Atlantic Aircraft Corporation set
about building the *America*. It had more wing spread than our
North Pole plane. With the extra wing surface we expected
to be able to get off the ground with at least 3,000 pounds more
pay load than we had been able to lift on the North Pole flight.

This extra capacity would permit us to take fuel for a long
flight and 800 pounds of equipment over and above that which
was absolutely necessary. We wanted to show that some pay
load could be carried across the Atlantic. We planned to take
a special radio set, as well as a water-proof installation in case
of a forced landing; two rubber boats for the crew; and emergency food and equipment of all sorts; Very pistols for night
signaling, etc. Also, I wanted to try to take two extra men to
see if passengers, as well as pay load, could be flown across
now. Here was another reason for taking a big three-engined
plane of a type that was still in a sense experimental.

I was sworn in by the Post Office Department as the first
trans-Atlantic air mail pilot, and we carried the first bag of
U. S. air mail from the United States to France.

In addition to the apparatus mentioned above, we also had
built a 1,200-gallon gasoline tank. The building of that great

gas tank designed to carry over 7,000 pounds of gasoline was an interesting experiment. We put a dump valve in it. This was the first time such a device was used in aviation. Its purpose was to empty our fuel in a few seconds in case we saw we were going to crash. Besides lessening the impact and fire risks of a forced landing on the ground, the empty tank would give flotation in case we landed in the ocean. Then it gave another great advantage: If one engine should stop, we could dump gasoline to a point where the diminished load would make it possible to fly on two engines.

Another important matter was meteorology. There was no suitable trans-Atlantic meteorological service, and this had to be devised. Long ago Lieutenant Commander Noel Davis and I had asked the Secretary of Agriculture for the coöperation of the United States Weather Bureau. This was granted. The bureau needed reports of conditions over the Atlantic; so we requested the Radio Corporation of America to procure radio reports from seagoing ships, which they did magnanimously and patriotically. For the first time in history, regular weather maps of the North Atlantic were developed, at the behest of aviation. This work was the beginning of a valuable meteorological service.

We devoted considerable time to the study of a proper take-off field for a trans-Atlantic flight. The biggest field available around New York was Roosevelt Field on Long Island. Mr. Grover Whalen, Mr. Wanamaker's representative, leased it, and we set about developing it for the heavy loads the long-distance plane must carry.

Next to the plane, the take-off field was the most important consideration; and in those days there were no large fields near New York. Lifting heavy loads into the air is what makes long distance flights difficult. A very long run and high speeds are necessary to get off the ground. The bigger and the more heavily loaded the plane, the longer the run.

René Fonck had used a three-engined plane in his attempted

trans-Atlantic flight in 1926, and one of the things that made for his fatal accident at the take-off (in which two of his companions were killed) was the irregularity and shortness of the runway he had to use at Roosevelt Field. We repaired this same runway and took out its worst bumps and soft spots. Day after day I personally went over every inch of the ground, striving for the same smoothness that we got on our Spitzbergen snow-way, which finally had made the North Pole flight possible.

But the field was not, we thought, big enough. Some one suggested building a little hill. We had taken off going down hill with skis on the North Pole flight. Surely it would work with wheels. So we built the hill, and in effect at least it added 500 feet to the runway by the fast initial start it gave us.

Things were going along merrily by the middle of March, when several other trans-Atlantic flights were announced. Noel Davis, Charles Lindbergh, Clarence Chamberlin, and nearly a dozen others were preparing for New York-to-Paris flights. Fonck was making ready for a second try.

This was not exactly news. I knew they had been preparing. Each had his own ideas. Some of them were competing for the Orteig Prize of $25,000 for the first pilot to fly between New York and Paris. *We* were not.

Despite this, the first thing I knew, I had been projected into what was euphemistically called by the press the "Great 1927 New York-to-Paris Air Derby." I admit, however, that it would have been very gratifying to be first across; but we were by no means sure our three-engined plane would fly the distance from New York to Paris; and, for the first three-quarters of the way across the Atlantic, on account of the weight of the fuel, we would come down in the ocean if any one of the three engines should stop.

On April 20th, 1927, our plane was ready for the factory test. It was through no special effort that we were many weeks ahead of all the others planning to fly the Atlantic. We wanted to make the flight in May when we would have the full moon.

Having received word from the factory at Hasbrouck Heights, N. J., that Mr. Fokker, the designer, was ready to take the airplane up for its first flight, I sent for Noville and Bennett to join me. We got off all right. Fokker was at the controls; the other three of us were passengers. We didn't want to fly the plane and be responsible if it should crack up.

So long as the engines were running everything went all right. But the moment they were cut off the plane felt nose heavy. Noville and I saw Bennett licking his lips. This was the only sign Bennett ever gave when he was nervous—which, I may say, was very rare. I nudged Noville and nodded toward Bennett.

Fokker brought the plane down for a landing. But, when he slowed up to touch the ground, again came unmistakable signs that the plane was nose heavy. He took her up again for another turn and to think over what we had better do.

As we had very little fuel, we couldn't stay up long. And, as there was no way to shift weights, we could not help ourselves. We couldn't get aft because the great 1,200-gallon fuel tank blocked off the way. Fokker brought the plane within a few feet of the ground. I caught hold of a steel upright just back of Fokker's seat—kept my gaze concentrated on the air-speed meter. We were going a mile a minute. The wheels touched the ground. Instantly, I saw Fokker rise and make frantic efforts to jump out the trapdoor that was directly over his head and Bennett's.

With all my strength I clung to the heavy steel upright. Abruptly the deck rose under us. In a flash we knew she was going over on her back. There came a terrific crash. It sounded as if every inch of the plane was being crushed to kindling. Something struck me a stunning blow on my head and in the small of my back. It was Noville thrown forward from the sudden stop. The impact snapped my arm like a match stick.

"Look out for fire!" cried a strained voice. I learned afterward this was Bennett, caught in the wreckage. Noville and I, jumbled together with broken rods, frames, seats, and other gear, scrambled to our feet to find ourselves trapped. With my broken arm and bruised body I was of little use. Noville broke a hole through the fabric with his bare fist, dove through the hole, and fell on the ground in great agony. There was no fire. Fokker had had the presence of mind to pull the switch, cutting off all three engines. He had succeeded in jumping clear of the wreckage and was uninjured.

I went to Bennett. He was hanging head downward, held by the wreckage of the pilot's seat. It certainly looked as if he had "got his" at last. His leg was badly broken and his face streaming blood. He was drenched with oil.

It seemed tough to get it on a trial flight after all we had been through.

I leaned over him and told him who I was.

"Guess I'm done for, Commander," he said weakly. "I'm all broken up. I can't see, and I have no feeling in my left arm."

"Nonsense, old man."

I noticed that his eyes were filled with oil. When I wiped the oil away he could see. It was a great relief.

However, for a week it looked as though Bennett might not pull through. But the fine attention he got from Dr. Sullivan and his own courage and grit saved his life. His leg took many weeks to knit. He was out of the ocean flight for good. That was heartbreaking for him and a very great disappointment to me at the time.

Later, some time after the flight, Bennett was taken with pneumonia. He had never regained his strength after that accident, and he didn't have a chance, and so I was to pay a price too big to measure for our decision to try to fly the Atlantic in a plane big enough for passengers and freight. Floyd Bennett was the finest man I have ever known.

Noville suffered a great deal, but in several weeks he was up and back on the job again.

I set my broken arm on the way to the hospital. Two bones were fractured, and there were many bruises; my arm was still bandaged when we left on the flight. But beyond being something of a nuisance the injuries did not interfere with our plans.

The damage to our plane was serious. It took a month of day and night toil to get her back into shape again.

In the meantime, other trans-Atlantic planes were being tuned up, and reports of the imminence of their hop-offs were in every edition of the daily papers.

What was wrong with Byrd? What would the crossing of the Atlantic be with his great plane as compared to the other smaller ones in the race? Why was he delaying the hop-off? Fearing that our crash would hurt aviation, we had kept the seriousness of it from the public. There was another decision for which we paid dearly.

Lindbergh and Chamberlin were ready to go. With much pleasure Mr. Whalen and I offered them the runway we had built at Roosevelt Field. Grover Whalen is, by the way, the most efficient man I have ever done work with. When Lindbergh hopped off early in the morning, we went down to the field to tell him good-by and to wish him luck. It was a wonderful experience to see his wheels just clear the telephone wire at the end of the runway.

Finally, after many trial flights, I was convinced that the *America* could make the distance, but it did not seem exactly the right thing to do to fly immediately to Paris while Lindbergh was still there. To delay a little would not hurt our flight; while to have gone might well have done harm to the fine work he was doing in cementing French and American friendship. We didn't know. We simply didn't want to take a chance of lessening in any way the value of what he was doing in France.

So I took things more easily until after he returned to the United States. But again I was not allowed to pursue my course without criticism. Letters poured in reproaching me.

At 1:00 A.M., June 29th, 1927, Dr. Kimball telephoned that, while conditions were not ideal, the weather was about as good as we could expect. I had determined not to wait because I felt that the trans-Atlantic plane of the future could not wait for *ideal* conditions. Moreover, we probably could gain more practical knowledge if we met adverse weather.

I had only about one hour's sleep that night, and I knew there would be at least two more nights to go through before I would have another chance to sleep. When I reached the field at 3:00 A.M., June 29th, the plane was at the top of our little hill, and by the aid of powerful lights, the crew was applying the finishing touches. It was dark, dismal, and raining slightly, but a large crowd had gathered.

We felt that probably the most critical period of the whole flight was at hand, that of getting into the air with our load of over 15,000 pounds. Every other multi-engined plane built for a non-stop Atlantic flight had crashed with fatalities on the take-off with heavy loads. Among them was my old friend, Lieutenant Commander Noel Davis. In those days big overloaded planes were bad things to fool with.

In order to lift this terrific load, we needed a speed of nearly a mile and a half a minute. If we should not quite make this speed, we should crash, as our great momentum would carry us over the end of the runway.

Now let us review our preparations in so far as they bore upon our plans to overcome whatever lay ahead.

First:—the take-off with a heavy load—an extremely hazardous undertaking on a field barely a mile in length. The smooth hard surface would help and the hill would add to the length of the runway; if these factors failed, the dump valve would allow us to lighten the load, and reduce the risk in the event of a crash.

If we got off, the next immediate hazard would be from an engine stoppage and a consequent forced landing. A forced landing with a load as heavy as ours would smash the plane to pieces. Besides the dump valve, we had run a cat-walk out to the engines, hoping in this way to be able to make small adjustments on the engines while in flight.

Another grave risk would be from ice's forming on the wing. We anticipated this by placing thermometers about the plane so that we could keep a sharp outlook for the critical temperature. We were careful about flashlights. We prepared to fly high so that if we should get into the critical temperature and not be able to climb out of it, we could dive down to warmer temperatures near the water.

We had two rubber boats, one large enough to accommodate the flight crew and all of the emergency equipment—the other to be used as a lifeboat for the larger boat. We carried along materials to repair these boats.

Another grave danger in those days was from coming down at night in a tail spin in the dark clouds. We were all right there, as we all had had experience with night flying.

In all of the years of thought we gave to the trans-Atlantic flight, the worst thing we could think of that ever could happen —and the only thing, we decided, that could prevent success after our thorough preparations—was to have the hard luck to reach our destination in the middle of the night during a storm with thick weather making for impossible visibility. All this, however, was speculation.

We warmed up the engines gradually and took our places in the plane. Lieutenant George O. Noville sat with his hand on the dump valve. Bernt Balchen, young Norwegian relief pilot and mechanic, made a final inspection. Acosta put the engines on full; the plane strained like a live thing against the line that anchored it to the crest of the artificial hill. Knife in hand, Tom Mulroy, who had been chief engineer on the North Pole voyage, stood ready to cut the rope that held the plane. The tug of the great engines suddenly broke the line, as I learned later, and we started a little sooner than we had expected. That was bad. The engines were barely warmed up, and it looked for a few moments as if we might not get into the air at all. Once Bert Acosta at the wheel raised his hand to Noville to dump. It was a tense moment—everything hung in the balance. But just then the wheels left the ground, and we set forth on one of the toughest flights ever made. I remember Balchen shouted with joy. Acosta had done a superb job.

Slowly the ship gained altitude with its tremendous load. I made notes in my log and remarks in my diary, the same diary which I had carried over the North Pole. I find this entry made a few minutes after leaving Roosevelt Field: "Altitude 300 feet, turning, after turn completed, altitude 400 feet."

With the engines turning up maximum revolutions we went through the air at 100 miles an hour. Naturally, for the same wing surface, it is necessary to fly faster with a heavy load than it is with a lighter one in order to keep in the air.

Slowly we climbed. Shortly afterward I find the following note in my log: "Raining, fog, clouds low, standard compass $83\frac{1}{2}°$, wind southwest on surface, drift 5° right, air speed 100 miles an hour, altitude 3,000 feet."

We had to change the course of the plane five degrees to the left to allow for this drift. With a drift indicator, I had estimated our speed over the ground and found that at 3,000 feet we were getting the maximum assistance from the winds.

The rain continued for several hours, and the weather was slightly foggy; but these factors were not particularly bothersome.

When we reached Nova Scotia, the weather became clear. However, the air was very rough. But we had expected that. Passing near Halifax, we flew over beautiful white clouds, but the sun was bright above us. The shadow of the plane was etched on the clouds, and around it was a rainbow. Here was a good omen.

The cabin was still cluttered with five-gallon cans of gasoline. Every now and then as I sighted on the ground with the drift indicator, I could see a white object shoot down, glistening in the sun. These objects were gasoline cans that Noville was throwing overboard after he had emptied them into our huge tank.

We were now near the air station I had built at Halifax, and for a while I flew over territory with which I was familiar. When we reached the beautiful Bras d'Or Lakes, I looked down on the rough shore where Walter Hinton and I had once been washed ashore after a forced landing in 1918.

At Newfoundland we found everything covered with fog. We had not expected such a tough break. Thereafter, for 2,000 miles we flew without even seeing the ocean.

Thus there was no chance of taking a navigation departure from St. Johns and being entirely certain of our position before striking out over the ocean.

At 2 P.M. all the gasoline cans had been emptied. I instructed Acosta to "lean" the mixture and to cut down engine revolutions as much as possible. We had been going with almost a full throttle on account of the heavy load.

Finding no break in the fog, we fought our way above it; and, in climbing with our heavy load, we again had to run the engines at full speed. Slowly we got altitude, and at 5:50 P.M. we found ourselves about a mile high, but in fog most of the time; the plane was drenched. It would grow colder as night drew on, and we would have to watch the temperature carefully because, within fifteen minutes, a plane so drenched could be precipitated into the ocean if the moisture froze on the propellers and wings.

Little did we realize, as we went into the fog, the hours that would pass before we should again see either the land or sea. I asked Noville to check gasoline consumption. His figures indicated that it was much greater than we had expected. One reason for this, I thought, was the struggle to get above the clouds and fog with our very heavy load. This had caused us to run the motors much faster than we had intended.

I made some careful calculations and showed Noville (in writing, of course, because the roar of the three engines prevented conversation) that, at this rate, with the slightest wind against us, we must drop into the sea for lack of fuel before reaching Europe.

We were at that time in storm clouds. It would be just as hazardous to go back as forward. I made the decision to stake our lives on a theory that if we flew at the proper altitude we should have favoring winds. If I were wrong, then we should fall into the sea.

Noville and I decided not to tell Acosta and Balchen of our grave predicament. What was the use?

I had studied the velocity and directions of winds over the Atlantic. So far as I could learn, no reliable data dealing with wind velocities at high altitudes were available; but several meteorologists of the Weather Bureau, as well as I, believed that if a plane flew high enough, it would get the benefit of strong prevailing winds from the west, even though there might at the same time be easterly winds near the surface.

Therefore, whenever one of us took the wheel he flew as high as possible. I also knew, from Dr. Kimball's weather map, spread before me on the chart board, that we were flying on the southern side of the storm area and that later on we would be flying on the northern side of a high-pressure area.

We were now flying nearly two miles above the ocean. Night had brought bitter cold; and we were plowing through storm clouds, so dark that we couldn't see our hands. I find notations made hour after hour in my log, as follows: "It is impossible to navigate." One notation in the log stated: "Ice is forming on the plane." We were at a dangerous temperature. I passed a note to Acosta warning him to make every effort to get out of the clouds, which he managed to do in a short time.

He and Balchen both deserve credit for their fine work during this critical period.

During the night, between turns at the wheel, Bernt Balchen

took brief naps. As he stirred restlessly in the restricted space from time to time, his foot nearly touched the handle of the gasoline dump valve. I watched him closely without awakening him; but, if his foot should kick that, we should lose our precious fuel.

Our night lights worked well. We did not use flashlights very much because every time we flashed them we were blinded. The luminous dials and figures on the instruments showed up well in the pitch dark. I had a special portable light for my chart board.

I had left behind my rather heavy thermos bottle of tea, but during the night Noville gave me some of his coffee. It was only lukewarm, but it tasted good. We had plenty of drinking water. I ate a little roast chicken, but did not want to eat too much, because I knew it would be necessary to keep awake.

From time to time during the night we fought clear of the clouds. It was a weird sight to look down from the pinnacle of black masses we were skimming. Around us were ominous, towering cloud peaks, some of which reached far above us. As we could not afford to go around those that lay in our path, we would dash through them in a darkness so intense that we could not see the wing tips. The fire from the exhaust pipes of our faithful engines, invisible in the daytime, shone vividly in the dark night. The 30,000 flashes of fire per minute through the exhaust pipes made a cheerful sight against the black.

I had another bad time when I discovered a leak near the bottom of one of the main gasoline tanks. We had provided against such an emergency by bringing along some of a patent putty-like substance. This nearly stopped the leak, but a little of the precious fuel kept dribbling out. An hour or so past midnight the leak stopped of its own accord. This I told myself could mean but one thing—that the fuel had got down to the leak. This meant further that we had only fuel in the four wing tanks. This checked with what Noville had told me about over-consumption of gas, and confirmed the disagreeable fact that we should never reach the other side.

I was living over again now the same sort of worry which had come to Bennett and me over the Polar ocean after we had discussed the oil leak; only this time I had the responsibility of three men's lives instead of one.

I'll admit that those were very bad hours riding the storm clouds in the blackness of the night, facing what seemed to be inevitable disaster. I felt no personal fear, but I lived a lifetime of worry. What an incredible mess I was making for the families of my companions and myself. The responsibility lay entirely and directly with me. Exactly seven years later I was to have the same infinite regret in the middle of another night —a night months long—in the shadow of the South Pole.

I saw no reason to tell even Noville this time the bad news. All I could do was to give instruction to cruise at the most economical possible speed.

On one occasion in a thick cloud the plane got temporarily out of control. We must have been going downward at a terrific rate, judging from the roaring of the engines. Balchen, with skill, finally steadied the ship again on her course.

Throughout the long night each man went about his duty efficiently and calmly, taking each crisis as if it were all in a day's work.

I note in our record that I sent the following radio at 6:50 A.M. on June 30th: "We have seen neither land nor sea since 3 o'clock yesterday. Everything completely covered with fog." As the second day came on, we had some terrifying views; there were fog valleys, dark and sinister, hundreds of feet beneath us. At times distant cloud peaks took on shapes and colors of rugged Arctic land and mountains.

I find this note in my diary: "Went forward at 3:15 A.M. to pilot and got stuck in the passageway." I had to tear off a sweater to get forward.

Hour after hour we had seen no land or water. "I sit here wondering if the winds have been with us," I wrote.

From time to time we sent and received radio messages; and it seemed miraculous that, flying two miles above the ocean, hidden in dense clouds, we could get messages from safe, comfortable places.

I did not ask for a check on the gasoline. I thought I knew the answer.

At one time Noville reported he had a message from a steamer somewhere beneath us, and our signals were so clear that we must have been very near it. We were in dense fog at the time. He asked for conditions of weather at the surface, and the ship reported fog. We got its position and a radio bearing. This showed we were on a certain line.

A little later we got the position of another ship, the S.S. *Paris*, and this information put us somewhere on another line. Where the two lines intersected was our exact position. We were certain then that we had drifted to the south; so, instead of bucking winds to go to Ireland, we set our course directly for Finisterre, France. Indeed, by allowing ourselves to go with the wind we had made better speed toward our objective. I could now allow for drift to a nicety and knew exactly where we would hit land several hundred miles away if we had enough gasoline.

Our position indicated that we had been assisted by a 30-mile tail wind all the way from Newfoundland. We had made splendid speed.

I wanted to find out the worst about the gasoline, so asked Noville for an exact estimate, if possible. He came to me in a few minutes and wrote: "I made a mistake in the first estimate. We have enough gasoline left to fly to Rome."

"Wish I had known that 18 hours ago," I wrote back.

Naturally, I experienced a tremendous reaction. All my black vision of the night gave way to a great elation that, after all, we had more than an even chance of coming through.

The error in the gas estimate was caused, I think, by the fact that the tail of the plane was considerably down on account of the weight and the gasoline gauge forward of the tank did not register accurately.

In the afternoon of the second day, we came out of the thick, solid cloud layers into broken cloud fields, and we could see the water beneath us. Though it was rough, it was a most welcome sight. We had only passing glimpses, but they were enough to allow me to get my drift and to verify the fact that the wind was blowing from the northwest.

What a great contrast was our situation now compared with what it had appeared to be a few hours earlier! We could see sun and water; by our navigation we knew exactly where we were; there was enough gasoline to get to Rome; and all engines were hitting perfectly. When I squeezed up into the pilot's compartment to take a turn at the wheel, I could tell from the faces of my shipmates that they, too, were much relieved.

Soon we were getting many radio signals. They began to increase rapidly in number, and Noville reported to me that he thought the whole of Europe was calling us.

We hit land at Finisterre about the time and at the place we had calculated, and I am sure France never looked so beautiful to anyone before. We passed over Brest and set our course for Paris.

We had fairly good weather now, but it looked thick ahead. I asked Noville to radio to Paris to find out the condition of the weather there. Paris reported thick fog and squalls. Another battle lay ahead.

It was a very great temptation to set our course for Rome. We had ahead of us another storm and another night with possibly impossible landing conditions at Paris. No one had flown from New York to Rome. I had pleaded with Mr. Wanamaker to agree to make Italy our destination. He had his heart set on Paris, and I had ended by giving him my promise to do my best to get there. I considered changing course for

Rome, but even as I did so I knew I would have to keep my promise to Mr. Wanamaker.

The worst that we had anticipated—fog and storm at our destination—had happened.

We were able to locate accurately our position by the cities beneath us and the coast line to the left. But before long darkness began to descend, and with the second night came thick, rainy, ominous weather. Soon we had only occasional glimpses of the lights of the towns; thick, low-lying fog or clouds drenched the plane; and again we were tossed about in the blackness without being able to see our hands before our faces.

It was so inky dark that every time we put on the flashlight to give an order it so blinded us temporarily that we could only dimly see the luminous instrument board. However, the personnel and the many mechanisms of the plane continued to function efficiently, and I had every confidence of hitting Paris.

Having raised Finisterre after almost 2,000 miles of blind flying, I thought we certainly ought to be able to reach Paris, a few hundred miles off.

About the time we expected to reach Paris we broke clear of the overcast weather. I saw bright lights ahead and a revolving light which I took to be Le Bourget. Our dead reckoning showed us to be just about at our destination.

Our troubles seemed over. It was a relief. I wrote out the following radio for Mr. Wanamaker: "Paris is in sight. It has been a great trip. I wish to tell you with enthusiasm that Noville, Acosta and Balchen have faced dangers with the greatest possible courage and calmness. They have been wonderful, and we all send our best wishes to you."

That radio was never sent. I looked down and saw the revolving light flash for an instant on water. It was a lighthouse. I knew there was no ocean lighthouse near Paris. We were somewhere on the coast of France!

The compass had gone wrong—had taken us in a great circle. By flashlight I conferred on paper with the pilots and concluded that we had made a circle to the left. The fault evidently lay with an experimental, earth-inductor compass we were using. I afterwards learned that our estimate as to where we were on the coast was correct.

I checked our steering compass with a standard ship compass I always carry astern on long flights. I made sure this time of our course, and again we set out for Paris and again were tossed about in the storm and darkness. I had repeatedly to correct the earth inductor compass with the standard compass. It was raining very hard on the coast, and visibility was bad, but it was much stormier inland. We afterward found that the center of the storm was over Paris. I watched the course carefully after that and checked compasses every few minutes. I knew we were heading toward Paris. The rough air made it a little difficult to steer, especially in the darkness; but we kept a pretty good general course.

Then arose the necessity of watching the gasoline very carefully, for a forced landing in the darkness would not only have meant certain disaster for us, but also, perhaps, for those who might happen to be beneath us. The gas was getting low.

Finally, our dead reckoning showed us to be over Paris, but we could see nothing—nothing beneath us—nothing but the luminous lights of our steering instruments. We dropped to so low an altitude that we had to haul in our radio antenna for fear of hitting a house. We couldn't go any lower without killing others as well as ourselves. We had come to a point beyond which, if we continued, we could not have returned to the coastal waters, on account of the diminished gasoline. We knew that we would need a few gallons of reserve in order to cruise around for a landing place that we might not find even then. I believe at the moment we turned we were near Paris; our motors were heard by many people at Le Bourget through a sound intensifier. Twenty-eight people have since told me that they heard our engines.

In a flash it came to me that the compass needle taking us

in a great circle right up to that lighthouse was an act of Providence.

A decision had to be made. The big job now was to make a landing without killing ourselves or the people beneath us. The only thing to do was to turn back and attempt a landing off the coast, a dangerous alternative in itself, but the best choice at hand.

We set a course for the lighthouse we had seen. The wind might blow us off a bit in the darkness; but, if the fog were not too thick there, we were confident of hitting it. We could see nothing beneath us, and we were flying so low that Noville had to keep in the antenna we had pulled up. Finally, when I thought we were near the lighthouse, I asked Balchen to get down lower. He was afraid of running into something, but we had to take the risk. We emerged from the mists, and there was the lighthouse ahead of us. That proves, I think, that we had not been lost—that we had been over Paris.

We cruised over toward the lighthouse slowly, but in spite of the beam the area around it was black, and we could only guess at the nature of the land. We could see no landing place. We had hoped there would be a beach and had attached to a weighted streamer a message asking the people to clear the beach and make some kind of light for our landing.

We then flew over the lighthouse and, by the quick flash of the revolving beacon, we could tell that we were over water and could dimly distinguish the shoreline. It was still raining and dismally thick. I wrote a note to my shipmates which I passed around with the flashlight; it read: "Stand by to land."

We decided to land near enough to the beach line to swim ashore, if necessary, and to salvage the plane, if it were not too badly wrecked. At the same time we had to be far enough away to miss any rocks on the shore.

The worst had happened to us. We had reached Paris in the night in weather too thick to land. Against that contingency we had brought with us navigation flares which ignite on striking the water and give light for a few minutes. I had thrown half of them overboard to rid us of the weight, but had saved enough for a landing.

We now dropped a number of flares in as nearly a straight line as we could, about 100 yards from the beach line. They all ignited; and, although they made nothing better than pin pricks of light in a pool of blackness, we hoped in this way to be able to judge the distance of the plane above the water as we descended.

Those hours in the storm had not been pleasant. I felt myself entirely responsible for the lives of my shipmates. I don't believe they thought there was much chance of getting down safely; but still they faced gallantly, with steady courage, whatever fate lay ahead. In a few moments the story would be ended, but to the last they calmly obeyed orders.

We did not wait for the gas to give out. Balchen was at the wheel. I gave orders to land.

We were landing with the plane in control and the engines functioning perfectly.

As we neared the water we could not see it; only the flares ahead of us and beneath us.

The wheels touched, and though the landing gear is secured to the plane with a tremendous factor of safety, it was sheared off, along with the wheels, with hardly a jar to the plane, as though a great knife had cut it.

Just a second afterward the crash came. I suppose I was dazed a little. I know I got a stiff blow over the heart that made it beat irregularly for many months afterward. I found myself in the water outside, swimming around in pitchy dark and rain. I could hear Noville calling for me, but not another sound in the extraordinary stillness which contrasted so vividly with the roar of the great motors which had been pounding on our eardrums for forty-two hours.

The plane instantly filled with water. Noville was getting out the window. I yelled at him that I was unharmed and asked him how he was but he did not answer—just kept on yelling for me. I was a little worried about him, but I knew that he could not have been badly hurt. Hearing nothing from Balchen and Acosta and worried beyond measure, I swam to the cockpit, which was settling under water. I shouted but got no answer.

I found Balchen caught under water and trying to extricate himself. He talked a blue streak when he got out but didn't answer any of my questions. I couldn't make it out exactly but concluded that he, too, was somewhat dazed.

Thinking that Acosta must have been caught in the cockpit, we dived down, but he was not there. A moment later he appeared, apparently from nowhere, swimming toward the wing, the leading edge of which was now awash. He must have been swimming around out there somewhere in the darkness all the time. Bert also talked a blue streak but not to either one of us. He mumbled something about breaking his collar bone.

With grunts and groans we dragged ourselves back upon the wing, which was slowly settling in the water.

So it must have happened with all the land planes that dropped into the ocean in the summer of 1927.

We were stiff and bruised, tired and watersoaked; and it was with some difficulty that we pumped up the rubber boat. As the wing was almost flush with the water, there was no difficulty in launching it.

We had placed our most precious cargo, which included some small American flags, and a piece of the original American Flag, in a compartment we had made in the great wing; this we thought was the safest place. We shipped the oars in the rubber boat, and wearily made for the shore in the dark.

It was then I learned why none of my companions had paid any attention to my remarks. They were temporarily deaf from forty-two hours of the pounding of the motors. I had used cotton in my ears and was not deaf.

We were a mile off shore from the village. Even after we

reached land, we spent much time going from house to house trying to arouse some one. But there were fences with locked gates around these houses and the occupants we managed to arouse took us for tramps. Suddenly, a boy on a bicycle passed us. We tried to stop him, but he took one look at us and kept on going. Wet and bedraggled, we certainly were not prepossessing.

Finally, we found the lighthouse keeper and his wife up in the lighthouse tower, but they wouldn't come down. Noville could talk French but was deaf. My French wasn't much and seemed to add to their idea that we were a gang of drunken roughnecks. But, when at last they realized that we had landed at Ver-sur-Mer, having come all the way from America, their astonishment and excitement were comical though natural. They could not do too much for us.

Balchen and I rowed back to the *America* to salvage what we could of the mail and records. In the meantime the tide had gone out rapidly; and, when we reached the plane, it was nearly high and dry. Some of the villagers appeared and helped us carry our belongings up to the village. So long as we live we can never forget the kindness of the people of Ver-sur-Mer, and before leaving France we motored back there to tell them "good-by."

Chapter IV

~~~~~~

ANTARCTIC ASSAULT

NINETEEN TWENTY-EIGHT was probably the busiest year of my life. So the journal which I had promised myself I should keep, day by day, suffered in consequence. The few hours of quiet and isolation I had, usually came after midnight, on top of an exhausting day; and these naturally found me wanting in the spirit to write; the morrow invariably brought tougher problems. Nevertheless, I did occasionally find time to make entries in my journal; and from these I have been persuaded to select the following, in the belief that they may show by reason of their immediacy some of the difficulties and hopes that attended us as we got ready to go south.

1 A.M. The Owl, en route Boston, Sept. 28, '28.

The time is up. The last dollar that I can beg is raised. Four ships, with most of our equipment on board, are already on their way, headed for New Zealand. In their holds and on their cluttered decks are over 500 tons of supplies and materials; there are at least 5,000 different kinds of things, ranging from thumb tacks to airplanes; and every single thing is essential, in one way or another, to our unrelieved stay in the Antarctic. I hope that everything is there. There can be no return now. We are going into the largest non-shop area in the world, more than 2,000 miles from the nearest human dwellings, and for nine months out of every twelve shut off even from these by the impenetrable pack ice. So we stand or fall according to our preparations here in Manhattan, nearly 10,000 miles away from our Antarctic base. A pity if we should become vitally dependent upon some trivial, forgotten things. Through my brain runs a provoking rhyme... "For want of a nail, the shoe was lost. For want of a shoe the horse was lost...." I seem to have forgotten the rest, but the moral is clear anyway. No matter. We have done our best; if something is forgotten, some trifle necessary to the support of 82 men, for nearly two years, then it will have to be one of those things with which Providence bedevils humans who reach out for too much.

It has been a real fight, this battle of New York. Minor crises fell hard upon major crises. None of us has rested. Nearly all are exhausted. We have been stimulated by the knowledge that the battle ahead in the frozen world will be won or lost by the battle of preparation. We are not done yet—not by any means. There is still an immense debt.—I owe more money than I used to think existed. . . .

October 16, '28, Aboard S.S. C. A. Larsen en route New Zealand.

Headed southward at last. After years of anticipation and months of preparation. . . .

This expedition brought me trying problems from the start. Of these, the problem of financing was perhaps the most difficult. My business manager met me at the office after a night with his reports. He did not hold his punch.

"I have a final statement to make on our debts," he said. "We have a deficit of $300,000."

I had not expected it to be half so much. The reasons for this deficit were soon forthcoming. The cost and outfitting of the *City of New York* and the *Eleanor Bolling* had amounted to a small fortune—$165,000 for the first, $125,000 for the second. To build new ships would have approximately cost three times what I put into them. There could be no cutting corners in the matter of strengthening the ships for the struggle in the ice: this expenditure was absolutely necessary. I owed a fortune. And here I was, at the bitter end of my resources, dead tired, sustained during the last crowded days by the hope I should have the last few days at home. Well, I had to get that money; though where, God only knew.

I am in no proper frame of mind, even at this distant date, to record that struggle here. From early morning until late at night, I was at the most disagreeable job in the world, money-raising, begging it really is. I was fortunate. The debt was reduced to $184,000. The job, I confess, could not have been done alone. Loyal friends went to the bat for me, not once but many times. And to them I give undying gratitude—small recompense indeed for what they have done. . . .

The situation, nevertheless, calls for determination and co-operation on the part of all members of the expedition; and from nature, the most favorable of circumstances. If, for example, we should fail to get our winter base established on the Barrier, there can be but one miserable ending—bankruptcy and disgrace. In expeditions of this kind success and failure are not nearly so far apart as the antithetical meanings of the words themselves would indicate. Failure of the pack ice to break up at a seasonable date, thus holding us back too long for the complete basing of supplies, or the presence of a speck of dirt on the airplane engines in flight —matters remotely beyond human control—may well bring disaster at the beginning.

The Plan.—My interest in the South Polar regions dates far back and seems always to have been synonymous with the names of Scott and Peary, of whom I had heard a great deal in my youth. But the plan, which I had secretly worked out, was not spoken of until the night of May 10th, 1926. It is a date not likely to fade from memory; for the two men who shared it with me are dead, having sacrificed their lives in an attempt to aid fellow pioneers.

That night saw the late Floyd Bennett and me at Spitzbergen. A few hours earlier we had completed the first flight by air to the North Pole and back; weary and glad, we had returned to our base, where we were greeted by my friends, Captain Amundsen and Lincoln Ellsworth, who themselves momentarily expected to fly in the *Norge* to Alaska, over our tracks to the Pole and then beyond. We had a splendid dinner that night. Toward the end, Amundsen and I drew together. "Well, Byrd," he said, smiling, "what shall it be now?" Half humorously, half seriously, I replied: "The South Pole." Amundsen's face instantly became serious.

"A big job," he said, "but it can be done. You have the right idea. The older order is changing. Aircraft is the new vehicle for exploration. It is the only machine that can beat the Antarctic. Look here!" And he began to plan; he talked soberly and gravely, as if the fatigue and the buffetings of his magnificent journey to the South Pole (1911-1912) were still on him, and naturally his advice was good. He suggested several capable Norwegian men; he offered the use of some of his equipment; he suggested the ship I was to use—the *Samson*, which I bought and renamed the *City of New York*—"The best bargain for that kind of a job you can find anywhere."

Most earnestly he warned me to look to my men: "Men are the doubtful quantities in the Antarctic. The most thorough kind of preparation, the shrewdest plan, can be destroyed by an incompetent or worthless man." In the same temper, but in different words, the warning was repeated to me by a distinguished British explorer, an executive officer on Scott's last expedition: "The first man who starts trouble of a disloyal nature deserves the worst death you can think of." On expeditions of this kind, a good man is priceless; a disloyal man is soon found out, and his comrades live to damn him and rue the day he was born.

The Preparation.—Actual formation of the expedition was held up until I completed the trans-Atlantic flight. That accomplished, the work of setting up the apparatus with which every expedition functions was begun.

Transport was, as always, the first consideration and the last. The difference between good transport and bad is the measure of the difference between great success and failure in polar exploration. Our plans proposed the enlistment of three types—sea, surface, and air. Each had to be selected with a view to its particular fitness to demanding problems.

There was no polar ice ship big enough to carry all our supplies; so we should have to take an ordinary, seagoing freighter with us. As a safeguard for the men on the freighter, we should have to have a polar ice ship with us.

The task of selecting a good vessel was much simplified by the kindly offices of Amundsen. On the strength of his recommendations, I purchased the *Samson* by cable at Tromsoe, Norway, and ordered her sailed at once to New York. She was a stout vessel, with the spirit and tradition that Conrad would have loved. She was old, as ships' ages are measured, but not in strength. Although built in 1882, she was nearly as strong in 1928, after we reconditioned her, as the day she first put out with the sealing fleet that plies in the pack ice north of Spitz-bergen. We rerigged her, and made her into a bark. She carried auxiliary steam power.

On this windjammer, then, the safety of our ice navigation rested. The second ship was the *Chelsea*, a freighter of 800 tons cargo capacity. She was not much larger than the *City*, having approximately the same length and beam. Her top speed was nine knots. We purchased her because she was cheap; otherwise, I must confess, she had little to recommend her. She was put in dry dock, where she underwent extensive repairs, principally looking to strengthening the forward part of her iron hull against a fatal blow from the pack ice. The choice of the *Chelsea*, which we renamed the *Eleanor Bolling* after my mother, was significant, in that, ours, so far as I know, was the first exploration party to risk a metal hull in or south of the pack.

Months of thought and experiment went into the selection of aircraft. Our largest plane was a Ford tri-motored metal monoplane. We mounted a 525 horse-power Cyclone in the nose, using two Whirlwinds outboard. This gave us a total horse-power of nearly 1,000—200 horse-power more than the stock plane, a top speed of 122 miles per hour, a cruising speed of from 110 to 116 miles per hour, an easy load capacity of 15,000 pounds. This carrying capacity was required for the scientific instruments and emergency gear needed for polar exploration.

Two other planes were acquired, for reserve, for use of the scientists in the field, for transport—in short to provide us with a surplus of effective machines to insure the carrying out of the program of scientific inquiry if one, or even two, machines were wrecked. These included a Fokker Universal monoplane with a 425 horse-power Pratt and Whitney Wasp engine, and a Fairchild folding-wing monoplane.

During the early stages of preparation, Bennett, despite his weakness, planned the aviation equipment which was used in the Antarctic. His death deprived me of a judgment, loyalty and determination in which I always had implicit faith. Had he lived, he would have been second in command. Hundreds were the times I was to feel his loss.

As the supplies accumulated, they were assigned to ships that were to carry them. The loading of the *City* began first. Owing to her low speed, it was necessary for her to leave the United States well in advance of the *Bolling*; we hoped—too optimistically, as it turned out—she would make the trip to New Zealand in less than three months. With 200 tons of material aboard, and a crew of 33, she put out from Hoboken, August 25th, 1928. Her master was Captain Frederick Melville, a sailing man of excellent reputation who, in the face of the times, had not deserted sail.

The *Bolling*, under command of Captain Brown, put out from Norfolk, Virginia, exactly a month later. She carried 300 tons of supplies and a crew of 28.

Another detachment of the expedition was with me on the *Larsen*. At Norfolk she took aboard the four airplanes, the aviation gas and oil, about 100 tons of supplies and the aviation personnel. The task of clearing up ultimate details as well as reducing the deficit left me no alternative save to remain in New York up to the last minute. We boarded the *Larsen* at San Pedro. October 10th, she put out to sea.

So the second week of October saw all of the units on the Pacific, widely scattered, but all hurrying southwestward as fast as their varied speeds would allow, toward the concentration points at New Zealand. I was reminded of a naval force converging for a distant action.

The Problem.—Any discussion of the Antarctic problem, except, perhaps, in scientific circles, soon comes up hard on the question: "... but what's the use of it? What's the value of snow and ice so many miles away?" It is often difficult to make clear the value of polar research to those who do not understand the value of scientific investigation in general. It

(© Wide World Photos)

WRECK OF THE *America*
After she had been hauled ashore by the local villagers

WHALES TRAPPED IN A CRACK THAT SUDDENLY OPENED UP AT THE
BACK DOOR OF LITTLE AMERICA

is not that the answer is necessarily lacking in logic or conviction; more often it is that the asking mind has not turned its thought in that direction; for the most unpracticed student in polar history must soon sense its great significance. It was the most fertile field left for science in the world.

Dr. Mawson has said: "The polar regions like any other point of the globe may be said to be paved with facts. We cannot ignore them without hampering scientific advancement."

Candidly, at this moment the Antarctic is sleeping, so far as we can calculate its value to modern civilization. But no one, except God, can tell how long it will remain sleeping. Immense beds of coal were hinted at by Shackleton's discoveries, Scott found copper, there was iron in the "red mountain" that Shackleton climbed in search of a highway leading to the Pole. Economic minerals were found by Mawson's party at Adélie Land; and Scott's Northern Party, under command of Professor T. Edgeworth David, found titanium on Depot Island, a place he described as "truly a most wonderful place geologically, and a perfect elysium for the mineralogist." These, to be sure, are remote possibilities. There is a much richer ore to be mined immediately in *terra incognita*.

The Antarctic is a continent still in the ice age, similar to that which gripped the northern hemisphere perhaps 30,000 years ago. Few people realize that the ice age long ago receded from the top of the world. The South Pole probably averages more than 40 degrees colder than the North Pole. The greatest ice mass in the world covers the Antarctic continent, and only the highest peaks emerge; bare rock is so unusual that explorers finding it, could hardly seem more delighted if they had come suddenly upon green meadowland. The continent is mainly uplifted tablelands of snow and ice, from 5,000 to 10,000 feet above sea level, and is traversed in places by mountain ranges of extraordinary size and beauty. Inland lie the Polar and South Victoria plateaux—level, vast, and elevated—which are central areas of the continental ice sheet; here the depth of the ice cap appears to range from a few feet, where it touches steep mountainous slopes, to from 1,000 to 5,000 feet on the plateaux. From these areas pour moving masses of continental ice, which, propelled by vast pressures in the interior, move down the valleys and passes of the encircling mountains in the shape of glaciers and ice falls of a size and grandeur found nowhere else in the world.

We selected the Bay of Whales as the best place to base because (1) it seemed to offer the likeliest circumstances for flying and (2) because it was surrounded by unknown areas. Here lay hundreds of thousands of square miles of territory utterly unknown to geography, a vacuum abhorrent to scientist and cartographer alike. What lay between the Pole and the Weddell Sea, no one could say. These avenues for pure science must benefit. And the advantage lay with us in that we possessed three of the most efficient instruments given to the explorer; radio, the airplane, with its wonderful speed and independence of surface obstructions that vex the foot-traveler, and the aerial mapping camera, which sees everything and forgets nothing.

We had reason to hope we might accomplish much. But as the *Larsen* forged south on a peaceful ocean, it was not difficult sometimes to imagine a very different ending. So many things might go wrong. So many important things that perhaps I had overlooked.

Chapter V

~~~~~~

LITTLE AMERICA IS BORN

THE *Larsen* docked at Wellington, November 5th; and before long my own two ships appeared, both brine-scarred from the long Pacific crossing. Though the meetings brought all units of the expedition together for the first time in months, precious little sentiment was accorded the incoming crews. Time was far too valuable. The *City* went into dry dock to have her hull scraped clean of the parasitical growths that a slow ship always accumulates on a protracted voyage. As soon as she was liberated, her crew joined the crew of the *Bolling* in the task of restowing cargo and taking aboard still more supplies and gear which had been dispatched to this rendezvous.

Mindful of Captain Nilsen's intention to take the *Larsen* into the pack at the first favorable opportunity, we labored night and day to be off to the rendezvous he had promised to keep if we did our part. It was important that we should keep this date in order to take advantage of the tow through the pack ice which he, in his much more powerful ship, had promised. Our own radiomen held regular schedules with the *S. S. Larsen,* and I was informed by Captain Nilsen that the pack was unusually heavy, too heavy in all events for him to attempt an early transit. He also reported good whaling north of the pack, and we prayed it would continue so. There was no telling, however, how long the pack would hold; from hour to hour my mind played with the thought: Perhaps she had already started through. So we strove, as it were, with one eye on the bulletin board, knowing that if we were tardy, we would lose the *Larsen* and, perhaps, our only chance of getting through the pack.

At last the hold was full: there was room for not another box below; so we began to load the decks. The crated fuselage of the Fairchild airplane was swung aboard and lashed in place amidships, between the main and foremasts. Food boxes and gasoline drums were ranged about it until the waist of the ship became so deep with things that, before the mainsail could be set, it must first be reefed. Seventy-five tons of coal were stowed forward. Then the dogs, in their clumsy kennels, were hoisted to the poop deck, and their crates ranged in rows; when the space was filled, the remaining dogs found haven on the top of my cabin and the airplane crate. Here they would be out of reach of water, which they cannot abide; and the yelps, the growls, and squalling with which they announced this change of residence were wonderful to hear.

My diary carried the following entry:

En route to Bay of Whales, December 2, 1928.

I think we may breathe more easily now. The last piece of loose cargo has been securely lashed, and it will take a pretty strong sea to do us much damage. The barest hint of a swell is running, otherwise sea and sky are all we could ask for. With all sails set and under steam, we are making about eight knots under the *Bolling's* tow. If we can keep this up, we ought to reach the northern edge of the pack within seven or eight days.

I have just made a trip of survey about the ship. There are fifty-four men aboard, making eighty-three men on the expedition all told. From the amount of congestion, one might imagine there were ten times that number. Below decks, everything is in great confusion. Every bunk is piled high with gear, which has overflowed to the deck. There is scarcely a place where one can set foot. Supplies of all descriptions so fill the deck that to get from fore to aft it is either necessary to do a perilous balancing act on the rail or else risk one's neck in an alpine assault over peaks and precipices of dog crates and food boxes....

Slowly we accustomed ourselves to the routine; and, as the congestion below was gradually relieved by the sorting out of gear, the ship became more habitable. There was still a chill in the air, but Wednesday, the 5th, brought continuing gentle winds and a smoking blue sky. With a few exceptions, all hands were in fine spirits. Among these exceptions were seasick seamen, of whom we had an abnormal casualty list. Another was Igloo, who, to my astonishment, developed a real inferiority complex. Igloo was (until his death a few years ago) the companion of my ventures, a fox terrier of doubtful pedigree but unquestioned integrity. Neither modesty nor humility, I regret to say, was in his attitude, and until this trip I fancied neither man nor beast could discompose him. He met his superiors, however, in the Eskimo dogs, and in admitting to himself their superiority, his spirit underwent an extraordinary change. He hardly dared venture out on deck alone. His mere appearance brought from the beasts a fearful medley of challenges and imprecations; they hurled themselves at the doors of their crates, and those chained on the deck dashed out at him with fangs bared and a tremendous rattling of chains as he streaked past. Nights, when they began their melancholy singing, which can unseat the composure of an imaginative man, he shivered behind a box in my cabin. Not until the last sound had faded away, as mysteriously as it began, dared he come forth again, and then only in the lee of a friendly human figure. Poor Igloo, I did not blame him. Those huge creatures would assassinate him on the spot, as he was shrewd enough to realize. It was he, indeed, who found adventure on the way south.

Monday, December 10th, a confused grayness in the sky indicated the pack ice was not far off. Soon the lookout reported it dead ahead, and not long afterwards it could be seen from the deck, a low-rafted rampart stretching east and west as far as the eye could see. Reluctant to force the *Bolling* into it, we sought a way around it and saw, to the eastward, a lane of fairly open water. Eight o'clock that night we were only about forty miles from the *Larsen*, but never had she seemed so far away. The pack ranged all about us, snow flurries from the west struck us continuously, and in the bad visibility we were repeatedly menaced by icebergs, weighing hundreds of thousands of tons, that challenged our path.

All that night and the morning of the next day (it was still December 10—having crossed the 180th meridian, we lost a day) we dodged shifting pack ice and bergs, working to the east in search of open water. Weather continued thick and snowy, with poor visibility.

The compasses, because of our proximity to the magnetic pole, now went completely "haywire." There was one hundred degrees difference between the standard compass and the steering compass. Because of thick weather neither our ships nor the *Larsen* knew our exact position. We were heading for a ship of unknown position with our own position doubtful and compasses confused.

In this situation our radio compasses proved invaluable. By means of a series of bearings we headed the ship in the direction of the wireless waves coming from the *Larsen* and thus bore steadily toward her. It was rather a problem, however, trying to keep on the elusive wave and dodge moving masses of ice at the same time.

Once we were caught between the main pack and an enormous field of floating ice, with floes half a mile long, distorted by pressure—a rather fearsome sight, but with a bit of jockeying we avoided dangerous ice. Sverre Strom and Johanssen, Norwegian ice pilots who had come all the way from Norway in the *City*, spent hours in the rigging conning the ship. We were greatly relieved when Strom called down from the lookout's barrel on the masthead that they had sighted the *Larsen* on the other side of an ice field. Captain Melville and I studied the situation, and decided that, by making easting, we could get into the sheltered bay of ice in which she lay. Here was a perfect ice-locked harbor in the middle of the pack, with upended ice offering a splendid lee. The ice pilots guided us safely around, and we stopped our engines a short distance from the whaler. For the moment, at least, our larger problems were solved, and you may be sure we were in a happy state of mind.

The *Bolling*, after transferring to the *City* all of the coal she could spare, cast off and made for Dunedin. There was no use risking her presence in the dangerous ice. Besides, she must make haste if she were to accomplish two more trips that season. We saw the last of her about noon, her smoke a gray plume in the northern horizon.

Noon, Saturday, December 15, 1928,
En route to Bay of Whales.

We have been in the pack since the midnight watch. It is a relief to be under way again. The *Larsen* has us in tow on a $3\frac{1}{2}$-inch single wire cable, and we slide along behind like a cockleshell in a narrow lane of shattered ice. It is tricky work keeping a strain on the line. A slight deviation to right or left might bring us up hard against a heavy floe, in which case something would have to give. The *City*, with her displacement of 500 tons, is just a chip compared to the *Larsen*, with her 8,000 horsepower and 17,000 tons, and, as we follow behind her, we have the impression of being drawn by an irresistible force. The *Larsen* goes at the job shrewdly. She eases up to a floe, pressing her bow gently against the ice, and then surges forward at full speed. She thus avoids a direct smash, and, instead of penetrating at a blow, she forces her way persuasively through. The pack has a tendency to surge back after the passage of the cleaving hull of the *Larsen*, and we have the constant feeling that it may come between us altogether. Behind us, the passage has closed down into a slim ribbon of black water, the edges of which now lip so closely together it is difficult to believe we got through it.

Monday, December 17, 1928.

We sighted our first penguins today. First, a lone Emperor penguin, nearly four feet tall. In attitude and action, he more than lived up to his reputation as the aristocrat among his kind. This most primitive of birds, which alone of all animals survived the glaciation of the once tropical or semi-tropical Antarctic, was standing erect, when we caught sight of him, and his attitude plainly implied a lordly proprietorship over the wastes he surveyed. His resemblance to a man in formal dress was so close as to be positively embarrassing. To see him standing so, dignified, unafraid—did I not also detect scorn?—gave one the feeling that one should address him in carefully chosen speech. Alas, he paid little attention to us. A scant bow, beak touching the breast, not at all the ceremonial bow for which he is distinguished, then off he went.

Presently we came across a batch of the smaller and more gregarious Adélies, and there was great hilarity aboard for a while. These comical creatures came to us unafraid, with friendly waves of the flippers, tobogganing with great speed on their bellies across the ice floes. As I write, three or four of them are following along behind me, swimming like fish through the water, diving under loose floes, and coming up with uncanny accuracy on the other side. Now and then they scramble on a floe and by prodigious use of their flippers race across it as fast as a man can walk briskly.

Tuesday, December 18, 1928.

A terrific tussle in the ice today. Captain Nilsen radioed us this morning that unless we do better—that is, unless we keep the line taut—he will have to cast us loose. Apparently he fears we shall either collide with him or else the line will foul his propeller. I can scarcely blame him, but I assured him, as forcefully as I could, that we shall continue to do our best. To lose the tow at this stage of the journey would be a real setback. Save for the lane behind us, we are shut in by a solid wall of ice. It would take us weeks to get out under our own power. The ice is hummocky, and is very much eroded—from the rigging it appears like the surface of the moon when viewed through a telescope.

We have been pounding all day. Down below, in the fo'c's'le, it is like standing in a chamber the walls of which are being pounded with giant hammers. There would come an impact, the deck would tilt alarmingly, then the ship would sag with groaning timbers and the shriek of cracking ice would sound outside. A good thing for us thirty-four inches of tough planking stand between.

Try as we may, we cannot avoid the thick ice cakes which close in behind the *Larsen*. When she makes a turn, the towline drags us into sharp ice corners. We go by fits and starts. It is wonderful to see the *Larsen* in action, but even she has had to draw upon her immense reserve of power to keep underway. Sometimes it is a matter of forcing a few floes apart. She knifes them at a thrust.

Sometimes she thus gains, at a single stroke, a mile or two of clear water. More often it is a matter of a few yards, when a stubborn floe threatens to resist every charge.

To add to our troubles it has been snowing hard.

The one solace our position offered was comparative immunity to storm: the pack effectively dampened the sea, despite the snow squalls that beset us, and the swell was the longest I had ever witnessed. We ceaselessly scanned the southern sky, looking for open water, but only the eternal high blink of ice, ice everywhere. But at last a change came. On the morning of Sunday, the 23rd, there was the merest suggestion of increasing stir in the ice, and from a distance came the muted sounds of some disturbance. A black line, that grew larger as we watched, spread across the southern sky. Open water!

Then, to the south, we descried a vast battlement of flat-topped bergs, stretching from east to west, with thin streaks of open water showing in between. It was the southern edge of the pack, and the gateway to the Ross Sea. We hurried on, making better time, as the floes became more scattered and the ice, a mushy, coagulated mass hardly more resistant than soup. At eleven o'clock we had the swell of the Ross Sea under foot, and with a blue sky over head and the tow line taut as a bow string, we pressed due south.

The *Larsen* towed up until two o'clock, when the appearance of whales compelled Captain Nilsen to turn to a more lucrative occupation. We bade good-by to this excellent friend; then with all sails set and under steam we drove south for whatever fate held in store for us. A last glance backward showed the *Larsen* in the shadow of the ice, and a chaser spurting madly, with white showing under her bow, after a plunging whale.

On our second Christmas Day (we had two because we recrossed the 180th Meridian) an imperceptible brightening in the southern sky—"barrier blink"—suggested the proximity of the Barrier. As the second was the official Christmas Day, I sacrificed a ton or two of coal for sentimental reasons, to speed up engine revolutions, hoping thereby to make the Barrier before the end of the day. I felt that a glimpse of it would be an exciting gift to the men. The Ross Sea was smooth as a mill pond, and the air so fresh and pure that breathing was a delight. Strom's voice from the crow's nest—"Barrier on the starboard bow"—fell with the abrupt intensity that long-awaited news always assumes. There was a clatter of dishes hastily dropped or pushed aside, the race of footsteps up the companionway and a wild crowding of men on the fo'c's'le head and in the rigging. The thing we had come so far to see was before our eyes, a far-flung reach of lifted ice, stretching east and west as far as the eye could see. In the distance it appeared low and flat, not yet impressive, but there it was, the Barrier.

We reached the Barrier at Long. 177° 25′ W., came alongside and cruised all night and part of the next day almost in its shadow. Caution stifled our curiosity, and we rarely ventured nearer than a mile from the base. The scarred and jagged wall commanded respect; one had the fear that an overhanging cliff might let go with scant warning. For here were the breeding grounds of the icebergs, and deep wounds in the Barrier walls told of the labor that brought forth the bergs that prowled the Ross Sea. Near the water's edge the front was honeycombed with caves of bewildering shapes and sizes, which, when the sun struck them at just the right angle, blazed with a rich blue coloration. We took soundings every hour, and they showed an average of 250 to 300 fathoms of water.

As we cruised along its lee, the Barrier constantly changed its outline. It is by no means of the formidable uniformity most people believe it to be. Its height varied from 70 to 125 feet, small inlets and fractures marked its profile, and scarred cliffs reflected the sun like great reflectors. The instability of the Barrier was forcibly impressed upon us. Occasionally there came from the distance a boom as of remote thunder—the sound of ice cliffs crumbling; and once, as I watched, the face of the Barrier miles away tore loose and fell in a showery cataract of ice. The sea, when we drew near, was littered with debris, in which several minor icebergs floated proudly in the newness of birth.

During the morning watch, December 28th, we sighted the western gateway to the Bay of Whales, and stood off the entrance some time later. West and east the northern portals of the Bay, which we knew were about twenty miles apart, were shrouded in a drifting haze; so we could see no more than a few miles in either direction. I strained with all my might to make out something in the mist shadows ahead; hoping against hope for clear water, then hearing the slap of waves against ice.

The Bay still held in its bosom a solid wall of ice that the impact of half a dozen vessels of the *City's* power could not bend aside. It was a disappointing finding. We changed course sharply, veering to the right, but progress in this direction brought no improvement. When wind brushed the haze aside, we saw that the bay ice, which in places was so heavily crossed and ridged by pressure as to appear impassable, stretched solidly from West Cape to the eastern wall of the Barrier. At least eight miles of it lay between us and the place where we hoped to establish our base. There was no doubting the fact the ice was far north of the point at which Amundsen had found it.

We moored to the edge of the bay ice with ice anchors, which were hammered into the ice some distance from the ship, and hastily made ready for a trip of inquiry. Our great need at the moment was to find a suitable place for a base: worry over getting supplies to it could come next. By seven o'clock we were ready to start. Two dog teams were ready, Walden's and Vaughan's. On one of them Petersen had packed a portable radio set, and with him, Balchen and Braathen, our ski experts, I started across the ice, striking for the eastern wall of the Barrier, where it sloped to within thirty feet of sea level.

Midnight, Dec. 30, 1928, Camp on the Bay Ice.

It is as quiet here as in a tomb. Nothing stirs. The silence is so deep one could almost reach out and take hold of it.

A moment ago I stepped outside the tent and was impressed anew with the deceiving effect of the Antarctic on the eye. Try as I could, screwing the eyes, I could not make out the distance of things from us, nor their shape. Skiing, it was the same. We glided smoothly over a surface and then all of a sudden came a cropper on a slight slope we failed to note. We sighted a mountain of snow, miles off, and it turned out to be a haycock twenty yards away. We strove to reach a pressure ridge close aboard and found it still miles away. Just as I wrote the last sentence there came a sharp cracking noise directly under us and a rumble from not far away. Pressure is working in the ice and no doubt creating wide cracks in the Barrier.

Jan. 1, 1929.

Having failed yesterday to find a suitable location for a base to the southward, this morning Bernt and I returned to the inlet we had followed down from the Barrier, and found that the slope at its head was a very gradual ascent to the Barrier. Visibility had slightly improved, and we found ourselves in a kind of a basin. We recognized instantly that here was an excellent place for our base and named it Little America. It is protected by a high ridge from the winds in all directions but west, and accessible from the point of view of loading operations. We have named the inlet Ver-sur-Mer Bay after the village that was so hospitable to us when we landed in France at the end of our trans-Atlantic flight.

There was much excitement aboard ship when we broke the news we had found a site for the base, and instantly preparations were begun to unload. The *City* was edged slightly to the east, to bring her nearer the Barrier and reduce the length of the trail by a few yards. Planks were run from the deck to the bay ice, and down this a stream of boxes, gasoline drums, crates and other articles commenced to pour in noisy confusion. There was a great to-do as the dog men got their teams ready, for the dogs seemed to realize their vacation was over and lively work was at hand. They rolled in the snow, dashed about in insane circles; and a number of them, at some fancied wrong, sprang at one another's throats. There was serious work with the handle end of the whips before peace could be restored. But in time Walden, the Three Musketeers, and Jack Bursey had five teams in harness, eager to go, and before lunch they started for Little America, sledges heaped high with supplies. An excellent way to start the New Year. They made a pretty sight snaking across the bay. The dogs' tails waved like plumes, and the drivers hurried behind, cracking their long whips and chattering incessantly in the mad monologue that passes as language between driver and dogs. We kept them in sight until they moved up the low slope on the Barrier, and then lost them behind a ridge. Some time later Gould, whom I had made second in command, radioed the ship that he had found the site, that several tents were up and that Little America, the most southern American community, was formally colonized.

We drove, now, as if our lives depended upon it.

Sunday, January 6, 1929, Bay of Whales.

Worked like devils today—and a miserable four tons ashore to show for our efforts. We must do better. With the time at our disposal before the *Bolling* arrives, six tons per day is the minimum we can allow for. Ten would be more to my liking. But how to do better is the question.

A big lead opened up in the ice about four o'clock this afternoon, not far from the ship, forcing us to move our berth a quarter of a mile to the west, which means a longer journey for the teams. We tried breaking the ice this afternoon in an attempt to reduce the distance to the base—backed the *City* and charged it, full speed ahead. Gave it a number of fearful wallops, but with no success. The force of each charge carried the *City* well up on the ice, where she poised a moment, every yard clacking and loose things pounding in the ship, and then fell back, her screw protesting and churning the water.

We had to give that up. Using too much coal. The best we did was to chip off a few slivers of ice.

Now we pray for a storm; whereas a few days ago we begged to be delivered from one. A walloping storm from the north might break up the bay ice, and give us a chance to tie the ship up alongside the Barrier.

We have had a really severe epidemic of influenza; about forty percent of the men are suffering. Doc Coman believes the germ was spread by the dogs.

Affairs were humming at the base. Two houses were up, a third was started, and about the place was a suggestion of security and coziness. Captain McKinley had the job well in hand. He is one of the most delightful as well as efficient men I have ever known. I decided to make him third in command and executive officer of the expedition. Boxes of supplies were

neatly assembled in orderly piles, and the exact whereabouts
of every item was recorded. Haste had not been allowed to
destroy efficiency. The dog teams were then averaging two
round trips per day, carrying from 700 pounds to 1,000
pounds per load. Only a person who knows dogs can appreciate
what that means. Knud Rasmussen once said, "I bless the fate
which allowed me to be born in an age when the Arctic dog
sledge was not yet out of date." And after seeing them race into
Little America, team after team, while the drivers fought top-
heavy loads which threatened constantly to tip over into the
snow, I could exclaim with him. Had it not been for the dogs,
our attempts to conquer the Antarctic by air must have ended
in failure. On January 17th, Walden's single team of thirteen
dogs moved 3,500 pounds of supplies from ship to base, a
distance of 16 miles each trip, in 2 journeys. Walden's team
was the backbone of our transport. Seeing him rush his heavy
loads along the trail, outstripping the younger men, it was
difficult to believe that he was an old man. He was 58 years old,
but he had the determination and strength of youth.

During the next few days, in spite of snow squalls, we drove
at top speed. But I never ceased looking for a way of short-
cutting that long haul from the ship to Little America. Sunday night, I decided to make a closer inspection of the Barrier.
The bay ice, however, was still much too thick to risk the *City*
in; so we reconnoitered in a small motor boat. With me came
Owen, Strom, Paul Siple, the Boy Scout, and John Sutton.

It was still snowing a bit, and the atmosphere was quite
thick. With the outboard motor arousing a medley of echoes
in the cliffs, we cruised along the edge of the bay ice, making
to the east. We followed a lead for about a mile until we were
stopped by the wall of thick bay ice. Half a mile away the
Barrier sloped almost to the level of the bay ice. Here it could
be approached by an incline formed by drifted snow, which
had packed hard and rose in a gentle slope. If we could get
the *Bolling* in that far, here would be an excellent place to

discharge cargo. But how to get her in? A cursory examination showed that the ice which lay between was much too hard and firmly set to be broken by the charge of either ship. We must wait until nature saw fit to move it.

Just then the motor, which had been kicking up wickedly, gave a final splutter and died. About the time we got it fixed, some one saw a whale sound about a quarter of a mile ahead. I turned in time to see half a dozen waterspouts rise in grayish vapor above the water; then a long, white and ebony body lunged out of the water and sank in a curving movement. Then another, and another, and still another, until I had counted about ten.

There was no mistaking the ominous, black, triangular fins, the ugly heads and the sickly yellow patches under the jaws. These were Killer whales. I do not consider myself a particularly imaginative man, nor am I impressed as a rule by the legends that accumulate about the habits of certain animals. Yet, I confess candidly that the sudden appearance of these ill-reputed creatures had a disturbing effect; and we became most sensitively aware of the flimsy character of our boat.

I was at the tiller at the time, and, deciding that discretion was the better part of valor, edged the boat toward the ice, looking for a shelf of ice where we might land. Meanwhile I kept one eye on the approaching whales, whose slow deliberate movements fascinated one as a serpent is said to fascinate its victim. Always they drew nearer, with a showing of glistening, oily backs. The measured progress was intimidating; but I was reassured when I saw that if they remained on their course they would pass astern; but, when fairly close aboard they rapidly changed course and headed directly for the motor boat.

The nearest ice was 300 yards away, and very ragged. At that moment, however, any kind of ice looked good. It was not necessary to order Sutton to open the engine at full speed. We raced for the ice, and the Killers, which seemed to be traveling twice as fast as the boat, gained rapidly. The thought was in my mind that one of them, coming up after a long dive, might capsize us. Each porpoising lunge brought them nearer, and the short dash to the edge of the bay ice took a long time. The hull scraped over an undershot tongue of ice and banged violently against the edge. I am sure that no boat was ever so quickly abandoned as this was. As we faced around the Killers came up not more than 15 feet from where we stood. Another dive would have brought them up with us. We had drawn our revolvers—a foolish gesture, I concluded later, for a battery of 75's would not have stopped them if they had meant business. They dived underneath the bay ice and we did not see them again. We waited quite a while after they disappeared before we put out again, and the journey to the ship was completed without incident. Serious as it was at the moment, the episode presently yielded its lighter side, and by supper time was subject for many a good laugh. It was Siple's unfortunate fate to have been appointed assistant biologist a few days before, with the duty of studying animal life in the bay, and his intimate introduction to his subject was the cause of much jesting.

Bay of Whales, Saturday, January 26, 1929.

It has been a real experience, lying here alongside the bay ice week after week, with the opportunity of watching the changes and caprices of this frozen world. It is not the rigid and immobile world that we imagined. All is movement and change. Day after day, hour after hour, the contours of the Barrier and bay ice change as fragments break off and float northward. The wind, the sea, the sky, and the visibility change with bewildering swiftness; the penguins and the seals are here in large numbers one moment and gone the next. I fancy that in Little America, after the sun has gone and the winter night brings cold and darkness, it will be the lack of change that will be conspicuous.

But what take my imagination are the regiments of ice fields and icebergs that drift past the mouth of the Bay of Whales. They come from the mysterious unknown area to the eastward. Sometimes these regiments pause at the mouth of the Barrier until a northerly wind starts the invincible mass in the direction of the *City*. We watch it carefully, for if it should catch and grind us between it and the bay ice, the *City* might be crushed to a pulp. Several times we have had to fight our way through these moving fields to the open sea beyond.

Chapter VI

~~~~~~

ESCAPE FROM THE
ROCKEFELLER MOUNTAINS

EASTWARD of Little America lay a first-rate geographical problem; and all the time that we were bending our backs to the monotony of unloading the ships and establishing a base, my mind was on it. Sunday afternoon, January 27th, my chance finally came. There was a lull in the unloading; and I seized it. The sky was a cloudless, perfect blue, and the temperature a few degrees below freezing. Exactly the kind of a day we had wished for. Haines looked up from his charts and with one of his rare smiles said, "We ought to have good weather here for at least twelve hours."

A run of thirty seconds lifted us clear of the snow, and a few minutes later Balchen, June and I were gazing down upon untrodden areas. To the left we had the curving coastline of the Barrier trending north of east: on the right we had the inner spaces of the Barrier rolling unbrokenly to the horizon. Visibility was about 40 miles. I laid my course directly for Scott's Nunataks, which were nearly 200 miles away.

Just before the Bay of Whales disappeared in the lengthening perspective, I glanced back, hoping to make out the masts of the *Bolling* against the horizon. But nothing moved on the blue waters of the Ross Sea, which glittered like a vast tray of diamonds tilted in the sun, except a column of icebergs, deployed like a regiment on the march.

At our altitude a hustling tail wind gave us a splendid boost. We averaged well over 120 miles per hour at cruising revolutions.

About an hour after the start of the flight we passed over

a beautiful bay, the mouth of which was several miles wide. From our great height it was no more than an exquisitely carved indentation in the Barrier. But actually it was a stern and rugged thing, with 150-foot ice cliffs, sheer and perfect as if cut out with a knife. Flying does deprive an observer of much of the awe that seizes the surface traveler. I could not help feeling, as we flew over this bay, that had we come upon it suddenly from the deck of the *City*, we must have marveled at its dimensions. But the vastly lengthened perspective that the airplane provides substitutes a different measurement. With so much to see, the things on the earth tend to diminish to their true cosmic proportions; and that which lifts itself above the rest and impresses must, of necessity, be truly striking.

Not long after passing the bay, I saw many miles to the right a few black peaks protruding from the snow, and beyond them a single peak which invited speculation. On consulting the charts used on this flight, I find that I wrote in the corner of one of them: "Small peak to the right—land may show— looks like it." I decided to investigate this peak later on.

Presently a snow peak lifted its white head dead ahead—an inconspicuous mound dancing slightly over the head of one of the cylinders. A patch of bare rock showed on the northern side. It was Scott's Nunataks. After Scott first saw it in 1902, three men, Lieutenant Prestrud, Johansen and Stebberud of Amundsen's Expedition, had fought their way to this lonely spur, in December, 1911. It gave one an odd sensation to rush at a rate of two miles per minute toward the spot which he and his companions had struggled weeks to gain, to be over it and gone in a very few minutes; whereas they had lain, shivering and wet, in a tent, beset by blizzards, while Prestrud, to pass the time, conjugated Russian verbs.

From a point a little beyond the Nunataks, we flew over land never before seen: and at the given speed of the plane, we were exploring snow-covered land to the right at the rate of 4,000 square miles per hour.

To the south of the Nunataks a chain of rather small mountains, trending to the southeast, lifted snow-capped peaks from the surface. It is doubtful whether any of them exceeded 1,500 feet in height. I was surprised to observe that several of them showed bare rock on the northern slopes.

Here the Ross Sea was solidly frozen over for miles to the north, and in the pancake smoothness we noted a number of odd-looking ice islands, the rounded domes of which were mostly split and broken, like tarts which had been toyed with. These domes, however, stood at least 100 feet above the level of sea ice, and their bottoms must have been deeply grounded. We also made out a lone glacier discharging its stream of pale blue ice into the sea, and around it, oddly enough in this hard frozen waste, lay a pool of open water. There were many indications that the sea ice here rarely breaks up, suggestive of the possibility of land to the northward which held it anchored in this place.

I had envisioned this as a probability, and peered ahead over Balchen's shoulder. In the gray opacity where ice met sky a dark, provocative ribbon held my eyes. Land, I was sure, lay there and beyond to the northeast. But before I could exclaim, Balchen lifted his hand from the wheel and pointed a gloved finger to the east. The whole sector of the horizon had disappeared in a thickish haze. We were catching up with the storm that had passed over Little America the day before.

Further inquiry was halted by an onrush of snow squalls. Actually, our rush of speed carried us into them; but the lack of things rapidly sliding past which we associate with motion gives the aerial traveler rather the impression of things advancing upon him. We saw long fingers of gray shadows stretch and feather along the snow; here and there a darker shadow blotted out the surface, and the restless, rapid rotations identified it as a "whirlie." The atmosphere about us thickened, the horizon was swallowed up in a gray indefiniteness, and the impression we had at the moment was like nothing so much as flying in a bowl of milk. How very easy, I thought, for a careless or intimidated pilot to fly his plane straight down into the snow. There was no point on which to pin the nose of the plane for steady, level flight. Only a milky, trembling nothingness.

June handed me a slip of paper. It was a message from the operator at Little America. "*Bolling* sighted." Receiving this encouraging news at this time was one of the most exciting incidents of the flight. Visibility to the south seemed to be good; so I headed the plane in the direction of the small peaks I had seen to the right on our way east.

In a little while, far ahead, but perfectly distinct, we saw a splendid mountain peak, with the slate gray of bare rock showing. Then, as we advanced, a second peak, then a third, and more lifted their summits above the southern horizon until we had counted fourteen.

This was our first important discovery. It was good to know that we were putting something on the map of the world that would remain there as long as civilization lasts.

I could not help thinking, as we approached them, what an immense advantage the airplane gives the modern explorer. Prestrud's sledges passed within a few miles of this range; yet in the restricted visibility had failed to see them.

We approached the mountains at an altitude of 4,000 feet. Here was a group of highly individualistic mountains, solitary and stern, many of them with patches of gray rock showing on their northern profiles, their spurs and crags clothed in snow. They lay in the shape of a crescent, and the northern-most peak we judged to be approximately 30 miles from Scott's Nunataks, in a west by south direction. We were impressed by the surprisingly large amount of bare rock exposed, in contrast with the Nunataks and the Alexandra Mountains. As we drew nearer, the gray overtone of the rock was modified, and some of it showed an interesting brown and black coloration.

Anticipating, as I was, the making of a preliminary aerial reconnaissance of the range, I was quite disappointed when Balchen handed me a note saying that fuel was running low, and suggesting we return to the base. We could not afford to extend our journey; so we pointed the nose of the plane for Little America, and raced home.

For a long time the peaks of this range danced across my vision, gradually growing smaller while the bare rock diminished to mere pin points, and I found myself wondering what we should name it. The names of several of the men who had befriended the expedition came to my mind; and foremost among these was John D. Rockefeller, Jr. And it occurred to me that his true inner life is as little known as these peaks which we had just seen. His character is in keeping with that of these austere mountain masses. He stands, steady as a rock, in the chaos of life, and the great power he controls is directed wisely and unselfishly for the betterment of the world.

I could do no better than to name this range after him— Rockefeller Mountains.

We drew within sight of Little America about eight o'clock, and from our lofty platform saw the two vessels, tiny and still, moored to the bay ice. I noted with pleasure that even during our short absence more ice had gone out of the Bay.

The scene, as we spiraled down, was one of wondrous beauty. An unbroken stillness, save for the hum of the propeller. The Barrier cliffs and slopes were rich with exquisite colors, which changed and shifted as we watched. The lofty arch of sky was a clear blue, with friezes of stationary cloudlets, some rose, some mauve. A few icebergs glittered on a sea washed with gold.

Now we hustled. Nature, after begrudging us our needs so long, relented a trifle, and during the flight sped out the ice between the ships and the low Barrier until only a few feet of ice remained. Our hours of ramming with the *City* had not been wasted. Captain Brown brought the *Bolling* into action, and with the aid of her sharp steel prow and superior horsepower she attacked the remaining ice and sheared off 150 yards of it. This gave us a fine pier on an ice foot about fifty feet from the Barrier. Directly opposite, the Barrier descended in an easy slope, and the snow was firm enough, and the incline sufficiently easy, to justify hauling stores up to the Barrier by means of block and tackle operated by the *Bolling's* winch. To the right and left the Barrier rose steeply to heights of sixty feet or more. This place was exactly suited to our needs. We were then only five miles by trail from Little America. Unloading operations were resumed at once.

Wednesday, January 30, 1929.

It happened after all. Shortly after supper, I was conferring with McGuinness in my cabin. Suddenly I felt a jar, followed by a succession of terrific shocks and then a tremendous explosion. The *City* heeled sharply to port—so sharply I thought she must capsize. As I flung the cabin door open I saw the *Bolling* heeling in the opposite direction to starboard. I was sure, for a moment, she was capsizing, for I could see her keel and masses of ice were still dropping on her decks from the place in the Barrier where a berg had "calved."

But even as I watched, the *Bolling* reached the peak of the heeling movement, standing almost on her beam ends, and then swung back. At the critical moment the lines from the *City* maintained the balance and offset the overbalance of the masses of ice and snow on her decks.

Huge blocks of the Barrier floated in the water, which was still boiling from their impact, rivulets of ice were still streaming down the face of the cliffs, and falling, with a hissing noise, into the sea. The break, then, had come very near the point where we had landed the Ford fuselage a few hours before.

Only fragments of the iceberg, I noted, had fallen directly upon the *Bolling's* deck, but they weighed tons and gave her a considerable list. She had escaped the main stream of the avalanche by a few feet. Thousands of tons had fallen, enough to obliterate her. An iceberg had been born almost on her deck.

High up on the Barrier was a man clinging to a thread of rope, his feet dangling helplessly in empty space. I recognized him as Harrison. And in the water, clutching a small piece of floe, was another man, Benny Roth, who, I knew, could not swim. He had grabbed a piece of ice and was holding on to it for dear life, but it was round and slippery and he could not get a firm hold; it spun in his hands. I asked Roth if he could swim and he said no. It seemed impossible to me that he could continue to hold on to that spinning ice.

While men on the ships rowed after Roth, the shore party set out after Harrison, who was clinging to a slippery line with bare hands. Coman, with real coolness, dropped a looped rope to him, in which he could put his foot and so relieve the strain on his hands. Then Thawley, with a line tied to his ankles, crawled out on the overhang, reached down, got a firm hold on Harrison's wrist and lifted him, unhurt and unruffled, to the top. And by this time another party in a boat had overtaken Roth, who was being swept around the stern of the ship. They reached him none too soon.

The whole incident took no more than twenty minutes, but it seemed hours.

When the second party came aboard, I ordered the ships to tie up to each other, and we discharged the *Bolling* directly into the *City*. It was a very fortunate thing that the unloading was nearly accomplished when the break came. I would never again tempt fate by trying to unload the *Bolling* on the Barrier. We returned to the old berth alongside the bay ice.

Saturday, February 2nd, we finished unloading the last of the *Bolling's* supplies into the *City*, while the *City* discharged more slowly on the bay ice. The same day, the *Bolling* put out for New Zealand, with the U. S. Mail Flag flying from her mast, carrying the first mail from an American colony in Antarctica. She went with our most sincere but none too confident hopes of seeing her again, with the last of our supplies, before the end of the month.

Bitter days followed.

With twenty-seven dogs hauling, we finally succeeded in hauling the Ford's fuselage to Little America. That task brought great satisfaction; the polar plane was at least safely berthed at the base. Yet the wind and blizzards and downcharging floes gave us little peace. Repeatedly gales drove the ship from her insubstantial docks. And time was forever running

THE FOKKER ON A FROZEN LAKE AT ITS BASE IN THE ROCKEFELLER
MOUNTAINS

VICTIM OF THE WIND'S FURY
The Wreck of the Fokker

(Photograph by Captain McKinley)

COASTING DOWN THE GLACIER, WITH RUTH GADE ON THE RIGHT, ON THE
RETURN FROM THE POLE

against us. It was getting colder, too; the ship's rigging was never free of ice. North of us the *Bolling*, again southward bound, had run into such fierce seas and heavy pack that I finally ordered Captain Brown not to try to reach us with his second cargo; though we could make good use of what he had aboard, we nevertheless already had at Little America enough food and material for our needs; so there was no need of exposing the ship to greater hazards. And finally, when a drop in temperature to 19° below zero covered the Bay of Whales with a glaze of hard, green ice, I ordered Captain Melville to start north before he, too, ran the risk of being beset.

With her canvas fluttering before a puffy wind and her blocks creaking, the *City of New York* moved into a solid mass of sea smoke which swallowed her even as we looked. With her going the forty-two of us who made up the Ice Party were alone with our future. Radio would still keep us in contact with the outside world, but the last physical connection, the one means of retreat, had disappeared for upwards of a year. The most stolid man could not stand and watch a ship go out like that and not feel oppressed; but almost at the same instant a subtle exhilaration and joy took hold of you; and you found yourself saying, "That's that, and now for the job." For the solid evidence of all that we had already done lay before us, and that was reassuring enough.

The winter night was in reality close at hand. The phase of the midnight sun was over; each night, when it was clear, we noticed how the sun set a little earlier, rose a little later; blizzards seemed to buffet you a little harder and the dogs, feeling the cold, were slowing up. But before we finally called a halt to the first season's operations and holed up for the four months' winter night, we determined, against my better judgment, to undertake one last job: an investigation of the geology of the Rockefeller Mountains. Dr. Gould was extremely eager to visit the mountains. The weather was stormy and cold; the winter night, near; and I thought there was too much risk for

the gain involved. Geology was only one of the many branches
of science we were to serve. The mountain party felt that it
would be necessary to use the Fokker plane, which was of tremendous importance to the success of the scientific work the
following year. The third plane, the Fairchild, was too small
to use effectively for the spring exploration. However, if an
expedition leader agrees to a project, either willingly or un-
willingly, the entire responsibility for that project rests squarely
upon his shoulders. He is responsible, in fact, for anything
that happens anywhere on the expedition, no matter how
large that expedition is.

Gould, Balchen and June left March 7th with the intention
of remaining several days.

Monday, March 11, Little America.

Gould radioed that he wanted to return today. Conditions here
were favorable, but changed suddenly in the mountains. Before
they could start, a snow storm came up and they were forced to
postpone the start.

The weather is up to all kinds of peculiar tricks. Haines told
me that he had never seen such rapid changes in the wind's direction as preceded the last storm. The barometer during the storm
had the worst drop I have ever seen; Haines himself confessed
he had never seen it so low. The graph of it looks like several
steep hills.

As the days slipped by and the weather continued foul, our
concern for Dr. Gould and his companions in the Rockefeller
Mountains became real. When we had good weather at Little
America, they had storm. And on the few occasions when it
was clear at the mountains, we had blizzards. It began to appear that good conditions might never be had at both places
at the same time; and, with winter steadily approaching, this
probability verged on being a certainty.

There was no word from Gould on the 15th. Nor the 16th.
Nor the 17th. And on the 17th, which was a Saturday, I became genuinely alarmed. The absence of radio communication

was peculiarly confusing. June had two complete radio sets—one on the plane, and an emergency set. How both of them could be out of commission, unless the plane had crashed, was difficult to understand. But how they could have crashed was even more perplexing. It had been definitely agreed that the Fokker would not start until we radioed a favorable weather report, which we had not been able to do. It was impossible to believe, then, that a start had been made. But there, on the other hand, was the silence. How could it be explained?

Thursday, I began to prepare for a flight of investigation. The Fairchild was made ready. The sun shone sullenly through thickish clouds, and there was a chance the weather would improve. But it became worse instead. Friday and Saturday were unfit for flying. There was still no word from Gould.

In an early report, Gould had said they had landed at the base of Chips Gould Mountain, which would place them at the northernmost peak. But a subsequent message had indicated that they were at the foot of one of the southernmost peaks. As the latter position was most likely the true one, I decided to set our course for it, when and if we started.

The long winter night was dangerously near. The situation was precarious.

Meanwhile, the radio men continued to stand an unbroken watch. Every hour we repeated a message that the Fairchild would fly at the first break in the weather, on the theory that June's equipment might be able to pick up messages even if it could not send. But the ether yielded no news for us.

The long-awaited "break" came Monday, March 19th. A small hole opened up in the cloud bank to the east, and widened gradually. A patch of blue sky showed through. A 22-mile wind stirred up drift, but we could not expect everything.

We took Hanson along as radio engineer.

Just about 5 o'clock, we started down the snow runway. The bumping was wicked, and the shock of the skis' striking the sastrugi caused the whole plane to shiver. But we rose finally in a flurry of snow and headed straight for the mountains.

The hour was later than I had wanted: at this season it became quite dark at night from 10 o'clock on. But beggars can't be choosers: we took what Providence offered, and were thankful.

It was a bit chilly in the plane, 10° below zero, and we were bundled up in heavy clothing.

The sun was behind us, and I could see it occasionally, a dull red disc surrounded by orange streaks. I laid a straight compass course for the southern end of the Rockefellers. The horizon was a blurred grayness, which presently gave way to masses of low clouds. It was one of the worst "flying" skies I had ever seen. The clouds were miles away, but seemed very near, and merged without a shadow to show where the horizon met the snow. The instinctive response of a pilot would be to fly lower and lower, trying to get underneath these clouds. Smith, however, kept his head and flew a straight, steady compass course. The sun was too low and too indistinct, besides, for us to use the more dependable sun compass, and we had to rely on the magnetic compass, which was not particularly reliable.

The clouds soon closed in behind, and we lost the sun. Things became quite dim, a confused, dirty-gray nothingness, through which we raced at a speed of 100 miles per hour.

Shortly after 6 o'clock, we sighted a mountain dead ahead. The other peaks slowly lifted their heads, and in the murk they were no more than vague, gray mounds. We approached the first peak at an altitude of 2,000 feet.

It was now dim, but we could see sheets of drift weaving across the snow, which indicated a stiff wind. Smith stared down, and moved his hand around to show the whirling character of the drift. "Pretty tough to land in that," he shouted. I thought so, too, but said nothing.

There was the more dreadful possibility we should not be

able to see anything. A shattered plane and three men would not be conspicuous against those dark ridges.

We flew over the mountain, circled it and then approached it again. We searched out the slopes, the valleys and the peak, but saw nothing. Could it be that Gould's position was inaccurate? If we failed to find them here, then we faced the heartbreaking task of combing seventy miles of mountain peaks. A more hopeless task I could not imagine.

A second survey yielded no traces of the party. I was about to ask Smith to turn north to search the other peaks when suddenly he touched my arm and pointed to the south. I saw a column of smoke bending indistinctly on the wind, then the flashing of a light.

We swung toward the light, and started to spiral down. Soon we could make out a landing "T" marked out with flags. We were apparently descending into a large basin at the foot of the mountain. In the dimness one had the sensation of dropping powerlessly into a porcelain bowl. The field, even from our altitude, appeared to be excessively rough. The pedestal of a landing "T" ran straight through it. But it looked bad, very bad.

We came in with a thud, bouncing on a wretched surface, with Smith nursing his engine and solicitous for his skis—an excellent and daring landing.

As the plane came to a halt in a smother of snow, I jumped out. At first I saw no one, and my heart sank. Then a figure came racing toward the plane—that gait could belong only to a Navy man, June; then I saw a man with bristling red whiskers advancing in our direction. No other face on the planet supported such a growth. Balchen's, of course. But where was Gould? In a moment I saw him as well. Even if I were capable of doing it adequately, which I am not, I would hesitate to describe my emotions at finding those men safe and sound. It was the same sort of feeling I experienced when

I found on the trans-Atlantic flight that we had enough gasoline to reach the coast of Europe.

Smith kept the engine idling. With less than an hour and
one-half before darkness, we could not afford to waste much
time in conversation. Balchen and June were ordered to take
Hanson's place and mine in the Fairchild, and return with
Smith to the base. As there was not room for everyone, there
was the inevitable dispute over who would stay behind, a gratifying demonstration of generosity on the part of every man,
but I was fortunately able to enforce my decision.

We removed from the plane some food and a small sledge.
Then Smith gave the Fairchild the gun, and it whirled off.
Soon we lost sight of it in the gathering twilight.

March 19, Tuesday, Rockefeller Mountains.

It is snug here in the tent, and I am peaceful in mind for the first
time in many days. A few minutes ago we received word by radio
of the safe arrival of the Fairchild at Little America. If weather
permits, they will come out for us tomorrow.

I now have the story of this episode—part of it from Larry,
part of it from June and Balchen, in the hurried talk before they
left.

They reached here after two hours and ten minutes of flying.
They taxied up the slope, which leads up to a kind of terrace at
the foot of the mountain, secured the plane with ice anchors, and
made their camp.

March 8th, the next day, a stiff wind blew, and that, combined
with the cold, kept them from doing much work out of doors. On
the following day, they laid a base line about a mile from the
tent, and by triangulation Gould fixed the positions of the various
peaks in the neighborhood. That done, they made a reconnaissance
part way up the nearest mountain, and gathered rocks for geological research.

This, I judge, was about the end of good weather during their
stay.

Saturday, the 10th, brought snow and a stiff wind. Too bad
to do any work, so they stayed in their sleeping bags until 11
o'clock. The wind rose steadily, carrying away the tent guys
which were secured to the airplane skis: that brought them tumbling out of the tent.

They found the ship banging up and down in spite of the ice anchors. Frantically, they began to pile snow blocks, which they cut out with knives from a nearby drift, on the skis, to keep them down.

The wind died down, and they were able to finish the anchorage with some comfort. Then, without warning, the wind rose again, more fiercely than ever. The plane began to pound once more, and they were hard put to it to keep it from blowing away. The difficulty lay in the fact that the plane rested on firm ice, and it was hard to get a firm hold on it.

When they tried to anchor the left wing, the force of the wind all but battered down their combined efforts. Several times, according to Gould, strong gusts lifted all three of them clear of the ground, while they held on to the wing, and swept their bodies out almost parallel to the ground. It was numbing cold, and Gould said the driving snow hit the face with the bite of red-hot needles.

"We could lean on the wind when we shoveled," June told me, "and if we didn't hurry, it whipped the blocks of snow from the shovel. We were constantly bombarded with lumps of snow carried down from the mountains, and believe me, they hurt."

How long did this keep up? "Hours and hours," Gould said, "we lost track of time."

Toward midnight there was a lull, and they crept into their sleeping bags, to gain what little warmth was to be had. The wind rose again, and they returned to the battle, painfully cutting out lumps of snow and dumping them on the skis. They would creep out on their bellies, cut a block, and then, they would stand up and let the wind blow them back to the plane. Balchen worked like a madman, and his strength helped to stave off the final blow for hours.

The anchors held. Toward morning they crept back to the tent. They could do no more. The issue was in the laps of the gods. When they turned in, the wind was still on the make, and the din, Larry said, was awful.

"Never saw anything like it," June said. "When I got in the plane to keep the radio schedule, the needle on the air speed indicator touched 88 m.p.h., and though she only banged up and down on the snow, the ship was certainly going through all the motions of flying. I looked out and saw Gould hanging on to a rope attached to one of the wing tips. He was blown straight out, like a flag. The prop was turning over very fast, and the lines on the 'dead men' were so taut you could play a tune on them. Mind you, the wind then was only working up to bigger and better things. It blew so hard afterward that Gould refused to let me enter the plane, to keep the regular 10:30 o'clock schedule. We could hardly breathe."

The end came suddenly while they were in the tent. A rush of wind, fiercer by far than any before carried away all the lines. The plane burst free, rose into flight and flew backwards for half a mile, then crashed upon the ice, a complete wreck. Balchen, a man who never gives up, battled against the wind to reach it, and came back with the news they had verified with their own eyes—the Fokker would never fly again.

Gould believes the wind reached a velocity of 150 m.p.h. (in gusts) and June said, "When it stopped it was so quiet that it hurt."

The wind dropped off the following day, and they went out to the Fokker. June reassembled the emergency radio set, which was badly battered, and tried to raise the base. He could hear the base operators sending, but apparently could not reach them.

The worst blow fell when the crankshaft on the generator broke. They could still hear with the set, but all hope of getting word of their predicament to the base was ended. It was the most depressing thing in the world, according to Gould, to sit in the shattered fuselage, and hear Little America discussing their absence with operators in New York.

The next day, I walked out to the plane, and saw how badly smashed it was. I was surprised to find that, save for the tips, the wing was undamaged. The plane had apparently landed on the skis. The ski pedestals, however, were split open, one ski lay clear of the plane, and the struts were bent and torn. The tail section was broken, the fuselage was ripped open and the cabin exposed. It seemed as if a great bird had come to grief, and this was its pathetic and broken carcass.

About 5 o'clock in the morning of the 22nd, Hanson was informed by Little America that the Fairchild was on its way, and an hour and a half later we sighted it. Smith landed neatly.

"Hop in," Smith shouted, "Room for everyone. Next plane leaves in six months."

We reached Little America about an hour and fifteen minutes later, and so far as we were concerned, the incident of the

Rockefeller Mountains was over. Balchen made a short flight over the Ross Sea and reported it frozen over as far as the eye could see. The aviation season was over.

With the incident at the Rockefeller Mountains thus happily closed, we were willing to relinquish the whole Antarctic Continent to the oncoming winter night, except for the few yards we had laboriously converted to our own devices. Even the surface above Little America we were willing to give up, in favor of the protected warm catacombs we had hewn out underneath. As the sun went down for the last time, and the darkness washed in, and the aurora jerked its fantastic patterns across a vast sky, we burrowed deeper and deeper still. Both planes were dragged into deep holes and covered with tarpaulins; the last of the tunnels was roofed over; and down in the shacks, now that the worst of the outside jobs were finished, was a cheerful sound of talk and planning.

Four months of darkness may seem a long time, and I suppose it was for many men. But I know that it did not drag for me nor for a good many other men. Even when the blizzards were pounding the surface and the darkness was a cyclone of sound and drift, we were snug enough below; life went on steadily in the shacks and in the tunnels; and we never wanted for things to do. For the aviation personnel had to work out the complicated business of getting the plane to the South Pole and back, and the Geological party had quite as formidable a task in working up schedules and packing gear and rations for their long trek with dog teams to the foot of the Queen Maud Range.

Chapter *VII*

∽∽∽∽∽∽∽∽∽∽∽∽∽∽∽∽∽∽∽∽∽∽∽∽∽∽∽∽∽∽∽∽∽∽

SPRING PREPARATIONS

ALL during August, save when the sky was overcast, a steadily enlarging shimmer of gold and red burned and waned on the northern horizon. Spring was in the air—but not the kind of spring of which poets sing in more temperate climes. From the 16th to the 18th raged a severe blizzard, turning the outside world into chaos. When it ceased, the temperature began to fall steadily. On the 19th the Antarctic equivalent of the robin —or shall we say the ground-hog?—a timorous Weddell seal— poked a brown head out of the thin ice over a blow hole, took one breath of the frigid air, and hastily drew it in again. He drew back none too soon, for a man hungry for the taste of fresh meat pounced at him with a pole.

On the 20th the radiance in the north grew and splashed the Barrier with a gold and yellow effulgence. The return of the sun was nigh. A few of us stole a march on it by climbing the radio towers, thus gaining a preview of its long-anticipated return. The sun was a gorgeous sight from this precarious perch, half a hemisphere of warm splendor suspended beneath a strand of coral clouds. In the south a moon that was green cheese was set, wan, pale and ethereal, in a vaporous purple firmament.

We began to dig out now with a vengeance.

September raced past, for all the cold, on the wings of expectancy. We were eager, all of us, to be off on our various missions: the Supporting Party to its depots, the Geological Party to the mountains, the Polar Flight Group to the Pole.

90

Wednesday, Sept. 11.

The houses are as busy as factories. The southern parties are making final preparations for the trail. Everyone is at work at something—sewing parkas and socks, repairing harness, testing tents, relashing sledges.

The quietest place in camp is Braathen's House, and Owen, seeking quiet for his literary productions, has fled there for sanctuary.

More seals have been in the bay, big, fat fellows.

Temperature today was 68° below. Can spring be far behind?

Friday, Sept. 20.

We have had a wild time with the dogs. They are so overjoyed to be above ground once more that they have forgotten all manners and training, and run about the camp like lunatics.

It is simply impossible to get them into harness. After a patient hour's work to get his team in line, Crockett finally gave up an unruly pair and started off with six dogs. Instantly they dashed around in a mad circle, slamming the sledge around as if it weighed nothing at all, while Freddy yelled and cursed and tried to hold on to the careening sledge. In the midst of these revolutions, the dogs suddenly sighted the entrance to their tunnel, and with impish perversity raced right down, carrying sledge, Crockett and all. It was a frightful tangle.

Bursey and Vaughan had no better luck. Vaughan's big black leader, Dinty, from whom we had been led to expect great things, was as wild as a stallion, and sooner than it takes to tell it his sledge was upside down in the snow and everything a noisy confusion. Braathen's team made a racing swing about the camp, but came to grief when the dogs ran head-on into one of the guy wires supporting the radio towers. The impact cut the harnesses, and poor Braathen had to chase two of the dogs down into Ver-sur-Mer. It is a wonder they did not break their necks.

With the sun climbing in the sky affairs moved at a steadily increasing tempo. The surface parties got off first. In the middle of October the Supporting Party, with the mission of breaking trail for the Geological Party and laying down food depots for its return, struck south across the Barrier. And a fortnight or so later, the main party consisting of six men and four dog teams, started the major advance.

The day after the Geological Party started south, we hauled

the Ford out of its underground hangar. It came out under its own power. Balchen, after a quick inspection, pronounced it undamaged. But the big wing had to be bolted on, and a thousand and one little things done before it would be fit to fly to the South Pole. First on the flight schedules was a series of local flight tests to determine the plane's speed and gas consumption. Without that data we could not be sure about the plane's performance; the success of the flight would depend upon whether we could lift the plane through one of the 10,000-foot mountain passes guarding the approaches to the Polar Plateau, a far more complicated problem than confronted me over the sea-level approaches to the North Pole.

Sunday, Nov. 17.

Have decided to make the base-laying flight tonight. The plane is being loaded and we shall take off within an hour. It is only necessary to fill the oil tanks and start the engines.

In addition to fuel and oil necessary for the flight, as well as other equipment, we shall carry 300 pounds of food, 200 gallons of gasoline, 25 gallons of oil and a large gasoline stove (for warming the engines) for the cache. We shall also carry 25 gallons of gasoline and a gasoline stove for the Geological Party. Smith will pilot, June will act as radio engineer and relief pilot, and McKinley will, of course, be the mapper.

Later.

No luck. We are too impatient.

Radio conditions have been absolutely dead all day. Every man in the Radio Division has tried his hand at the main set, but failed to raise a station. We have been unable to make contact with the *New York Times*, the ships at New Zealand, the Geological Party—in fact, for the past few hours we have been cut off from the world.

It would be stupid to undertake the flight without radio. So we shall sit still until the ether returns to normal....

9 o'clock A.M., Monday, Nov. 18.

The mysterious enervation of the ether is over, and we shall make the flight at once. Engines are turning over, and Mulroy has put aboard the fuel cans for the base.

Temperature—several degrees above zero and rising: sky—cloudless: wind—on the surface a 6-mile wind from the southwest, and a quartering 20-mile wind at 2,000 feet according to Haines's balloon runs.

A perfect day for the flight.

Haines said: "You might wait another year for a better one."

We took off at 9:40 o'clock A.M., with Smith at the controls. Thirty seconds after the start, after a run of less than a thousand feet, the three engines lifted our 14,300 pounds of dead weight from the snow, and the plane climbed rapidly, bearing to the south. As the engines took up a steady rhythm under Smith's deft synchronizing touch, my thoughts and hopes raced ahead. What would we find at the foot of the mountains? A firm, smooth surface? Or a surface torn and marred by crevasses and sastrugi? So much—everything—hung in the balance.

Little America, a few dark roofs and a mass of trodden snow, dropped steadily astern, the radio towers became black pins against the white, and the Ross Sea, open, black, and strewn with icebergs, stretched indefinitely to the northern horizon.

Our altitude was 1,200 feet, and Smith kept the plane at this height for some time. For more than a year we had been wondering if we could follow the dog team trail from the air. We had discussed the problem backward and forward and were now about to find the answer.

Down below, the southern trail wound through the crevasses southwest of Little America, but we could not see it. Reaching the Barrier, we had to search for the trail, and for a time I thought we were not going to be able to follow it. Finally we sighted it—a thin, broken ribbon.

We saw 20-Mile Depot, a few snow blocks surrounded by a welter of footsteps. Over the beacons the western sun threw long gray shadows.

Visibility was excellent, the atmosphere wonderfully smooth.

Snow, snow everywhere, rising and falling in swelling folds, meeting the blue of the sky with a sharp clear line.

We passed Depot No. 2 at a speed in excess of a hundred

miles per hour. We could see the crevassed area long before
we reached it. I had been intent on navigating when suddenly
Dean turned in his seat and wiggled his finger. Dark shadows
appeared in the smooth floor of the Barrier ahead—the crevasses. As we approached, the pattern evolved. What a frightful
mess it was! It was a frozen whirlpool. Even under the soft-
ening influence of vertical vision and altitude, the horrible nature of the surface was apparent. The area was traversed by
massive pressure ridges and crevasses, the sides of which showed
black and blue in the sun.

To the east a mass of crevasses was spread fanwise, furrowed
and partly drifted over.

Here for two days the Supporting Party had risked its
necks; and we were over it in two, perhaps three, minutes.

Amundsen had reported two high peaks to the eastward in
Latitude 82°. He did not name these peaks, but thought
they were part of Carmen Land. I searched the horizon with
binoculars, but could not see them.

Smooth and undulating, the Barrier stretched to the south.
The crumbled dome of Depot No. 4 was soon underneath.

"We ought to meet the Geological Party any minute," I
shouted.

"I see them now," said McKinley.

Five teams, far apart and each making its way alone, were
headed up a long rolling rise in the Barrier.

"They haven't heard us yet," McKinley shouted.

That was apparent, for they had not turned. Smith brought
the ship down in a long, curving glide. The poor devils, we saw
quickly, were having a hard time. Some of the men were in
harness, pulling with the dogs, and the sight of their bending backs, the separation of the sledges, the very, very slow
progress told everything. They had picked up a maximum
load at Depot No. 4, and the men had their toes dug in, and the
dogs had their bellies to the snow, trying to keep the sledges
moving.

"Must be cold down there," McKinley yelled. "They have their parkas up—can't hear the engines."

We passed them at 300 feet, swinging low in salute, and caught sight of two or three white faces lifted up.

If ever a conclusive contrast was struck between the new and the old methods of polar traveling, it was then.

We dropped them a bag of letters and miscellaneous equipment and continued on. A little later to the southwestward a magnificent peak appeared in the sky. It was the strangest mountain I have ever seen. It lacked body and base. It was a towering, truncated, gray-black peak pinned against a cloudless sky. Halfway down it ended, with a clear line of breakage, against the shimmering brilliance of daylight, as if the agency responsible for its structure had started to build it from the top, grew tired when the job was half done and left it there, like Mahomet's tomb, between earth and heaven. A mirage, I thought.

Then another peak, a third, a fourth, then a whole line of them popped suddenly in the sky, at least 150 miles away, trending laterally across our path; and the same shimmering light played underneath. Could they be—why, surely they must be—the mountains between the range that Amundsen saw on his polar journey (Crown Prince Olav) and those which Scott and Shackleton saw from Beardmore Glacier.

Fold upon fold, peak upon peak, the range rimmed the polar plateau, bending in a broad sweeping curve to the east. I studied them through my glasses. Here and there the blue-white stream of a glacier cut through the ebony; and one glacier, larger and more beautiful than the rest, which could be seen almost at the limit of vision, I took to be Beardmore Glacier, up which the parties of Scott and Shackleton had climbed, with infinite patience and pain, in search of a highway to the Pole. But of course I could not be sure; looking from the ground, it is often difficult to identify a mountain from a written description; but from the air it is well-nigh impossible.

Slowly, now, the Queen Maud Range came into view: first a few lone peaks dancing above the cylinder heads in the arc of the propeller; then dark shoulders of rock draped with snow; then, finally, a solid mass of mountains riven by glacial streams. Here, indeed, was what we had come so far to see.

Spread out on the navigation table were Amundsen's charts, a number of photographs ripped from his book, and scribbled notes taken from his descriptions.

Here was a subject which de Ganahl, one of the expedition's navigators, and I had discussed exhaustively on many occasions. Would it be possible to recognize from the air the mountains which Amundsen had seen and described according to their characteristics as seen from the ground? Amundsen had repeatedly confessed that under different conditions of visibility he failed to recognize mountains which he believed he knew well.

I searched first of all for Mount Fridtjof Nansen—"15,000 feet ... a blue-black look ... a mighty hood of ice that raised its shining top ... the immense Mount Nansen" and then for its eminent companion Don Pedro Christophersen ... "farther to the east ... more covered with snow ... but the long, gabled summit was to a great extent bare," and for Axel Heiberg Glacier ... "that rose in terraces along their sides ... fearfully broken and disturbed ... the great main ice field ... stretching right up from the Barrier between the lofty mountains running east and west."

But I recognized nothing. We were heading for a glacier which I at first took to be Axel Heiberg because I had confidence in Albert Bumstead's sun compass. One great mountain mass rose ahead, on the starboard bow, and an even larger mass loomed to the right of it. There were huge mountains on the port bow too. At the foot of these high mountains were rows of even, pyramidal, black foothills like Arab tents pitched at their feet.

But another mountain had shouldered its mass in sturdy

prominence against the rest, a stately, glittering cone. Could this be Ole Engelstad? I studied Amundsen's description of it. ". . . Ole Engelstad's a great cone rising in the air to 19,000 feet" . . . Mount Wilhelm Christophersen and Mount Ole Engelstad formed the end of Axel Heiberg Glacier, "two beehived-shaped summits, entirely covered with snow." No, this peak did not fall into that description. It must be—I hastily riffled the photographs, refreshing my mind with detail in them as we advanced steadily toward the range.

A queer thing happened as we approached. The cone of the mysterious mountain gradually separated itself from the mountain mass on the port bow and the shape of the mountain changed before our eyes. It had ceased to be a cone. From the northern peak a ridge ran far back, to the south, and the effect then was that of a tented arch. I saw, at the moment, a definite structural similarity with the picture of a mountain on my table—ah, Ruth Gade. It was a gorgeous mass, rising 14,000 to 15,000 feet.

There could be no doubt that the photograph I held in my hand and the one I was looking at were the same. From it I worked to locate the other mountains. The big mountain mass on the starboard bow must be the great Nansen. But, there was an even greater mass to the right of Nansen, seen in its length, perhaps, for the first time. I concluded that Don Pedro Christophersen and Ole Engelstad must be hidden behind Nansen. Axel Heiberg Glacier was ahead and Liv Glacier to the right. Good! Now we knew where we were.

Ever since we had passed the crevasses, I had searched for signs of Carmen Land and the mountain range which Amundsen believed connected Carmen Land to King Edward VII Land and South Victoria Land. We not only failed to see the "two lofty white summits" or the "appearance of land" to the southeast "in about 82°," which he reported on the return journey from the Pole, but we had not yet caught sight of the chain of mountains which he first saw at 84°, on the way in, and later as he stood halfway up the mountains and paused, before he renewed the ascent, for a backward glance at the Barrier.

Of this fascinating area not a trace had yet appeared.

Smith edged slightly toward the western portal of Axel Heiberg Glacier, where we planned to make the base. The Barrier underneath became more rolling, its level stretch giving way to a series of swelling undulations.

Anxiously we studied the surface. It was not at all promising. Everywhere the Barrier was scored with wave-like sastrugi, and these, for the most part, appeared to be so high and rough as to forbid a landing. However, several miles north of Nansen's foothills, the western peaks of which served as the eastern portal to Liv Glacier, we sighted a stretch of fairly level snow; there we decided to lay the base. As we turned and came into the wind, I had a fair view of Liv Glacier. Amundsen had wondered what this glacier was like. The main channel, which was astonishingly wide, curved behind Nansen's foothills and rose, in a series of escalated ice falls, some of which were at least 200 feet in height, to a great elevation. Far up it seemed to bend slightly to the west, disappearing behind the arm of Nansen and the bulking shoulder of Fisher Mountain.

The moment which we had looked forward to with apprehension was at hand. Everything depended upon this landing, and Dean Smith carried a heavy burden on his shoulders. When such moments come, the time for worry is passed. One feels calm, calmer than when planning for such a critical project. We had gone as far as mere planning could carry us, and the result rested with Fate. There was no thought of physical danger. We were oppressed only by the fear that if things went wrong now the whole expedition would suffer.

Just before the skis hit, Smith nosed the plane into a power stall. We landed at a speed of about fifty miles per hour; and the Ford was severely tested on the rough, very hard snow before it came to a stop. Smith's landing was perfect.

Smith remained in the cockpit, carefully nursing the engines, while June, McKinley and I prepared to build the depot. I paused long enough to take several sights of the sun, which gave us a longitude line on the chart and indicated that we were about where we thought we were. That done, I pitched in and helped the others unload.

Building the depot took very little time. We simply piled the cans of fuel and oil and the bags of food in a high mass. The food, however, we covered with snow blocks. The gasoline stove for which the Geological Party had asked was set on top of the mound, which was several feet above our heads. We finished with some satisfaction this southernmost base in the world.

The engines purred constantly. Smith, who was anxious about fuel, slid back one of the windows in the cockpit and yelled: "We'd better not hang around here too long."

We hustled into the cabin, and rose in a long climb and headed east. With the first phase of flight operations successfully accomplished, I was eager to make a thorough investigation of Carmen Land. It was my intention to fly at least 100 miles to the east. McKinley's camera went into action again, mapping the face of the Queen Maud Range as we flew parallel to it.

The Ford had risen to an altitude of 3,000 feet, and we had visibility to the east for at least 50 miles. Again I looked for Amundsen's Carmen Land, but in vain. I could see only the Barrier rolling endlessly to the east. A great pressure ridge or perhaps a mirage may have misled Amundsen into believing that land was there. So, from a geographical point of view, the base-laying flight had great significance in that we were now able definitely to extend the known limits of the Barrier at least 100 miles to the east. But I did not want to announce this until we had made still further investigation.

At this moment, as we stood again on the threshold of discovery, June, who had been sounding the fuel tanks, moved down the cabin and told me, with a grave face, that the fuel supply was dangerously low.

I shouted: "How can that be! Surely we must have gas for nearly seven hours' flying."

June took off his glove and raised four fingers, "Very heavy consumption. Don't know why."

When we were about an hour out from Little America June had discovered a leak near the hand fuel pump underneath the pilot seat. He had plugged this with chewing gum and then dammed it with heavy tape. At the time, he believed it had stopped the flow.

There was nothing to do but turn back at once. We should have to run for it, as it was. Smith turned the plane, and as it wheeled I stared up the valley of a steep mountain glacier which debouched from Nansen's flank. Far up, over a saddle where Nansen appeared to merge with a second mass of foothills, I caught sight, for a moment, of the blue-white flooring of Axel Heiberg. From it a mighty ice fall descended to the mountain glacier.

Studying it, I was moved to wonder if we could hurl our heavily loaded plane over its pass, which we could not see. I looked at it anxiously, and wished that I might be able to see what lay hidden in the heights.

We swung over the cache, turned north, and I laid a straight course for Little America. There could be no following of the southern trail on the return trip. With a diminishing fuel supply, a straight line recommended itself overwhelmingly. Fortunately the weather continued excellent, the sun was visible, and, as long as it was there, I could navigate with the sun compass.

I glanced for a last time at Liv Glacier, and the idea occurred that it might offer better passage over the "Hump" than Axel Heiberg.

We were over the crevasses shortly before 7:00 o'clock, and

just beyond sighted the trail. We were then about 150 miles from Little America.

About fifty miles on, the engines began to miss. Directly ahead was an area which Thorne and de Ganahl, both of them flyers, had reported, on their return from a sledging journey, was impossible for landing. It was furrowed with sastrugi, and we could see that the surface was still very rough.

Smith worked the throttles anxiously, trying to restore the engines to their former fluency, but to no avail. All three stopped at once. June looked up from the main gas tank. "No gas," he yelled in the quiet that followed the stopping of the engines.

Smith squeezed the last possible inch of altitude from the glide. We barely crept over the edge of the worst area and landed with a bump. Nevertheless, everything held. Luck and a fine piece of work by Smith saw us through.

It was then 7:29 o'clock.

The moment the plane stopped, all hands scrambled out, snatching empty cans from the racks in the fuselage, and made ready to drain the oil from the engines. We pulled out the plugs and caught the warm oil as it fell. A goodly percentage of it went into the cans, but a considerable amount fell on us. In a very short time we were reeking with oil and unquestionably the dirtiest persons within thousands of miles. The oil congealed on our clothes, and we were very uncomfortable.

June assembled the emergency radio set and tried to send an S. O. S. to the camp, but could not raise the operator.

We then set up a tent not far from the plane, and tried to get some rest. But we dared not remain for long, for we were greatly concerned as to the safety of the plane. The weather, however, remained perfectly clear and calm.

About 11 o'clock, when we were on the verge of giving up the hope of establishing communication with the camp, and when McKinley's arm was about used up in cranking the hand generator, we heard the sound of an airplane. It was the Fairchild, with Balchen and Petersen. To our delight Balchen reported that he had 100 gallons of fuel aboard.

"When we heard the transmitter stop," Balchen said, "we knew you had come down and figured you were about 100 miles out. Haines waited to hear from you by radio, and then decided to send the Fairchild out."

The return to the base was uneventful. The mechanics took over the Ford, and we turned in. We were ready then to tackle the polar flight.

Chapter *VIII*

FLIGHT TO THE SOUTH POLE

THANKSGIVING DAY, November 25th, brought what we wanted. At noon the Geological Party radioed a final weather report: "Unchanged. Perfect visibility. No clouds anywhere." Harrison finished with his balloon runs, Haines with his weather charts. The sky was still somewhat overcast, and the surface wind from the east southeast. Haines came into the library, his face grave. Together we went out for a walk and a last look at the weather. What he said exactly I have forgotten, but it was in effect: "If you don't go now, you may never have another chance as good as this." And that was that.

The mechanics, Bubier, Roth and Demas, went over the plane for the last time, testing everything with scrupulous care. A line of men passed five-gallon cans of gasoline to several men standing on the wing, who poured them into the wing tanks. Another line fed the stream of gear which flowed into the plane. Black weighed each thing before passing it on to McKinley and June, who were stowing the stuff in the cabin. Hanson went over the radio equipment. With de Ganahl I made a careful check of the sextant and the watches and chronometers, which were among the last things put aboard. For days de Ganahl and I had nursed the chronometers, checking them against the time tick broadcast every night from the United States. We knew their exact loss or gain.

The total weight was approximately 15,000 pounds.

Haines came up with a final report on the weather. "A twenty-mile wind from the south at 2,000 feet." I went into my office and picked up a flag weighted with a stone from Floyd Bennett's grave. It seemed fitting that something connected with the spirit of this noble friend, who stood with me over the North Pole, on May 9th, 1926, should rest as long as stone endures at the bottom of the world.

There were handshakes all around, and at 3:29 o'clock we were off. The skis were in the air after a run of 30 seconds— an excellent take-off. A calm expectation took hold of my mind.

Had you been there to glance over the cabin of this modern machine which has so revolutionized polar travel, I think you would have been impressed most of all—perhaps first of all— with the profusion of gear in the cabin. There was a small sledge, rolled masses of sleeping bags, bulky food sacks, two pressure gasoline stoves, rows of cans of gasoline packed about the main tank forward, funnels for draining gasoline and oil from the engines, bundles of clothing, tents and so on *ad infinitum*. There was scarcely room in which to move.

June had his radio in the after bulkhead on the port side. From time to time he flashed reports on our progress to the base. From the ear phones strapped to his helmet ran long cords so that he might move freely about the cabin without being obliged to take them off. His duties were varied and important. He had to attend to the motion picture camera, the radio and the complicated valves of the six gasoline tanks. Every now and then he relieved Balchen at the wheel, or helped him to follow the elusive trail.

McKinley had his mapping camera ready for action either on port or starboard side. It was for him and the camera he so sedulously served that the flight was made. The mapping of the corridor between Little America and the South Pole was one of the major objectives of the expedition.

Balchen was forward, bulking large in the narrow compartment, his massive hands on the wheel, now appraising the engines with a critical eye, now the dozen flickering fingers on the dials on the instrument board. Balchen was in his element. His calm fine face bespoke his confidence and sureness. He was anticipating the struggle at the "Hump" almost with eagerness.

It was quite warm forward, behind the engines. But a cold wind swept through the cabin, making one thankful for heavy clothes. When the skies cleared, a golden light poured into the cabin. The sound of the engines and propellers filled it. One had to shout to make oneself heard. From the navigation table aft, where my charts were spread out, a trolley ran to the control cabin. Over it I shot to Balchen the necessary messages and courses; he would turn and smile his understanding.

That, briefly, is the picture, and a startling one it makes in contrast with that of Amundsen's party, which had pressed along this same course eighteen years before. A wing, pistons and flashing propellers had taken the place of runner, dogs and legs. Amundsen was delighted to make 25 miles per day. We had to average 90 miles per hour to accomplish our mission. We had the advantages of swiftness and comfort, but we had as well an enlarged fallibility. A flaw in a piece of steel, a bit of dirt in the fuel lines or carburetor jets, a few hours of strong head winds, fog or storm—these things, remotely beyond our control, could destroy our carefully laid plans and nullify our most determined efforts.

Still, it was not these things that entered our minds. Rather it was the thought of the "Hump," and how we should fare with it.

Soon after passing the crevasses we picked up again the vast escarpment to the right. More clearly than before we saw the white-blue streams of many glaciers discharging into the Barrier, and several of the higher snow-clad peaks glistened so brightly in the sun as to seem like volcanoes in eruption.

Now the Queen Maud Range loomed ahead. I searched again for the "appearance of land" to the east. Still the rolling Barrier—nothing else.

At 8:15 o'clock we had the Geological Party in sight—a cluster of beetles about two dark-topped tents. Balchen dropped overboard the photographs of the Queen Maud Range and the other things we had promised to bring. The parachute canopy to which they were attached fluttered open and fell in gentle oscillations, and we saw two or three figures rush out to catch it. We waved to them, and then prepared for a settlement of the issue at the "Hump."

Up to this time, the engines had operated continuously at cruising revolutions. Now Balchen opened them full throttle, and the Ford girded its loins for the long, fighting pull over the "Hump." We rose steadily. We were then about 60 miles north of the western portal of Axel Heiberg, and holding our course steadily on meridian 163° 45′ W. with the sun compass.

I watched the altimeters, of which there were two in the navigation department. The fingers marched with little jumps across the face of the dial—3,000 feet, 3,500, 4,000, 4,500. The Ford had her toes in, and was climbing with a vast, heaving effort.

Drawing nearer, we had edged 30° to the west of south, to bring not only Axel Heiberg but also Liv Glacier into view. This was a critical period. I was by no means certain which glacier I should choose for the ascent. I went forward and took a position behind the pilots.

The schemes and hopes of the next few minutes were beset by many uncertainties. Which would it be—Axel Heiberg or Liv Glacier?

There was this significant difference between flying and sledging: we could not pause long for decision or investigation. Minutes stood for gasoline, and gasoline was precious. The waste of so little as half an hour of fuel in a fruitless experiment might well overturn the mathematical balance on which the success of the flight depended. The execution of the plan hung on the proper choice of the route over the "Hump."

Yet, how well, after all, could judgment forecast the ultimate result? There were few facts on which we might base a decision. We knew, for example, from Amundsen's report, that the highest point of the pass of Axel Heiberg Glacier was 10,500 feet. We should know, in a very few minutes, after June had calculated the gasoline consumption, the weight of the plane. From that we could determine, according to the tables we had worked out and which were then before me, the approximate ceiling we should have. We should know, too, whether or not we should be able to complete the flight, other conditions being favorable.

These were the known elements. The unknown were burdened with equally important consequences. The structural nature of the head of the pass was of prime importance. We knew from Amundsen's descriptions and from what we could see with our own eyes, that the pass on both sides was surrounded by towering peaks, much higher than the maximum ceiling of the heavily loaded plane. But whether the pass was wide or narrow; whether it would allow us room to maneuver in case we could not rise above it; whether it would be narrow and running with a torrent of down-pressing wind which would dash a plane, already hovering near its service ceiling, to the glacier floor —these were things, naturally, we could not possibly know until the issue was directly at hand.

I stood beside Balchen, carefully studying the looming fortress, still wondering by what means we should attempt to carry it. With a gesture of the hand Balchen pointed to fog vapor rising from the black rock of the foothills which were Nansen's high priests—caused no doubt by the condensation of warm currents of air radiated from the sun-heated rocks. A thin layer of cloud seemed to cap Axel Heiberg's pass, and extended almost to Liv Glacier. But of this we were not certain. Perhaps it was the surface of the snow. If cloud, then our difficulties were already upon us. Even high clouds would be resting on the floor of the uplifted plateau.

There was, then, a gamble in the decision. Doubtless a flip of the coin would have served as well. In the end, we decided to choose Liv Glacier, the unknown pass to the right which

Amundsen had seen far in the distance and named after Dr. Nansen's daughter. It seemed to be broader than Axel Heiberg, and the pass not quite so high.

A few minutes after 9 o'clock we passed near the intermediate base, which, of course, we could not see. Our altitude was then about 9,000 feet. At 9:15 o'clock we had the eastern portal on our left, and were ready to tackle the "Hump." We had discussed the "Hump" so often, had anticipated and maligned it so much, that now that it was in front of us and waiting in the flesh—in rock-ribbed, glacierized reality—it was like meeting an old acquaintance. But we approached it warily and respectfully, climbing steadily all the while with maximum power, to get a better view of its none too friendly visage.

June, wholly unaffected by the immediate perplexities, went about his job of getting the plane in fighting trim. He ripped open the last of the fuel cans, and poured the contents into the main tank. The empty tins he dropped overboard, through the trapdoor. Every tin weighed two pounds; and every pound dropped was to our gain. June examined the gauges of the five wing tanks, then measured with a graduated stick the amount of fuel in the main tank. He jotted the figures on a pad, made a few calculations and handed me the results. Consumption had thus far averaged between 55 and 60 gallons per hour. It had taken us longer to reach the mountains than we had expected, owing to head winds. However, the extra fuel taken aboard just before we left had absorbed this loss and we actually had a credit balance. We had, then, enough gasoline to take us to the Pole and back.

With that doubt disposed of, we went at the "Hump" confidently.

We were still rising, and the engines were pulling wonderfully well. The wind was about abeam, and, according to my calculations, not materially affecting the speed.

The glacier floor rose sharply, in a series of ice falls and terraces, some of which were well above the (then) altitude of the plane. These glacial waterfalls, some of which were from 200 to 400 feet high, seemed more beautiful than any precipitous stream I have ever seen. Beautiful yes, but how rudely and with what finality they would deal with steel and duralumin that crashed into them at 100 miles per hour.

Now the stream of air pouring down the pass roughened perceptibly. The great wing shivered and teetered as it balanced itself against the changing pressures. The wind from the left flowed against Fisher's steep flanks, and the constant, hammering bumps made footing uncertain in the plane. But McKinley steadily trained his 50-pound camera on the mountains to the left. The uncertainties of load and ceiling were not his concern. His only concern was photographs—photographs over which students and geographers might pore in the calm quiet of their studies.

The altimeters showed a height of 9,600 feet, but the figure was not necessarily exact. Nevertheless there were indications we were near the service ceiling of the plane.

The roughness of the air increased and became so violent that we were forced to swing slightly to the left, in search of calmer air. This brought us over a frightfully crevassed slope which ran up and toward Mount Nansen. We thus escaped the turbulent swirl about Fisher, but the down-surging currents here damped our climb. To the left we had the "blind" mountain glacier of Nansen in full view; and when we looked ahead we saw the plateau—a smooth, level plain of snow between Nansen and Fisher. The pass rose up to meet it.

In the center of the pass was a massive outcropping of snow-covered rock, resembling an island, which protruded above and separated the descending stream of ice. Perhaps it was a peak or the highest eminence of a ridge connecting Fisher and Nansen which had managed through the ages to hold its head above the glacial torrent pouring down from the plateau. But its particular structure or relationship was of small moment then. I watched it only with reference to the climb of the plane;

and realized, with some disgust and more consternation, that the nose of the plane, in spite of the fact that Balchen had steepened the angle of attack, did not rise materially above the outcropping. We were still climbing, but at a rapidly diminishing rate of speed. In the rarefied air the heavy plane responded to the controls with marked sluggishness. There is a vast difference between the plane of 1928 and the plane of 1937.

It was an awesome thing, creeping (so it seemed) through the narrow pass, with the black walls of Nansen and Fisher on either side, higher than the level of the wings, and watching the nose of the ship bob up and down across the face of that chunk of rock. It would move up, then slide down. Then move up, and fall off again. For perhaps a minute or two we deferred the decision; but there was no escaping it. If we were to risk a passage through the pass, we needed greater maneuverability than we had at that moment. Once we entered the pass, there would be no retreat. It offered no room for turn. If power was lost momentarily or if the air became excessively rough, we could only go ahead, or down. We had to climb, and there was only one way in which we could climb.

June, anticipating the command, already had his hand on the dump valve of the main tank. A pressure of the fingers—that was all that was necessary—and in two minutes 600 gallons of gasoline would gush out. I signaled to wait.

Balchen held to the climb almost to the edge of a stall. But it was clear to both of us that he could not hold it long enough. Balchen began to yell and gesticulate, and it was hard to catch the words in the roar of the engines echoing from the cliffs on either side. But the meaning was manifest. "Overboard—overboard—200 pounds!"

Which would it be—gasoline or food?

If gasoline, I thought, we might as well stop there and turn back. We could never get back to the base from the Pole. If food, the lives of all of us would be jeopardized in the event of a forced landing. Was that fair to McKinley, Balchen and

June? It really took only a moment to reach the decision. The Pole, after all, was our objective. I knew the character of the three men. McKinley, in fact, had already hauled one of the food bags to the trapdoor. It weighed 125 pounds.

The brown bag was pushed out and fell, spinning, to the glacier. The improvement in the flying qualities of the plane was noticeable. It took another breath and resumed the climb.

Now the down-currents over Nansen became stronger. The plane trembled and rose and fell, as if struck bodily. We veered a trifle to the right, searching for helpful rising eddies. Balchen was flying shrewdly. He maintained flight at a sufficient distance below the absolute ceiling of the plane to retain at all times enough maneuverability to make him master of the ship. But he was hard pressed by circumstances; and I realized that, unless the plane was further lightened, the final thrust might bring us perilously close to the end of our reserve.

"More," Bernt shouted. "Another bag."

McKinley shoved a second bag through the trapdoor, and this time we saw it hit the glacier, and scatter in a soundless explosion. Two hundred and fifty pounds of food—enough to feed four men for a month—lay strewn on the barren ice.

The sacrifice swung the scales. The plane literally rose with a jump; the engines dug in, and we soon showed a gain in altitude of from 300 to 400 feet. It was what we wanted. We should clear the pass with about 500 feet to spare. Balchen gave a shout of joy. It was just as well. We could dump no more food. There was nothing left to dump except McKinley's camera. I am sure that, had he been asked to put it overboard, he would have done so instantly; and I am equally sure he would have followed the precious instrument with his own body.

The next few minutes dragged. We moved at a speed of 77 nautical miles per hour through the pass, with the black walls of Nansen on our left. The wing gradually lifted above them. The floor of the plateau stretched in a white immensity to the south. We were over the dreaded "Hump" at last. The Pole lay dead ahead over the horizon, less than 300 miles away. It was then about 9:45 o'clock (I did not note the exact time. There were other things to think about).

Gaining the plateau, we studied the situation a moment and then shifted course to the southward. Nansen's enormous towering ridge, lipped by the plateau, shoved its heavily broken sides into the sky. A whole chain of mountains began to parade across the eastern horizon. How high they are I cannot say, but surely some of them must be around 14,000 feet, to stand so boldly above the rim of the 10,000 foot plateau. Peak on peak, ridge on ridge, draped in snow garments which brilliantly reflected the sun, they extended in a solid array to the southeast. But can one really say they ran in that direction? The lines of direction are so bent in this region that 150 miles farther on, even were they to continue in the same general straight line, they must run north of east. This is what happens near the Pole.

We laid our line of flight on the 171st meridian.

Our altitude was then between 10,500 and 11,000 feet. We were "riding" the engines, conscious of the fact that if one should fail we must come down. Once the starboard engine did sputter a bit, and Balchen nosed down while June rushed to the fuel valves. But it was nothing; to conserve fuel, Balchen had "leaned" the mixture too much. A quick adjustment corrected the fault, and in a moment the engine took up its steady rhythm. Moments like this one make a pioneering flight anything but dull; one moment everything is lovely, and the next is full of forebodings.

The drift indicator showed a variable wind from the east. To compensate for it, we had to point the nose of the plane an average of about 12° to the east, in order to steer a straight course for the Pole. The influence of the drift on the course was always a bothersome element. It had to be watched carefully, and any change in the angle of drift detected at once, so as to make good a straight course south. Fitted in the floor of the plane was a drift indicator which McKinley used in connection with his photographic work, and during the flight he constantly checked the drift with me. Whenever I noted any change in the direction or strength of the wind, I would steady Balchen on his course with the sun compass, first shaking the trolley line to attract his attention, then waving him on to the new course.

The character of the plateau surface varied from time to time. There were stretches of smooth, soft snow, colonies of domed haycocks and arrow-headed sastrugi. From the time we had first struck across the plateau its level appeared to slope gently toward the Pole; the altimeter showed that the *Floyd Bennett* was maintaining a fairly steady altitude at approximately 11,000 feet, and the plateau fell farther below. We had named the Ford after my gallant friend and companion on the North Pole flight.

While the mountains on the left were still in view, I attempted to shoot the sun with the sextant to get its altitude. This would give us a sun line which would cut our line of flight and at the point of intersection tell us what the sun had to say about our progress. The air, however, was fairly rough. The powerful center engine, laboring to keep the heavy load at an altitude of two miles, produced a weaving in the plane; and the most patient efforts failed to bring the sun and the bubble together long enough for a dependable sight. This was bothersome, but relatively unimportant at the time; we were quite confident as to the accuracy of the dead reckoning.

From time to time June "spelled" Balchen at the controls; and Balchen would walk back to the cabin, flexing his cramped muscles. There was little thought of food in any of us—a beef sandwich, stiff as a board from frost, and tea and coffee from a thermos bottle. It was difficult to believe that two decades or so before the most resolute men who had ever attempted to carry a remote objective, Scott and Shackleton, had plodded over this same plateau, a few miles each day, with hunger, fierce, unrelenting hunger stalking them every step of the way.

Between 11:30 and 12:30 o'clock the mountains to the eastward began to disappear, dropping imperceptibly out of view, one after another. Not long after 12:30 o'clock the whole range had retreated from vision, and the plateau met the horizon in an indefinite line. The mountains to the right had long since disappeared.

The air finally turned smooth. At 12:38 o'clock I shot the sun. It hung, a ball of fire, just beyond *south* to the east, 21° above the horizon. So it was quite low, and we stared it in the eye. The sight gave me an approximate line of latitude, which placed us very near our position as calculated by dead reckoning. That dead reckoning and astronomy should check so closely was very encouraging. The position line placed us at Lat. 89° 4½' S., or 55½ miles from the Pole. A short time later we reached an altitude of 11,000 feet. According to Amundsen's records, the plateau, which had risen to 10,300 feet, descended here to 9,600 feet. We were, therefore, about 1,400 feet above the plateau.

So the Pole was actually in sight. But I could not yet spare it so much as a glance. Chronometers, drift indicators and compasses are hard task-masters.

Relieved by June, Balchen came aft and reported that visibility was not as good as it had been. Clouds were gathering on the horizon off the port bow; and a storm, Balchen thought, was in the air. A storm was the last thing we wanted to meet on the plateau on the way back. It would be difficult enough to pass the Queen Maud Range in bright sunlight; in thick weather it would be suicidal. Conditions, however, were merely unpromising: not really bad, simply not good. If worse came to worst, we decided we could out-race the clouds to the mountains.

At six minutes after one o'clock, a sight of the sun put us a few miles ahead of our dead reckoning position. We were quite close now. At 1:14 o'clock, Greenwich civil time, our calculations showed that we were at the Pole.

I opened the trapdoor and dropped over the calculated position of the Pole the small flag which was weighted with the stone from Bennett's grave. Stone and flag plunged down together. The flag had been advanced 1,500 miles farther south than it had ever been advanced by any American or American expedition.

For a few seconds we stood over the spot where Amundsen had stood, December 14th, 1911; and where Scott had also stood, thirty-four days later, reading the note which Amundsen had left for him. In their honor, the flags of their countries were again carried over the Pole. There was nothing now to mark that scene: only a white desolation and solitude disturbed by the sound of our engines. The Pole lay in the center of a limitless plain. To the right, which is to say to the eastward, the horizon was covered with clouds. If mountains lay there, as some geologists believe, they were concealed and we had no hint of them.

And that, in brief, is all there is to tell about the South Pole. One gets there, and that is about all there is for the telling. It is the effort to get there that counts.

We put the Pole behind us and raced for home.

The mountains to the eastward came into view again, one by one. But whereas before the southernmost peaks had stood out clear and distinct, they were now confused by haze and clouds. The clouds were traveling fast, threatening to close in ahead of us; and, if we valued our skins, it behooved us to beat them to the pass.

We were then riding the 168th meridian to Axel Heiberg Glacier. It was my intention to return somewhat to the eastward of the original course, in order to bring within range as much new territory as was possible. McKinley, who had photographed the area to the eastward on the way to the Pole, was then mapping the area to the westward.

Time began to crawl. It was a case of hitting the pass of Axel Heiberg Glacier ahead of the clouds or being sorry. The wind was now astern and helping us considerably. Of course, its direction varied from time to time. Our speed increased. About two o'clock, seeking a still stronger wind aloft, we climbed several hundred feet and found a fairly stiff following wind. With that boosting us, we hurried over the plateau. At three o'clock Balchen opened the throttles wide and a short time later we climbed about 400 feet higher. At this level the wind was even stronger. We commenced to make better than 125 miles per hour. Our altitude was between 11,500 and 12,500 feet.

About 3:30 o'clock Balchen's face broke into a smile. Ruth Gade's conical turret was off to the starboard bow. There was Nansen off the port bow. Soon W. Christophersen came into view, a small rounded dome between Ruth Gade and Nansen. The charts, photographs and descriptions which I had culled from Amundsen's book, as well as the photographs which McKinley had taken on the base-laying flight, were before me; and as each new prominence appeared and fell neatly into its expected place, we were delighted. Our return course had been straight, and our position coincided with our dead reckoning position. The flight was almost done. Best of all, the pass was clear.

A few clouds were beginning to gather in the passes to the right and left, but we had outstripped the main advance.

By 3:50 o'clock we had passed over the head of the glacier, sinking lower all the time, and glided down the shattered terraces between the precipitous sides of Nansen and Don Pedro Christophersen. The air in places was very bumpy, and the loose gear in the plane was tossed about rather wildly.

We emerged from the glacier shortly after four o'clock.

June finished with his calculations of the fuel supply and reported there was a slight margin over needs. There was

enough, then, to make further inquiry into Carmen Land; so
we continued to the eastward. McKinley, I decided, ought to
photograph this area.

We were now over the Barrier, and we could see how the
shearing movements of the Barrier, where it pressed against
the feet of the mountains, had produced deep and extensive
crevasses in several areas. What mighty pressures must be at
work, to rip that tough fabric as if it were silk. The extensions
of the Queen Maud Range and the new mountains which we had
seen on the base-laying flight were on our right, a solid rampart
extending to the south or east. They were almost wholly covered with snow, and some were broken by glaciers of considerable size and beauty.

The flight proved what I already knew to be true: Carmen
Land does not exist. McKinley photographed the Barrier where
Amundsen believed it lay, and we then turned westward, land-
ing presently at the base.

Taking the fuel aboard was quite a problem. Each can had
to be broken open and poured, one by one, into the wing tanks,
and we soon tired of lifting them to June, who was doing the
pouring. It was 6 o'clock before we rose from the Barrier and
headed north, on the last leg of the flight. By that time the
outriders of the storm clouds were creeping over the mountain
rim to the east.

We steered a straight course for Little America, and made
no attempt to pick up the trail, which was to the east. But
our course converged with the trail a few miles north of Little
America. We flew by sun compass and drift indicator and made
a perfect land fall. Again the sun compass had done its job.

We had Little America's radio spires in sight at 10 o'clock.
A few minutes later we were over the Administration Building,
swinging west to come in for a landing. A last survey showed
that the Bay of Whales was still choked with ice, the northern
edge of which extended almost to West Cape.

Sunday, Nov. 29.

Well, it's done. We have seen the Pole. McKinley, Balchen and June have delivered the goods. They took the Pole in their stride, neatly, expeditiously, and undismayed. If I had searched the world I doubt if I could have found a better team. Theirs was the actual doing. But there is not a man in this camp who did not assist in the preparation for the flight. Whatever merit accrues to the accomplishment must be shared with them.

Chapter IX

~~~~~~

EASTWARD BEYOND THE HORIZON

THE completion of the polar flight left the expedition, as far as operations were concerned, with only three major objectives unachieved—(1) the geological and geographical survey by the Geological Party, (2) an accurate ground survey of the Bay of Whales, and (3) the further investigation of the new land to the eastward. The first of these was on the threshold of accomplishment. Sunday, December 1st, the Geological Party notified the base by radio that they were camped at the foot of Liv Glacier, having spent the previous day in negotiating crevasses which "made the memory of those back between 81° and 82° seem like playthings for children." As for the third, we were already preparing for an extended flight.

Apart from the attraction which any unknown area holds for an inquiring mind, the land to the eastward drew us, as it had drawn many before us, with a magnetism peculiar to itself. It is the central mystery in a continent of mysteries. For many years a school of geologists and geographers had held the theory that the Antarctic is not one continent, but two. Hence, our desire to get over there, in spite of the fact we had been driven back thrice by sea and twice by air during the first season.

Thursday, Dec. 5, Later.

I think we shall make the eastern flight tomorrow. Haines believes that weather conditions are improving. No announcement will be made, however, until we are absolutely certain. The false starts before the polar flight were very hard on the personnel.

Parker will be the pilot, and June and McKinley will go in their accustomed capacities. We will use the Floyd Bennett.

This flight may be the most important flight of all.

119

On the morning of the 5th, Haines made a series of balloon runs which showed a slight southerly drift up to 10,000 feet. The day was clear and warm, with a light southwesterly wind on the surface. The plane was ready, and at 10:50 o'clock in the morning we took off. In the tanks was fuel for 12 hours' flying. I laid a course which would bring us about five miles to the north of Scott's Nunataks.

We climbed to an altitude of approximately 2,000 feet.

The Ross Sea was open, except for scattered pieces of pack and a few icebergs in the distance. During the previous weeks the wind had blown rather steadily from the south, and this, no doubt, had driven the pack farther north. It was a perfect time to send a ship through, but the *City,* alas, was still in New Zealand.

A little before noon we had the Rockefellers abeam. We were cutting across Cape Colbeck on a great circle course. South of Colbeck the continental ice sheet was rough and undulating. To the north the fine, glittering clarity of the snow's edge met the burnished copper of the sea. The water was slightly ruffled, and here and there an iceberg floated suspiciously near a jagged break in the Barrier, suggesting recent "calving."

To the north the continental ice sheet ended in a most unusual formation of ice tongues, which licked into an outer band of shelf ice. From our great height it was difficult to believe that these out-jutting tongues rose probably 200 feet above sea level. Under the vast pressures exerted from the hinterland they had pushed out over the sea, and huge pieces had broken off, forming ice islands, some of which were grounded and others imprisoned in the layer of shelf ice which was anchored to the coast line. These islands were terribly crevassed and split.

We could now see into the great blank space on the chart which I had studied hundreds of times and wondered about.

About 12:40 o'clock the thing we were looking for emerged grudgingly from the translucent horizon—first a mountainous

THE *City* IN HER TOUGHEST BATTLE

This photograph was taken on her last journey to the Bay of Whales, when nearly 200 tons of ice accumulated on her

THE *Jacob Ruppert* APPROACHES THE BAY ICE

(Photograph by Joseph A. Pelter)

A STATELY PROMENADE

mass a few degrees to the right of our course, which at the moment was 55° right of north. It was a considerable distance to the eastward. As we drew nearer other peaks loomed up, and there was the suggestion of a long range. It was, we knew, a first-class discovery.

Steadily we bore away from the coast. When we were 20 miles out, June, looking down at the open sea, turned and went through a series of gestures which plainly indicated swimming. True, there had been little enough bathing in Little America during the winter; but the suggestion left the rest of us cold. The engines sang without a break, and their music was the sweetest and most satisfying sound that we wanted to hear.

A few minutes after 1 o'clock, we reached the edge of the shelf ice and soon afterwards were over the 150th meridian, the eastern boundary of the British claims. We were advancing at the rate of 100 miles per hour over an area which had been unseen before, unknown and unclaimed. Here was the romance of geographical exploration; and seeing this land at last, after so much hoping and trying, brought deep satisfaction. The mystery to the eastward was beginning to yield. Aviation was doing what surface craft had for many years been failing to do. Best of all, every foot of this area was being recorded precisely and in its full detail by McKinley's camera.

The mountain masses to the eastward had been steadily enlarging. Against the horizon they extended north and south as far as the eye could see, an irregular, steel-gray bulwark. The nearest peak was at least sixty miles away, but at our altitude could be seen quite distinctly.

Most important of all, what I took to be the white elevated floor of a plateau showed behind the range. In this new land, then, there was perhaps a counterpart of the mighty plateau in South Victoria Land and about the Pole.

Our northerly course took us approximately parallel to the mountain range, which ran north and south, and we continued

in this direction for about sixty miles, then changed course
again to the eastward to bring the mountains nearer.

McKinley's delight was beyond words. Everything of which
an aerial surveyor dreams were before his camera in one grand
profusion—a new and undiscovered land, excellent visibility, a
well marked coast line which would give him a fixed altitude
(sea level) for constructing a map and a scenery unlike any
other known to man.

At 2:10 o'clock we swung to the southward and flew again
approximately parallel to the mountains. Just as we made the
turn, June was certain that he saw the sea to the northward
of us turn sharply to the eastward. If it did, I failed to see it.
The mountain range continued on to the northward and some
of the mountains curved to the eastward as far as I could see
with the glasses, and that was at least about seventy miles.
Though we were still a great distance from these mountains,
they stood out clearly and beautifully. The peaks of some of
them were surely 5,000 feet high. Bursting through this rampart, was a superb glacier. Cold and blue, it lay between two
gray-black walls, and in the center of the stream stood a high
black peak.

After paralleling the coast line for a while, we steered
various courses to investigate and photograph a number of ice
islands and rock islands which we thought we saw in the Ross
Sea. But they were too far off, and we finally desisted. What
they are I do not pretend to know. So many explorers more experienced than I have made mistakes in the claiming of lands
that I was determined to claim discovery only of those things
which could be, and were, recorded by the unforgetting and
unassailable memory of the camera.

About 3 o'clock we turned south again.

Dim shapes began to loom up in the southeastward, suggestive of land. They were not unlike the pyramids of Egypt in
the odd looming which is characteristic of Antarctic visibility.

Of all the flights I have ever made, none was so full of excitement and profit as this one. An air of impending drama foreshadowed every mile of progress. North, east, south and west—everything that was there was unseen and untrodden and unknown. It seemed to be very important, and yet one could not exult. Nature had worked on such a large scale and with such infinite power that one could only gape at her handiwork with open mouth and say: Holy smoke!

For here was the ice age in its chill receding tide. Here was a continent throttled and overwhelmed. Here was the lifeless waste born of one of the greatest periods of refrigeration that the earth has ever known. Seeing it, one could scarcely believe that the Antarctic was once a warm and fertile climate, with its own plants and trees of respectable size.

There was great beauty here, in the way that things which are also terrible can be beautiful. Glancing to the right, one had the feeling of observing the twilight of an eternity. Over the water and submerged land crept huge tongues of solid ice and snow, plowing into the outer fringe of shelf ice and accomplishing wide destruction. There were cliffs that must rise hundreds of feet. Once I caught sight of a cliff as it fell into the sea. From the great height of the plane it was just a small pellet falling from a toy wall. Not a sound penetrated through the noise of the engines. Yet thousands of tons must have collapsed in one frightful convulsion. To the right were the mountains, cold and gray, and from them fell, in places, ice falls which were perhaps 500 feet in height. The figure is arbitrary. They may have been more, or less.

By this time, we were well inland, homeward bound. Presently the Rockefellers were in view, a scattering of peaks throwing long shadows. A few stratus clouds floated near them.

Parker opened up the engines, and we struck across familiar territory.

At 6:20 o'clock we landed at Little America.

Friday, Dec. 6.

The flight to the eastward was more successful than I had dared to hope.

From a geographical point of view it was eminently satisfactory. It proved the existence of land in that area—an immense landfall.

It extended the outline of the coast and lifted a great section of it from the realm of fiction. McKinley has now surveyed and mapped a 400 mile stretch of the Barrier line and coast line.

It provided the new land first discovered on the flight of February 18th with a coastal access.

The survey photographs which McKinley made will be interesting and important to glaciologists fifty and one hundred years from now. For they are a permanent record of ice conditions in 1929, and the extent of the changes which will undoubtedly occur during the intervening years can be clearly drawn. Here, again, is an example of the new precision in modern exploration. . . .

To the new escarpment I have given the name Edsel Ford Range. Mr. Ford has been a consistent supporter of my efforts in exploration and aviation. More than that, he is a dear friend.

To the new Land I have given the name Marie Byrd Land, after my wife, who has backed and helped me every foot of the way, who has shouldered much of the burden of the expedition and whose understanding has made my many expeditions possible.

With the discovery of Marie Byrd Land our flight operations closed. The few short flights we made thereafter, such as the mapping of the Bay of Whales, were of no large geographical importance. Indeed, the field work of the expedition was approaching the mopping up stage. The Geological Party, striking brilliantly along the foot of the Queen Maud Range, penetrated the eastern margin of Marie Byrd Land, claimed it for the United States, thereby becoming the first Americans to set foot upon a land discovered and claimed by Americans in the South Polar regions. On January 18th, after a journey of 1,500 miles, they finally returned to Little America. We were all proud of what they had done.

That should have been the end of my anxieties. Nothing to do now but wait for the ships to come in and take us home.

Practically everything done as planned, all the parties back, no casualties—it was a situation from which a leader could draw deep satisfaction. Yet my troubles, it seemed, were only just beginning. The *City of New York* and the *Eleanor Bolling* had started in, but the pack guarding the Ross Sea refused to break up and disperse; for days and finally weeks they cruised and stabbed fruitlessly for an opening south. And, as the radio reports from the skippers steadily grew more discouraging, a sense of uncertainty, then of fear, then finally a mood bordering upon hopelessness took hold of Little America.

It wasn't just the thought of the hardships of a second winter that oppressed us. Though we were short of coal and certain kinds of food, we could still have lived through a second year at Little America with no great hardships; the hundreds of seals in the Bay of Whales meant meat to eat and blubber to burn. What made the waiting and the uncertainty so hard to bear was the knowledge that several men were ill, and one of them, Mason, was threatened with an operation for appendicitis. For that reason it would have gone hard with us if the ships failed to break through. And yet there was nothing we could do but wait. Only God and the winds and the tides could break up the billions of tons of ice between the 68th and 70th parallels. And so, having little else to do, the men watched for the radio bulletins posted in the mess hall, telling of the skirmishing between the vessels and the pack.

January dragged into February. The *Bolling*, having emptied her bunkers of coal, was obliged to steam back to New Zealand. But the *City of New York*, her bunkers replenished by the loan of coal from a Norwegian whaler, decided to attempt a break-through on February 6th. She met heavy ice, and a message from Captain Melville said that she "just hammered and hammered." But thirty-seven hours later her lookout sighted open sea ahead through the swirling sheets of fog and snow. "Severe southerly gale of hurricane force," Captain Melville warned. "Have passed through 60 miles of new pancake ice.... With low temperature and calm, the ice pack will become impassable. Therefore, strongly urge that base party be prepared to leave on arrival as any delay might prove serious. With more favorable conditions we should arrive at Bay of Whales in five or six days."

With the posting of that news Little America began to disintegrate before our eyes. Men were busy packing clothes and gear. The scientists were crating their records and instruments. The sound of hammering continued with unabating enthusiasm. And with the dissipation of uncertainty, spirits mounted wonderfully.

The *City*, however, found the Ross Sea in an evil mood. A few minutes after Captain Melville gained open water, the wind stiffened to hurricane force, and gusts reached velocities in excess of 100 miles. The air ran with snow, and visibility shut down to zero. The *City* met the storm head-on and managed to steam six miles south of the pack. Here her engines could not prevail against the seas, and she was driven back. A small storm trisail was set to keep her head to the seas.

As she retreated slowly, a new danger appeared. The ship was driven into a spur of the pack, and in the darkness, immense floes, rising and grinding under the combined force of wind and seas, towered menacingly at the crests of the waves. Because the rudder and stern sheets are the most vulnerable points of the *City*, it was necessary to head her into the ice. Melville swung her to port. Although the engines were full on, she failed to come around quickly in the face of the tremendous seas, and in a moment tons of green water swept over the rail. The deck cargo shifted, heavy steel fuel drums broke away from their lashings and charged into the bulwarks and rails, smashing them; the bags of coal washed into the companionways, blocking them so that the men below were trapped; and the decks were swept unceasingly by a cross sea.

In the darkness, they were driven into the pack. The stern, poised high, came down with fearful violence on a floe. A moment later another large mass of ice smashed against her starboard quarter. "I thought, for a moment, the blow had finished her," Captain Melville said later. But the *City* took it with no more than a shiver, and Melville stopped the engine to save the propeller. "Had one of those floes, sliding up and down those towering seas, crashed on the deck, it would have crushed it to pulp," the radio operator, Berkner, said.

The sky cleared, and for two days the *City* drove south at a goodish clip. Then the gale struck her again, and this time nearly finished her. On the night of the 10th a southeaster sprung up, cold and raw. By morning it had reached almost hurricane force. Snow fell continuously, and the spray whipping from the choppy sea froze on the decks and rigging as fast as it fell. Captain Melville, recognizing the danger, ordered the crew to clear the ship with axes and hammers; but the ice formed faster than they could chop it away. A cylinder of ice, ten feet thick, covered the bowsprit and the martingale; and the mass of ice on her decks brought her so low that every other sea boarded and raked her fore and aft.

The gale continued for four days, and during that period, the *City's* plucky crew never wavered once. How hard the battle was we did not realize at Little America. There were hints of it in the meager messages that flew between the base and ship, sandwiched in between discussions over mattresses, knives and forks, bedding, food, plates, bunks and the like—things we should have to take along to eke out the supplies of the *City*, which was scarcely equipped to handle sixty men.

February 15.

The vessel is iced up in the worst condition I have ever seen a vessel. We have been running under full steam in a living gale of wind ever since we left the ice pack. We have had no sun for a week and our positions are only approximate. Our head gear is so heavily iced up that at present we are looking for the first shelter to clear ship of ice. On the outside of her hull from the water line up there is approximately two feet of ice. Heavy pitching. We are hampered by heavy seas in our efforts to keep the ship clear of ice. The leak in the stern remains unchanged, but it is not serious. I am in full control of the situation and will advise you of any change.

MELVILLE

On the night of the 15th the situation reached a crisis. The men were worn out. Everything that could be spared had been thrown overboard to keep her afloat. And Captain Melville, after a conference with Johansen, reached the conclusion that unless a haven was gained before morning, they would be forced to run with the gale in search of shelter to clear ship. Johansen went on watch, and toward the end he made out land to the westward through a break in the clouds. It was the cone of Mount Erebus, a volcano, with a feathering vapor streaming from her crater; and the land which they sighted was Ross Island. They had been driven *more than 300 miles off their course.* Presently they could see to the westward the lower peaks of South Victoria Land. Melville edged the ship in toward the shelter, and in the morning had her in the lee of the Barrier. Her decks were then nearly level with the sea, and her hull, rigging and spars were encased with a solid coating of ice which, in places, was three feet thick. More than 200 tons of ice lay above the water line of this 500 ton ship. That the *City* did not go down, I think, is due to the skill of Captain Melville and ice pilot Johansen, the courage and unswerving loyalty of her crew, and the stout heart of the ship herself.

Sunday, Feb. 16.

Little America is about ready to pass out of existence.

For the past eight days the sledges have been moving in a steady line to Floyd Bennett Bay. McKinley and Black have the stuff gathered in three piles. Nearly half the camp is now living there. Feury has built a mess hall from dog crates, and an upturned ski from the Ford serves as a mess table. Two lines of tents face each other, and with tons of gear piled behind them it is like a refugee camp.

Winter cannot be far off. The temperature has been falling steadily, and the Bay has been full of sea smoke for days. We shall get out just in time. And yet, with the end so near, I am rather sorry that it is over. I shall miss most of all the informal life and the understanding of men which only an expedition of this kind can bring out. Nowhere else can the qualities of friendship and unselfishness be so fully nurtured.

Monday, Feb. 17.

The *City* is making excellent time, with clear sky and open sea, although contending with a strong westerly set in the current. She will arrive some time tomorrow afternoon.

The last things were moving out of Little America today. The camp is very quiet tonight—there are just a few here—the rest are at Floyd Bennett Bay. "Doc" Coman has remained, to keep watch over Mason. Mason is doing quite well, although in constant pain, and we have decided not to attempt to move him until the *City* is fully loaded and ready to go.

It is a pity that we cannot take the airplanes. However, the aviation gang has anchored them securely on the top of a wind swept ridge about three-quarters of a mile to the eastward of the camp. They faced the planes into the prevailing winds and we hope that they will not be buried by the snow for several years to come.

Tuesday, Feb. 18, Eight o'clock.

The *City* is in.

An hour ago Melville radioed that the ship was in the Bay of Whales, making for the West Barrier. A few minutes later the camp at Floyd Bennett Harbor radioed she was in sight, her topmasts showing through a heavy mist. She came alongside the ice a few minutes ago, and June has begun to load her.

The place has never been so quiet, nor has it seemed so large and barn-like. The bunks are empty and stripped of everything. The fire in the stove has gone out. Mason is curled up in a bunk and the "Doc" is talking quietly to him. Vaughan is sitting near-by. Ten miles away the loading is in full swing. In all frankness, I hate to see it end.

Wednesday, Feb. 19, At Sea.

At 9:30 o'clock this morning Melville gave the order to cast off. The *City* nosed her way through loose ice in the Bay of Whales and then stood out to sea. We are now making our way along the Barrier.

Early this morning, I came down to the ship on Vaughan's sledge. As we rounded the entrance of Ver-sur-Mer Inlet, we met Blackburn on his way back to pick up Dr. Coman and Mason.

The air was quite raw and cold. We saw the *City* moored alongside the bay ice, and the loaded dog teams scurrying between it and the camp in Floyd Bennett Harbor. The *City* still bore the marks of her struggle. Her bow, rigging and decks were still swathed in ice, and the sheathing was scarred where heavy floes had struck her.

McKinley, Gould, June and Black had the loading problem well in hand. They had been working all night, and most of the important records and scientific equipment were already aboard. All hands pitched in, and the supplies marched up the wooden plankings in a steady stream.

At 9:30 o'clock the last piece was put aboard. Then the dogs were released from the sledges and taken on the ship. We cast off.

Now that we have started the Antarctic is showing its most beautiful side. The sun is shining, lighting up the Barrier cliffs, bringing out its lovely blue shadows and tints. It seems to say: "You see, I am not half so bad as I am painted."

Friday, Feb. 28.

Homeward bound.

The voyage is almost run. In a few days we shall see Dunedin and our friends. Then home. The mission is done, and well, I hope.... I hope it sincerely, principally for these men who have gone each step of the way with me. They have given two years of their lives to the service of science, a hard and grudging master, and it would be a pity if their sacrifice were neither understood nor appreciated.

Chapter **X**

RETURN TO ANTARCTICA

My decision to return to Antarctica with a second expedition was not so much a spontaneous thought as a maturing compulsion bred by the work of my first expedition. Problems of large geographical and scientific importance remained to be investigated, and it seemed desirable—more than that, imperative—to attempt to close them while we still had the momentum of one successful effort, the advantage of a more enlightened public interest in Antarctic research, and while there was still available an Antarctic-trained personnel from whom could be drawn the nucleus for a second and stronger expedition. And, finally, there was, at least for me, the intangible attraction of the white continent itself, the pull of discovery, of seeing new lands and fitting into the jig-saw of geography the missing pieces beyond the horizon. No one who has ever seen new lands rising above the prow of a ship, or above a running dog team, or through the shine of a propeller, can easily deny the pull they exert.

Anyhow, that was the way I looked at it. When I walked out of Little America, in February, 1930, to go down to the ship, it was with the firm resolve to go back.

"We'll be back, Bill," I said to Haines, the meteorologist.

"Not me," said Bill, "once is quite enough."

Well, four years later both of us were to stand again over Little America, in the rare sunshine of its sheltering valley, and Bill was digging furiously down to our old quarters. When at last his chunky frame slid and disappeared into the depths of the Balloon Station, I drew a sigh of relief such as I have rarely had opportunity to indulge.

For a long time the odds were three to one we'd never get back.

The Second Byrd Antarctic Expedition was assembled and departed in the travail of the depression. Indifference, its own poverty, even actual hostility were among the obstacles it had to overcome. In my own files are letters—not the most agreeable correspondence—berating me for stupidity and selfishness in setting forth on such an enterprise when the country was in a bad way. What they were driving at wasn't very clear. I'm quite sure they couldn't have measured Little America as a haven for spirits too sensitive to endure the economic agonies of civilization.

Looking at the matter in the broad way, there are few divisions of science, or sections of human knowledge that cannot be profitably explored in Antarctica. Geology, glaciology, meteorology, botany, biology and zoölogy, astronomy, physics, geography, terrestrial magnetism, oceanography, geophysics and paleontology—these and many others hold open broad avenues of research. In all, the second expedition was equipped to investigate and did investigate some twenty-two divisions and subdivisions of scientific research.

The geographical program was as complete as our ingenuity, skill and perseverance could make it. Perhaps in this connection a statement of policy is in order. Geographical discovery is still, as it always was, the brightest weapon in the explorer's armory; but in the new philosophy of exploration it is principally a tool for getting at something deeper. It attains the dignity of a science only when, rising above the superficial glory of a first penetration, it brings the apparatus of science to bear upon the unknown for a truer understanding of a multiplicity of problems.

In the program of the second expedition there was no spectacular objective, no *tour de force* such as a polar flight, that would create great public interest. The nearest we came to that sort of thing was a proposed flight from the vicinity of

Peter I Island and across the unknown coast to Little America. This project, however, had to be canceled. The burden of nearly every main flight, surface journey or ship's penetration was exploration of the Pacific Quadrant. Therein is the key to the network of tracks traversing the reconnaissance maps of the expedition.

The Pacific Quadrant is the great region of unknown land and sea lying east of Little America, including the unknown seas of the South Pacific Ocean that beat against the unknown coast; back from the coast it extends up through the unknown interior to the Pole. Clear to Hearst Land, south of Cape Horn, discovered by Sir Hubert Wilkins, on the opposite side of the continent, the region was a geographical vacuum. If the interior was completely blank, the coast and its ocean approaches were hardly less so. In the South Pacific between the 150th and 130th meridians West, for example, the horizon of knowledge had barely been pushed beyond the Antarctic Circle —and, astonishingly the record was Cook's penetration of 1773. The region drew my interest throughout the first expedition. We succeeded in making two successful aerial casts to the east, the first of which located the Rockefeller Mountains, and the second, northeast along the uncharted coast, yielded up the Edsel Ford coastal range of Marie Byrd Land. I considered the results of this flight far more important than the results of our flight to the Pole.

Against the Marie Byrd Land region, holding as it did the most substantial American gains on the continent, we proposed to throw virtually the full weight of our field resources—to run over it a geographical network of an intensity and range impossible to previous expeditions. With ships, airplanes, dog teams and snow tractors, a broad plan seemed feasible. The idea was to launch a double attack by ship and plane on the way in, having for its principal object the exploration of the unknown coastal regions of the Pacific Quadrant. In the second season (that is to say, the second Antarctic spring and

summer) we would press the attack into the interior from Little
America, using dog teams, tractors, and aviation on a broad
front between the coast and the Queen Maud Range, which
buttresses the Polar Plateau.

To fulfill the broad program of geographical exploration
and scientific research which alone would justify a return to
Antarctica, we required a vast quantity of things—planes,
dogs, tractors, food, clothing—all the innumerable things
indispensable to the setting up of an expedition on a continent
which offers nothing toward existence except seal and penguin
meat.

We needed ships also, two of them—an ice-breaker plus a
big steel ship to transport the bulk of the stores, and to carry
on her deck a twin-engined plane with an 82-foot wing spread.
The United States Shipping Board had laid up at Staten
Island a number of freighters, mostly of wartime construction, which hadn't been able to earn their keep on the seas. For
a dollar-a-year we got the loan of a three-island, oil-burning
outcast from the Pacific lumber trade, named *Pacific Fir*. She
looked her age, and her engines hadn't turned for some time.
Rechristened the *Jacob Ruppert*, after my friend Colonel
Jacob Ruppert, she left the graveyard with a creaking and
groaning in her stiffened members, for a fleeting resurrection
in the ice of the far south.

Locating a trustworthy ice ship was more difficult. Not many
are available. The barkentine *City of New York* of the first
expedition was past her usefulness; she was reduced to the
state of a floating museum, towed ignominiously from one ex-
hibition mart to another. Out in Oakland, California, I came
upon another old ice-breaker, the celebrated barkentine *Bear*,
which in April, 1884, had relieved the six survivors of the
Greely expedition at Cape Sabine and subsequently served
brilliantly in the Arctic. She was the "White Angel" of the
whaling fleet, and she policed the gold rush to the Yukon. The
city of Oakland let me have her for the nominal sum of $1,000.

Edsel Ford paid the expense of getting her to Boston. In appreciation for the kindness of the city of Oakland in letting me have her on such generous terms, I renamed her *Bear of Oakland*. She was 200 feet long, with a draught of 18 feet, 2 inches, beam of 32 feet, and of 703 tons net register. In her prime she could make 9 knots under steam, according to a report written by Captain Cochran, who commanded her on 8 cruises. Well, she never quite did that for us.

At the critical moment my friend William Horlick came forward with a substantial cash donation. With what he gave and what we were able to borrow, we got the plane the job called for—a Curtiss-Wright Condor, powered by two supercharged Wright Cyclones (725 h.p.) fitted with skis and floats, and wonderfully handy for exploring. It was, in fact, an exploring instrument with special fuel tanks for long-range flying, unobstructed vision from all windows, ports for the mapping camera. Capable of lifting a gross load of 19,000 pounds on either floats or skis, it provided the essential elements of load (mapping cameras, repair kits, emergency rations and camping gear, etc., for the flight crew in the event of a forced landing away from base) and range (approximately 1,300 miles with a full load.)

Besides stores and ships and airplanes, we needed tractors. Ever since I had first looked upon the firm, undulating surface of the Ross Ice Barrier, the idea had been evolving in my mind that a properly designed tractor, equipped with caterpillar treads, could safely navigate it. Now tractors had been tried before in the Antarctic; indeed, we had used one, though with no great success, on the first expedition. The fault, however, was not with the idea but rather with the vehicle itself; it was short of power, for one thing; and not long enough, for another, to span crevasses. This time I was resolved to give mechanized transport another test. On account of lack of funds, we could not do what I really wanted to do—design and build machines especially for Antarctic navigation; instead we had to take and adapt as best we could vehicles already on the market. Mr. Edsel Ford gave us two light snowmobiles; the Cleveland Tractor Company presented a Cletrac, a mighty land dreadnaught which could haul a ten-ton load; and from M. Andre Citroën, whom I had met in France after the trans-Atlantic flight, we got three fast intermediate cars, called Citroëns.

Planes and tractors are superb instruments, but there is no getting away from dogs. The Eskimo husky still is, as he always has been, the one absolutely reliable means of polar advance. He can overcome terrain which a tractor can't penetrate and a plane can't land on. We drew in all directions for dogs —the north shore of the St. Lawrence, Labrador, Manitoba and (indirectly) from Alaska. At Wonalancet, N. H., Milton Seeley had crossed the Alaskan breed of the first expedition with Siberian and wolf, producing a stout sledging dog—short, stocky, well-formed, with good shoulders and paws, the extra speed of the Siberian, and weighing about 65 pounds. We selected some 50 of them. From the north shore of the St. Lawrence and the Labrador region we collected 76 huskies, typical Labrador dogs, motley in coat and blood history with a distant wolf strain, stocky dogs with wide foot pads and strong legs, averaging between 70 and 75 pounds. From John Is-feld at Gimli, Manitoba, came 30 Manitoba huskies, descendants of the dogs used by Sir Ernest Shackleton's second expedition—magnificent animals, large-boned, deep-chested, heavy-shouldered and strong-legged. They weighed between 80 and 100 pounds.

The *Bear of Oakland*, being slower than the *Ruppert*, had to get away first. She left Boston, September 25th, 1933, under command of Lieutenant (J. G.) Robert A. J. English, U.S.N. The *Ruppert* with the planes, 153 dogs and the bulk of the stores aboard, put out from Newport News about a month later. Commander Hj. Gjertsen, of the Norwegian Navy, was in command with the title of Commodore.

Except for storms which harassed the slower footed *Bear*, the Pacific crossing was uneventful. The *Bear* made her westing down via Tahiti, stopping there only to coal. We on the *Ruppert* took a more southerly course. On the morning of December 5 (having meanwhile crossed the 180th meridian and lost a day), the lookout shouted "Land," and the serrated peaks of North Island, New Zealand, welled over the horizon. Bucking a full gale, we made for Wellington.

There we lingered only long enough to take aboard various supplies which had been forwarded by commercial steamers to this rendezvous. The aviation unit meanwhile got the big plane ready for flight. The huge wing sections were mounted, the variable pitch propellers were removed and replaced by fixed pitch propellers, heater hoods were installed for warming the engines in cold temperatures, and a stanch, tiered platform, seven feet high and fabricated of pine balks a foot square, was constructed over No. 5 hatch, on the after well deck.

On this tiered pedestal, directly abaft the mainmast, the plane was cocked fore and aft. The whale-like tail ran high across the poop. The pedestal, which covered the whole square of the hatch, was made fast to the hatch coaming by steel rods; and as a safeguard against the wrenching force of the ship's roll it was further strengthened by long 1½-inch steel rods —three to a side—bolted to the bulwark stanchions. Cocked on this eyrie, the plane's lower wing was some twenty-seven feet above the water line, well out of reach of any seas we were likely to encounter. Altogether the structure seemed solid enough. Still, I must confess that I never breathed easily until the plane was safely berthed at Little America.

Of course, these and other preparations took time; but at last, on the night of December 11th, they were done. At 7:38 o'clock next morning we cast off.

So it was Southward Ho! again; I couldn't restrain a feeling of satisfaction as I felt the deck strain to the pulse of the engines. All that had gone before was in the nature of a prelude. Now we were squared away on our mission. As the ship stood out from Cape Palliser we were like a man-o'-war clearing decks for action. The last stray cargo was whisked below, hatches were battened down, and in the holds and on the shelter deck the lashings securing the small mountains of cargo were inspected and reënforced. The decks were nakedly bare. Up forward the engineering force was hurriedly lagging with asbestos the steam lines to all winches, to keep the lines from freezing up in the south.

"All secure to sea," Commodore Gjertsen reported that afternoon. With the engines wide open and turning up a brave nine knots we steamed toward one of the most formidable areas on the face of the earth. In this same area other expeditions had tried and failed. Yet, somehow, as I contemplated the heaving metallic sea, I was quietly confident of the outcome. Where the others had staked all on a single thrust, we had two strings fitted to our bow. The first was the ship. We would speed her to the limit of her penetrating powers. Sooner or later it was inevitable that ice would stop her, as it had stopped every other vessel in the past. When that happened we should fit the second string—the plane. The "mountains of ice" which had flung back Captain Cook and his successors would be trifling barriers to a plane. Soaring in its natural element it could venture with impunity where no ship could live. In the expiring twilight I studied the structure of the plane: the enormous upper wing, 82 feet long, shrunk the 54-foot beam of the ship: and the bulking outline in the shadows conveyed an impression of power that was reassuring.

My diary reports:

Wednesday, Dec. 13, 9:50 P.M.

A heavy fog closed in during the middle watch this morning, and visibility was reduced to half a ship's length. Nevertheless, being well out of the steamer lanes, we are running at full speed. The air is calm and colder. At noon mess Commodore Giertsen remarked that it has the look of "iceberg weather." It's hardly likely that we should encounter bergs this far north, but to be on the safe side lookouts were stationed in the eyes of the ship.

We lost our seventh dog today—Watch. He died of strangulation—fell, unobserved, over the side and strangled in his collar. It is always a tragedy to lose a good dog, but no blame attaches in a case like this. I can't praise the dog department too highly. The mortality rate among the dogs has been surprisingly low—only 7 out of 153. We had expected to lose upwards of twenty per cent in the tropics.

The fog was somewhat disquieting. We were still in it on the 16th, twelve hundred miles southeast of Wellington. Sometimes it would lift a bit for a few hours, then shut in again, thick as wool. The telegraph moved fretfully from full speed, to half, then slow, then back again to half and full. Commodore Gjertsen and Captain Verleger were constantly on the bridge. Decks, spars and rigging dripped with oozing moisture, and the dogs, hating wet, laid back their ears and whined, night and day.

Tuesday, December 19th, was a notable day. That day, on the given course, we broke past Captain Cook's track for a record southing; and, in the early watch, raised the first icebergs. We were at last on the rim of the unknown sea. One hundred and fifty years had passed since a keel had furrowed these blue waters. Instinctively my eyes sought the southern horizon for the yellow-white effulgence of ice blink. No, still a water sky. For a while at least the road south lay open.

Shortly before midnight, just after the sun set for the last time, we marked the creamy glow of ice blink on the southern horizon. That meant pack ahead. The ship was running south-southeast. At 6:30 A.M., December 20th, at Latitude 65° 55′ S., Long. 151° 10′ W., 35 miles north of the Circle, we fetched up against the northern rim of the pack. Great fields of loose, pancake ice curved irregularly to the east and west. Southward they extended to the limit of vision. It looked none too promising; neither did it look too bad.

We worked eastward through scattered floes, looking for a feasible passage. Remember, we had an old iron ship which for years had lain unused in a Government graveyard. Her plates were only seven-eighths of an inch thick; they were rusty, and there was no telling how much of a strain her rivets could withstand. We went cautiously, side-stepping the heavier floes.

By mid-afternoon it was evident that the ice massing in front of us was too heavy to be taken by assault. The shocks of impact came more frequently; several times, when we struck masses of hard, blue-green ice, the *Ruppert* trembled the length of her keel. Down in the engine room you could hear the hollow sound of the ice banging against the plates.

Commodore Gjertsen shook his head. "She's an old ship," he reminded us. "It's not as if you had a wooden ship, built for ice. Her plates won't stand much punishment."

So we made ready to fit the second string to our bow.

Twenty-eight miles astern I had noticed a wide lake of open water in the pack. It was sheltered, and wide enough to give us a long take-off in any direction. So we turned back to this lake. Here the ship hove to. The aviation crew worked all night to make the big plane ready for flight. When they were done, it was swung over the side, test-flown by pilots June and Bowlin, then gassed. Shortly before noon next day, with the two pilots, radioman Petersen, and airmapper, Pelter, I set out on the first flight over the pack.

The day was perfect—ideal for a flight, with one of the steadiest barometers I have ever seen in the polar regions. The thermometer stood at 40° above.

Making one hundred knots, we roved over the pack, climbing to 2,000 feet. At that altitude we had vision of about 59 miles. In all directions the pack lay upon the sea, like a curiously tesselated ivory plain, with coal-black lanes of open water twisting through it, filling the interstices. It was mostly light, loose pack. I looked in vain for the heavy, rafted pressure ice which I had expected to find in this region. And this puzzled me, for awhile, until the explanation leapt to mind.

A theory, growing out of my observation and study of the best scientific opinion, had already matured.

The absence of pack—on the contrary, the comparative openness of the sea—strongly argued against the existence of an archipelago or a peninsula of the continent, supposed by some to project into this area. If land existed, there must have been larger quantities of heavy bay ice than we had seen. After all, a steady current with a westerly set was continuously wafting pack down from the ice coast to the eastward; and any extensive land mass lying athwart that current was bound to accumulate and dam back the immense pack for which this region was fabled.

At 1:40 p.m., having reached the outward limit of our gas, we turned at Lat. 69° 51' S., Long. 149° W., and headed back for the ship. At our altitude we had visibility of at least 50 miles, and, therefore, well beyond the 70th parallel.

No, it seemed to me, as I turned the facts over in my mind on the way back to the *Ruppert*, that the first explanation was apt to be the right one. The huge lobe of uncharted white space bulging between the 140th and 160th meridians West must be nearly all Pacific Ocean. With a little effort later on, perhaps with a fair measure of luck, it could be erased from the map and the land be defined as falling within the then known coasts of Marie Byrd Land and King Edward VII Land. This had already been forecast by the best geographical opinion.

A more profitable point of attack was in the vicinity of the 120th meridian West, where a deep embayment in the pack seeming to persist year after year and shoal soundings indicated the proximity of the unknown coast.

Time was the controlling element. We couldn't afford to delay arrival in the Bay of Whales later than the middle of January; and, taking all things into account, I didn't see how we could spare more than a fortnight to take up the attack farther east. Besides, the ship's oil reserves allowed no greater margin. The region was notoriously inhospitable. The seas were rough, and earlier navigators had reported that the sun was rarely seen through the fog. Maybe we were off on a wild goose chase.

However, exploration is less a matter of waiting for breaks than of creating them. It was decided that immediately after landing, the plane would be hoisted aboard and the ship sent eastward.

The flight was completed without incident. The sun being obscured by clouds, we asked for a radio direction bearing from the ship. It checked nicely. Then, dead on our course, a smudge of smoke on the horizon—the *Ruppert*. At 2:55 P.M. we raked over it, fore and aft, and at 3:03 P.M. landed in the quiet water.

Three hours later, with the plane cradled on its tier, the *Ruppert* was steaming northward at full speed through a widening breach in the pack.

At last we extricated the ship and, breathing easier, bore north of east through lighter ice, past which we gained the open sea. Coasting the pack, which now curved irregularly on our starboard hand, we steered eastward, altering course occasionally to evade the tentacle-like streams, and belts of ice extending from the main mass.

Chapter *XI*

∿∿∿∿∿∿∿∿∿∿∿∿∿∿∿∿∿∿∿∿∿∿∿∿∿∿∿∿∿∿∿∿

THE DEVIL'S GRAVEYARD

THE respite was short-lived. The glass dropped sharply. The wind, which had been holding in the east, whistled into east northeast and stiffened. Then a white fog arose, and wet snow came slanting through it. The night turned sodden. Out of the mist, heaving on the long swell, lurched the outriders of a ghostly fleet of icebergs. Speed dropped to half, then to slow. All night long the chilled men in the crow's nest and up in the eyes of the ship, were calling: "Berg off the starboard bow," or "Berg close aboard to port."

Though the name was to come later, we had entered the frontiers of that region which the members of the Second Byrd Antarctic Expedition will forever remember as the Devil's Graveyard.

You'll probably never see that name on any chart. Like Scylla and Charybdis, or the Symplegades—the Clashing Rocks—of the Euxine Sea, it is one of those fabulous, terrifying aspects of Nature which lie in ambush for sailors at the ends of the earth. What we called the Devil's Graveyard lay, roughly between the 147th and 135th meridians, along the Antarctic Circle. It was a mood of nature. For days a sleet-oozing, dripping oppressive fog, so thick that the bow at times was lost from the view of the bridge, lay over the sea. And through that smoking pall, like phantom fleets, prowled icebergs past numbering, with the sea sobbing in their basement grottoes. Like a cornered thing, the ship stood among them, stopped and drifting, or maneuvering, with swift alarums and excursions, to evade towering cliffs, emerging with formidable clarity out of the gloom, which bore down upon her. Fog alone

143

is oppressive enough at sea, but when it is a veil concealing hordes of preying enemies it becomes malevolent. The telegraph was cocked at standby; lookout watches were doubled; on the bridge, in the eyes of the ship, in the crow's nest, and deep down in the engine room, men waited and watched uneasily. Those days in the fog left a spell on us that will not be lightly shaken off. Months later, George Noville told me, he'd break, with a start, from a sound sleep, with sweat on his palms and forehead, his body braced against an invisible blow, listening for the cry of the lookout and waiting for a reeling impact. That's the way it was in the Devil's Graveyard—a deep brooding fog which, in Conrad's phrase, was one great circular ambush.

Sunday, Dec. 24, 11:38 p.m.

Christmas Eve. A more god-forsaken place could not be imagined. Ship stopped and drifting all day. The fog still holds, robbing us of irreplaceable hours. It lifted a bit this afternoon, when the wind shifted into south southwest, but soon closed in again. Snow squalls swirling around the ship every few hours. The bergs about us seem to be increasing in numbers. Our position is really critical. Visibility at times drops to zero, and the bergs rise out of the fog with alarming suddenness. You stare into the shifting vapor, seeing nothing, only dim, uncertain shadows. The cliffs upwards of 150 feet high, cleaves through, scarcely four ship-lengths away. Then the cry floats down from the crow's nest, echoed almost simultaneously from the lookout in the eyes of the ship: "Berg on the port bow." Down in the engine room the engineers on watch spring to their posts, the screw turns, the decks tremble to the motion, and the ship sheers away from the menace. This darting to and fro has been going on all day.

We nearly lost one of the dogs—a wolf dog, Olaf. Buckley and Paine were exercising a team up forward. Lewishon swore that the dog, having lost all interest in polar expeditions, simply jumped overboard. Anyhow, there he was in the water, paddling violently. Dustin went over the side on a line and tried to grab him by the collar, but the dog, being badly frightened, escaped him and rounded the bow. He couldn't have lived long in that water. Fortunately, he swam into the current of warm water discharging from the circulating pumps, and had the good sense to paddle around there until the men were able to reach him in a small boat. Innes-Taylor gave the dog artificial respiration, and tonight Olaf appeared to be suffering less from exposure than from a hang-over produced by too much excellent whiskey. When Innes-Taylor revealed the cure, it was all we could do to restrain the entire ship's company from jumping overboard.

Monday, Feb. 25, Midnight.

Christmas. In spite of the fog we had a very satisfying day: the tables in the forward and after saloons groaned under an amazing variety of food; there were movies on the shelter deck, and Christmas boxes, bought months ago, were opened with eagerness and their contents shared all around. Except for those on watch, the rules were relaxed, and I doubt if there was anywhere on this earth a gayer Christmas than was celebrated in the Devil's Graveyard.

For a while it looked as if the elements had released their own gift. The fog lifted at 6:15 this morning, and we got under way again, steering east and southeast along the front of the pack. Shortly after 4 o'clock the fog closed in again, thicker than ever. An hour later the air cleared enough to tempt us into a slow advance. With the edge of the pack about two miles off on our right hand, the ship crept ahead for two hours, feeling rather than seeing the way.

Suddenly the fog drained into the sea. It was an eerie experience. One moment we were sliding down a narrow gray corridor, thankful for the lack of bergs. The next moment the fog was sucked away, and hundreds of bergs, many of immense size, cropped up as if by magic. Closely ranked, they extended as far as I could see, so numerous that the sea was broken into rivers coursing among mountains of ice. It was Scylla and Charybdis multiplied a thousand times.

Commodore Gjertsen signaled for a slow speed astern. We backed out a way, then turned. The fog closed in, and we stopped at 9 o'clock. We've been drifting ever since. The barometer is dropping. Wind and sea are making.

A gale struck during the night. The Cape pigeons, more reliable than a barometer in that area, had given warning. Higher and higher they flew, till they were cutting across the truck of the foremast—a sign of bad weather. The seas piled up, breaking across the forward and after well decks.

Shortly after 7 o'clock the lookout up forward sang out:

"Big berg dead ahead!" almost the same instant Captain Verleger and Chief Officer Bayne, who were on the bridge, raised a big berg on the starboard bow. The sides were lost in the fog, but two hundred feet in the air, white spires stood clear.

Not caring to steer between them, and unwilling to lay the ship in the trough of the sea to pass them to leeward, Captain Verleger decided to pass them to windward. Heaving on the gale, the ship lunged forward. Just as she drew abeam of the larger berg, her speed fell off. Came a whistle in the speaking tube behind the helmsman. Commander Queen, in the engine room, reported the fires were out. In some way water had gotten into the starboard oil tank; with the pitching and rolling of the ship it had worked up through the oil, been pumped under pressure to the burner nozzles, and put the fires out. Queen had instantly switched to the port tanks and started the fires again, but steam pressure was dropping fast.

Pressure dropped in short order to less than ninety pounds— barely half normal pressure. It wasn't enough to hold her in the wind. She lost steerage way. Slowly the seas cuffed her bow around; then she fell off, beam-on to the storm, and swiftly drifted down wind, rolling like a drunkard.

Just 200 yards—maybe a little more, maybe less—to the good, we fell past the big berg. Then the mists enveloped it; we saw it no more. "Gorblime," muttered Chief Officer Bayne, under his breath, "I'd just made up me mind where to jump." We weren't clear yet—not by a long shot. The ship fell in among a mess of growlers, scarcely less formidable than the giant bergs of which they were shattered remnants. Masses of hard, blue-green ice, they lay strewn everywhere, heaving with loud crashings on the sea. It was impossible to tell which way they were bearing. The waves would throw them up, revealing twenty feet of green basement, then suck them into the hollows until they were barely awash. You found yourself watching them with a curious fascination. It was like being among countless agitated reefs. If the ship in her helplessness had ever grazed her plates against one of those things, it would have been too bad. We passed some with nothing to spare.

Providence must have been with us that day. Slowly steam pressure rose, and the ship groped her way back into the wind. All the afternoon and evening, and until the storm abated at 6 o'clock in the morning of the 27th, we held her in the eye of the wind, following it as it hauled into the westward. And all the while these malevolent fleets of ice—with bergs two, three, four miles long and more, and of every conceivable shape and form—came wallowing out of the gray mists, stood briefly in view, then vanished, as new ones emerged to take their places. The waves welled and crashed and gushed against their smooth flanks, sending spray clear over their tops. Sometimes the mists would wrap around them, so that you saw only the dripping domes, strangely truncated and floating with baffling buoyancy in mid-air. The sea was littered with brash ice, bergy bits, growlers and half-shattered bergs, as though two giant fleets were fighting an action somewhere in the dark.

Whence came these phantom fleets? And whither were they bound? To destruction, of course. For this was a march of death, and in all nature there is nothing like it.

That night, when he took his place at the head of the wardroom table, Commodore Gjertsen spoke soberly: "Gentlemen, you can thank God that you still have a deck under you tonight."

Wednesday morning, the 27th, the sun shattered the fog like a golden lance. The seas moderated, and the ship was able to resume her easting. Several sights—the first shots of the sun since the 22nd—fixed our position as Lat. 65° 50′ S., Long. 139° 30′ W. Though we had been driving at close to full speed against a northwest wind all the day before, the ship had actually been driven about sixty miles east.

Under a cold breeze pouring in from the west southwest, the fog vanished, and in the sunlight we had our first full view of the Devil's Graveyard. The sea was almost lost for the bergs. There was no end of them. They rose, one upon the other, like skyscrapers in a metropolis.

As the day wore on the bergs, instead of diminishing in number, actually increased: and the wonder we had felt in the morning increased to amazement. Every mile forward brought new columns into sight. They seemed inexhaustible. We had discovered the greatest iceberg area in the world. In a twenty-four hour period ending December 28th Dr. Poulter estimated we sighted 8,000 bergs. In that single day we passed among nineteen times as many bergs as the International Ice Patrol reports in a normal year.

Still, now that the fog had lifted and we were once more driving toward our objective, we could look at these things with greater equanimity. In the evening the sun strove clear again, bathing the sea with amber warmth, and all the delicate, latent lights—the fine blues, the lavenders, the greens—were awakened in these floating creations. You saw whole cliffs glow with that rare, lovely beauty you associate with the light falling through old stained glass in ancient cathedrals. Softened and transformed by the warmth of sunlight and the shy emergence of colors, the Devil's Graveyard was very different from the death prowl it became in the fog. Even the bridge players in the saloon put down their cards and went on deck to watch. It was the ultimate compliment to Creation.

New Year's Day, 1934, found us cleaving southward into the pack, though at greatly reduced speed. Sometimes we profited by stretches of open water, but more often we crept through loose, mushy ice, interspersed with heavy floes. Often the ship hardly had way on her, though you could feel the screw thrashing and the poop trembling as the blades fought for a foothold.

As always, when we approached the limits of discovery, the excitement over the possibility of sighting land got the better of the new hands. The flying bridge was clustered with hopeful Columbuses. And there were beguiling hints to whet their hopes

—a solitary Emperor penguin moodily measuring his fate on a drifting floe, and a giant petrel wheeling like a startled thing in the fog. These are not often found far from land. Bergs, too, often carry the illusion of coast; in mist they are especially deceptive, and so there were frequent cries of "Land Ho!" which were repudiated almost in the same breath. "Don't get me titillated," complained Second Mate Dempster, "till ye see the smoke curlin' from the chimneys."

By mid-afternoon it was manifest that the *Ruppert* had reached the limit of her southing. The ice got heavier; even with the shaft turning up forty revolutions, the ship's speed dropped to nothing. The lookouts, conning the pack from the crow's nest, reported heavy ice fields in all directions.

At 3:30 o'clock, at Lat. 70° 02′ S., the ship stopped, backed cautiously and commenced to retreat.

Six miles back the *Ruppert* glided to a stop in a stretch of slick black water. The aviation crew made ready to lower the plane for another flight. But shortly after we swung the plane overboard, a gale arose and we had a bitter struggle to bring it aboard again.

Still we lingered, seduced by the promise of the thin wafer of sun gliding past the overcast. All that night, while the ship lay sleeping, Haines, shivering in sheepskin coat, kept his finger on the weather's pulse.

Next morning, January 3rd, we flew. No sun, limited visibility, low ceiling, a barometric height of 28.54 inches, and a steady snowfall. Poor conditions for any sort of a flight—abominable for a flight of exploration. Maybe we were just being obstinate. Anyhow, the plane went over the side shortly after 10 o'clock, and at 11:22 A.M. we took off. The start was made from Lat. 69° 57′ S., Long. 116° 35′ W. The flight crew was the same—Chief Pilot June, Bowlin, Pelter, Petersen and myself.

I dare say that much harder flights have been made, but none with the peculiar perils of this one.

Before we squared away we made three quick navigation runs over the ship, to determine the compass error. The sun was obscured; so the sun compass was useless. We'd have to rely on the magnetic compasses. And the ship, surrounded by mist, was a pretty small target to hit upon our return.

At 11:33 we struck south along the meridian of 116° 35' W.

Conditions were anything but encouraging. At 400 feet scud was flying under the floats, and 600 feet above the great orange wing the air was solidly roofed with stratus clouds. It was snowing, too.

Five minutes later, when I looked back, the ship was lost to view. The gray mist had closed in around it.

My last instructions to Haines were to flash us a weather bulletin by radio every fifteen minutes, even if it meant just saying: "Unchanged." Polar meteorology is a curious thing. Local conditions change very rapidly, sometimes without apparent rhyme or reason. And when you're on a flight away from base, no matter how reassuring your own horizon may be, one thought is always uppermost in your mind: What's happening back there?

On the run south visibility was rarely better than ten miles and often less. The ceiling was never higher than 1,000 feet. Most of the way we flew at 400 feet. Even at that altitude we burst through heavy cloud fields.

About 110 miles south we cut across an enormous stretch of ice. At first it had all the appearance of shelf ice, anchored, perhaps, to continental Barrier. In the mist we couldn't tell what lay beyond. We crossed it at an altitude of 300 feet, and presently discovered what it was: a perfectly flat floe of extraordinary size. We estimated it was 20 miles wide. How long it was we couldn't tell; to right and left it extended as far as we could see.

In the middle of that immense slab, on which an army could have maneuvered without being cramped, were two huge Emperor penguins, the only living things we saw. They must have heard our engines, because, after glancing wildly around, they dropped to their bellies and scuttled off. Probably it never occurred to them to look up. For no reason at all I was suddenly bemused by the thought that here was the loneliest couple on the face of the earth. I never realized how well off most of us are until I saw my first Emperor penguin.

We were still pressing south when June beckoned me forward. The southern horizon ran black with snow squalls. No sense sticking our necks into that. We turned sharply.

At the turn our latitude was 72° 30′ S., with a vision ten miles south of that, say to Lat. 72° 40′. The pack, hard and compact, continued unbrokenly.

On the homeward leg our work was cut out for us.

The sodden clouds pressed down. A brace of snow squalls swelled darkly across our course. Blobs of mist streamed past the windows. The wing tips wallowed in it. Bowlin, whose trick it was at the wheel, rose into the cloud level in search of quieter air. For a little while we flew blind, holding a course by instruments. It was colder at that level. The air speed indicator stopped—ice, of course. Then I noticed the beginning of the thing I was waiting for: ice crystals forming on the fabric of the wing, like dew on summer grass. Bowlin saw it immediately. He bore down through the clouds and leveled off at 100 feet, where the air was warmer.

No great comfort at that level, either. Directly on our course we remembered seeing at least three bergs, two of them over a hundred feet high. Others lay scattered through the pack. Another squall swirled around the plane. Snow fogged the windows. Visibility fell to nearly nothing.

Out of the mist a black shadow loomed and sprang forward. Bowlin yanked up the bow. The plane rose, like a ship's bow flung up by a long wave, and the full force of 1,500 horsepower poured into the climb. Some of the rations and gear stowed on the long side seats came loose.

Between the pontoons and the shattered summit of a berg there was just enough room for daylight and a prayer.

After that we held an altitude of 300 feet. Toward the end of the flight the air cleared a bit.

About twenty miles south of the *Ruppert* we passed a monstrous berg, twenty-five miles long if it was an inch. Another great berg, tilted and splintered, lay jammed against it. They had evidently collided.

At 2:18 o'clock we were over the ship, landing three minutes later. The plane was immediately taken aboard. Two hours after we landed a thick snowstorm blotted out the whole horizon, and simultaneously the stretch of open water in which we had landed filled with pack and bobbing growlers.

"You fellows stole one that time," Haines had said to the flight crew as it came aboard. As indeed we had.

Chapter XII

∽∽∽∽∽∽∽∽∽∽∽∽∽∽∽∽∽∽∽∽∽∽∽∽∽

LITTLE AMERICA REGAINED

EVER since leaving New Zealand, indeed at every spare moment, the whole ship's company had been preparing for the big job—disembarkation. With the ship retracing her steps through the fog of the Devil's Graveyard and Little America only a fortnight distant, these preparations now became our complete concern. Mindful of the difficulties and hazards that had attended the unloading four years before, I had put Vic Czegka in charge of the operation. He was assisted by June and Innes-Taylor, both veterans of the first expedition; and by Noville and Rawson. There were seventeen different departments within the expedition, and each was responsible for the packing and identification of its gear and equipment. All stores had to be distinctly marked and identified, with symbols designating their relative importance, to facilitate handling on the ice. All items were divided into three categories: absolutely necessary, necessary, and least necessary. They were to be unloaded in that order or precedence. The wisdom of this segregation was obvious.

Now, miraculously, the skies cleared. Under a fine Capri sky we completed our southing. After days of sunless voyaging, the air suddenly filled with flying life—clouds of snowy petrels like white arrows flying, latticed groups of brown Antarctic petrels, checkered mantled Cape pigeons darting across the bow, and overhead, like flights of bombers wallowing among swift pursuit ships, the heavily flying skua gulls. The Ross Sea was blue as a tropical sea. The wind moved into the southwest, and brought a hint of ice. The temperature dropped to + 23°.

At 6:15 o'clock, on the morning of January 17th, we raised

153

the white palisades of the Ross Ice Barrier on the starboard bow. And men who had been working all night in the holds, getting the last things ready, swarmed up the ladders to have their first glimpse of the Antarctic Continent. Marbled cliffs under a cloudless blue, it was as beautiful a thing as you could wish to see, like a white cloud resting on the sea. Three hours later we passed West Cape and stood into the mouth of the Bay of Whales. A voyage of 13,323 nautical miles was ended.

Looking back on the events of that day, I find it hard to tell exactly what did happen; and in what order. Events were crowded, and we moved from one fresh excitement to another. Of one thing I am sure: the day belonged, properly enough, to the veterans. For they had the memories; remembered things came flooding back, to be confirmed or contradicted by what they saw. Anyone looking over that wide bay, with its fine sheer cliffs, its gentle rolling swales and smooth eminences, and gleaming, glistening snow, the soft roundness of everything, the infinite reaches of sky, would understand why one is pulled back.

Carl Petersen, scanning the western side of the Bay, suddenly exclaimed: "There's a flag—a flag, by golly, that Blackburn left there!" One could make it out with the help of glasses, a bamboo pole, with a wind-torn shred of orange pennant still clinging to it, showing above a haycock on the heights of Chamberlin Harbor. A moment later Bill Haines marked the beacon atop the north cape of Ver-sur-Mer Inlet. Four years ago it was a square turret of snow blocks, standing twenty-five feet high. But the winds had torn it down until it was now just a smooth dome barely awash.

If the discovery of familiar things excited the others, it was the changes that bewildered me. Outwardly the Barrier seems as enduring as mountain rock, but is scarcely more permanent than desert sand. Every season, every month, every day, indeed every hour works its change. A cliff shears off under infinite pressure, altering the configuration of a bay. The accretion of snow gradually transforms an inlet into a valley, a valley into high barrier. Capes and harbors born by the calving of bergs are obliterated by the same violent circumstances. In the South Polar regions nature is forever shaping and re-shaping, creating and destroying, striving in an infinite variety of ways towards ends we cannot foresee.

Not only was the entrance to Ver-sur-Mer Inlet blocked off; the Inlet itself appeared to have filled in until it had become merely a shallow depression. Once the north cape had been an almost sheer wall fifty feet high. Now the Inlet had filled in with drift, the cliff had disappeared, and only a gentle slope remained. But what appalled me was the pressure in along the east side of the Bay—miles of it, thirty to forty feet high. We should have a devil's own time, I saw, trying to move supplies through that stuff.

Five hundred yards off the east Barrier wall Commodore Gjertsen stopped the ship. The motor sailer was lowered, and fifteen of us went aboard. About three miles north of Little America we made the landing, bringing the boat alongside a gentle incline of ice foot. Haines, Petersen, Noville, and I started on foot for Little America. Sinking to the knee at every step we toiled up the slope. Now three black specks slowly lifted above the glistening ridge—the three radio towers! On the crest Little America was revealed—the shallow valley at the head of Ver-sur-Mer Inlet, the tall steel towers one of which was leaning out of plumb, a cluster of low bamboo antennæ poles, and strange, unremembered things that the snows of four winters hadn't covered. A crystal quiet lay over the place, over the smooth and rounded swales running to the horizon; not a snow crystal was out of place, and the surface was smooth as the slickest satinwood.

In a little while we stood over the Administration Building. The snow had deepened three or four feet. The ventilators and the stovepipe were barely awash, but the cleated anemometer pole stood a good five feet above the surface; and, curiously, a

broom, stuck in by the handle, was there, an irrelevant suggestion of domestic felicity.

Neither Haines nor I was exactly certain where to start digging. We paced off the distance from the stove pipe, trying to
remember how many steps we used to take from the stove to
the vestibule opening into the tunnels. However, after an
argument, a large hole was started. Three or four feet down,
Haines broke through a shell of hard blue ice, and uncovered
the tarpaulin roofing the old balloon station. In short order
he drove a hole through that, and disappeared. In a little while
we heard him chuckling. We plunged in after him.

Fourteen feet down, at the bottom of the square balloon station, with its ledge for the theodolite tripod still intact, we
turned left into the vestibule. Bill had left the door open. We
could hear him stumbling around in the dark. A faint ghostly
fluorescence illuminated the ice packed around the windows.
Petersen struck a match. By the light of it I found a fruit
jar, half-full of kerosene. The wick burned; and, as the glow
strengthened, the shadows fell back.

It wouldn't be right to say that the place looked as if we had
left it only yesterday. The roof had sagged under the crush-
ing weight of ice. Several of the main beams had cracked. They
lay splintered across the top bunks. A film of ice lay over the
walls, and from the ceiling hung thick clusters of ice crystals,
which were brighter than jewels when the light caught them.
The haste with which the building had been evacuated was
everywhere in evidence. Torn parkas and windproofs, un-
matched mukluks, dirty underwear and odds and ends of all
sorts were scattered about. By the looks of it you would have
thought a tornado had struck the place. I was a trifle ashamed
that we had left that mess behind us, and glad we could do our
own housecleaning.

On a table stood a coffee pot, a piece of roast beef with a
fork stuck in it, and half a loaf of bread. Four years before,
Dr. Coman had lunched off them while he waited for the last

sledge to come back for Mason, who lay ill with appendicitis. It evoked queer memories to come upon that. On the bunk walls were 1929 calendars, with the days scratched off. Haines found a tinfoil medal, big as a pie plate, which the camp had presented to Vanderveer, the cameraman. It was a medal for hardship—hardships that he had managed to escape.

Meanwhile the others had dug down into the Mess Hall, breaking through the roof of McKinley's photographic laboratory. This building lay about two hundred yards west of the Administration Building. The rest of us hurried over to have a look. They told me that the door from the photo lab to the main house was open when they got to the bottom. Well, that was another reality out of the past. McKinley was never one to close a door behind him. In the old days you could always tell when Mac was in the shack by the cold draught on the back of your neck.

While we were standing there the telephone rang. I'm not joking: it actually rang. If the Lion of Judah had crawled out from under one of the bunks, we couldn't have been more taken aback. Nobody moved for a second. "Did somebody miss the boat?" asked George Noville with raised eyebrows. Petersen had found the telephone and pressed the buzzer. We heard him laugh. Poulter answered in the Ad Building. "By yiminy," said Pete, "she works!"

Then the most amazing thing of all happened. Petersen idly flipped a switch. The lights went on. Not brightly—just a dim, faint glow in the bulbs, but undeniably they burned.

On the stove were cooking pans full of frozen food. There was coal in the scuttle. A fire was made in the kitchen stove, the food was warmed, and found to be as good as the day we left, four years ago. The seal and whale meat and beef in the tunnel were perfectly preserved.

So much for the rediscovery of Little America. It was an agreeable—more than that, an affecting—experience for the men who had wintered there in 1929-1930. It left a spell that lingered for many days, and I dare say that many will remember it long after the larger discoveries in the field have slipped their minds.

Before leaving I put Dr. Poulter in charge of the job of reclaiming the base and handling the stores which, I hoped, would soon be pouring in from the ship. His fine talents had already impressed me, and I had him in mind for second in command. Then I dispatched Ronne, the best man we had on skis, and Blackburn, because of his intimate knowledge of the Bay of Whales, to make a quick exploration of the pressure ridges along the east shore of the Bay.

"Look for a feasible passage near Ver-sur-Mer Inlet," I instructed them. "Remember that it will have to accommodate tractors as well as dog teams."

On the way back to the ship I passed half a dozen dog teams already hauling food, camping equipment and other gear in to the base party. Though the temperature was well below freezing, men were stripped to the waist. In the loose, soft snow the dogs made heavy going of it. Obviously they were badly out of condition. Well, their holiday was ended. From now on it would be all heart and sinew, for them as well as the men. A polar expedition moves forward and survives mostly by brute force and by its capacity for punishment. And the impending struggle to unload would tax these things to the limit.

At 10 o'clock that evening I rejoined the ship. An hour and a half later the *Ruppert* was brought alongside the bay ice and moored. She lay, then, about two miles east and somewhat south of the mouth of Floyd Bennett Harbor. East and west of her the front of the bay ice ran elliptically between the high barrier walls. This white flooring was from eight to ten feet above the water's edge: soft white snow on top, more densely packed as you went down, and hard blue-green ice at the water level. The total thickness was probably close to thirty feet. This was our unloading platform, our natural dock.

Little America, hidden by the barrier shoulder north of Ver-sur-Mer Inlet, was about three miles, as the skua gull flies, from the ship's berth. But there was no assurance that we could gain it from this position, not unless Ronne and Blackburn could unravel a trail through the glittering chaos of pressure. From the flying bridge I scanned it with field glasses. A belt of pressure, from a quarter to half a mile wide, ran irregularly along the eastern shore of the Bay. It had neither unity nor symmetry: just great misshapen blocks and ridges and boulders of ice, upheaved and twisted into tortured attitudes by the incalculable pressures of glacial action. Some of these ridges stood thirty feet high; deep crevasses gaped in the troughs. Where the bay ice ran up to the edge of the disturbance the surface was grossly disturbed, rising and shelving to form a series of mighty bulges, like arrested waves. From where I stood I could see no way through.

From that night on sleep was a dimly remembered pleasure. The winches were squealing, and hand trucks were rumbling on the iron decks. It was the first job of unloading all over again, with the same endlessly repeating gales and fog, the ice breaking up and forcing the ship out of her berth, and the same dogged straining for vantage points. What we did was to establish caches at various points along the trail which Ronne marked through the pressure ice, between the ship and Little America. Dogs and tractors relayed between these caches. So long as the weather held good and the ship could hold her berth, we discharged directly into the nearest caches. In the bad spells, while the ship waited out the storms, the shore parties would take advantage of each let-up to move the stores which had meanwhile accumulated at the unloading berth, farther and farther along the trail. In this way we lessened the risk of having precious material lying for long near the edge of the constantly crumbling bay ice.

Yet it was brutal work. For the trail to Little America was seven miles long, more than a mile of it through badly unheaved pressure ice; and the dog teams and the tractors literally had to carve and pound their way through. The currents and tides working under the pressure, together with the expansion and contraction of the ice itself, seemed to contort the trail from day to day. Two bridges, made of telephone poles and hatch covers, which were thrown across two of the widest crevasses, were forever being heaved out of position by the shifting of the ice; and time after time a call would come from up the trail for men to move the bridges into a new position.

Somebody called the unloading a white nightmare. The description fitted it perfectly. For we lost track of the days; and exhausted men, lifting themselves from one task to another, ceased to heed or remember anything but the compulsion of work. Fed by the mainstream pouring off the ship, the heaps of stores in the caches deepened; and between them the tractors and dog teams, like prodigiously active centipedes, scuttled to and fro, running out loaded and flying back empty for another load. Literally we inched our way along Misery Trail, hauling and relaying, making uncountable thousands of small journeys in this wise, like so many ants engaged in a stupendous transfer. I don't know what it is that gives that aspect of frantic industry to ants: hunger, probably, and a dim sense of doom. What drove us was the thought of the ice crumbling behind our backs, and the sea creeping hour by hour nearer toward our caches. It was with such drudgery that Little America was regained.

At the end of January the *Bear of Oakland*, with bare sticks and yards aslant, rounded West Cape. With her coming the expedition was once more reunited. Fresh from their long voyage, the crew of the *Bear* leaped into the struggle; and three days later the *Ruppert* was practically empty.

Saturday, Feb. 3, 11:20 P.M.

Today, with Lieut. English and Captain Verleger, I made a tractor trip into Little America for the first formal broadcast from the Antarctic Continent. It took us two hours to reach

(© Paramount Pictures, Inc.)

ADMIRAL BYRD STEPS ASHORE

FOUR YEARS OF ICE CRYSTALS IN THE OLD TUNNEL

(Photograph by Joseph A. Pelter)

BLAZING A TRAIL THROUGH THE PRESSURE

ON THE MAIN HIGHWAY TO LITTLE AMERICA

Little America. Dyer, Hutcheson and Pierce had everything in readiness. The apparatus was housed in a tent on the surface. A strong westerly was blowing, causing the tent to flap violently and sifting drift inside.

"Think it will go through?" I asked Dyer. Dyer chuckled. "No reason why not," he said, "if nothing blows up." "And if something blows up. . . ?" I suggested. Dyer chuckled again. "It will be just too bad." Outside Pierce, dancing up and down to keep warm, stood by the power plant which chugged bravely in the blizzard.

Well, we gathered in the old Mess Hall, by the dim light of kerosene lanterns. Hutcheson fiddled with controls on a monitor board, snapped his fingers across the microphones to test them.

And I thought, as I watched these mysterious preparations, how much things had changed: how, twenty-two years before, Scott and his whole party had silently died of hunger while his base party, just 160 miles away, awaited his homecoming at Cape Evans; and here we were casually making ready to tell of our prosaic doings to a vast audience in the United States. A momentary misgiving swept over me. When too much talk seems to be the cause of much of the grief in the world, no man could break the isolation of the Last Continent of Silence without a twinge of remorse.

Anyhow, a thing called a cue finally came; each of us went to the microphone to say his piece: and ten thousand miles away (so Dyer reported) the voices came through clear as a bell. Somehow, in the shadows of the Mess Hall, fifteen feet or so beneath the surface, it didn't seem possible.

That afternoon, before returning to the ships, I took stock of the rehabilitation of old Little America. The improvements that Dr. Poulter had accomplished in a fortnight, with only a handful of men, were remarkable. The old buildings were restored, the old caches excavated, and the stores which had lately been hauled in were neatly segregated, each in its proper cache near the center of the camp.

Bowlin, Smith and Schlossbach had meanwhile dug down to the old planes—the Ford and the Fairchild—which in 1930 we had anchored on the ridge to the eastward. Both planes were completely buried: there was just a pale shadow to mark the submerged wing of the Fairchild; of the big Ford only the rudder post and the starboard wing tip were awash. I decided, however, to let them lie there until next spring. We had no need for them, and no time to spare for digging them out.

Contemplating this activity I ceased to despair over our seemingly desultory progress. All this had been done in little more than a fortnight. It was something to be proud of. The teeming trail, the regular movement of teams and tractors, the fattening caches, the rebirth of Little America—all these things were proof of a stupendous effort. Sweat, blood, risk and doggedness had gone into the making of the road to Little America. Before the business was done, some men would feel that something of their souls, too, had gone into it.

Even the *Ruppert* when I boarded her, seemed to wear the dowdy dress of fatigue. Her decks were full of debris, her lavatories frozen, odds and ends of rejected things thrown everywhere. The winch packings were all blown out: and either too weary or too hard-pressed to make repairs, the winchmen preferred to stand in clouds of steam, which froze as it struck their faces and hands. Well, it wouldn't be long now. A few more hours and they could go. In the year's waiting at Dunedin both men and ship could rest and refit.

I cannot in truth say that her departure meant a lessening of my problems. Captain Verleger fell ill with pneumonia the night before she sailed; the fact that the expedition surgeon, who, because of high blood pressure, was also returning to New Zealand, meant that the Captain would have as good care as was within our power to give; but it also put the Ice Party in jeopardy, since fifty-six men would have to face the prospect of a year in the Antarctic without the services of a physician and surgeon unless I could find some means of getting another one down from New Zealand. At the moment the problem seemed impossible of solution.

It was too late in the season for the *Ruppert* to make it to New Zealand and back.

I watched the *Ruppert* leave with despair in my heart that

weighed as heavily as dishonor. I felt that in some way I had betrayed my men. So I determined to get a doctor regardless of cost or consequences, or else cancel the expedition.

New Zealand was nearly 3,000 statute miles away and the winter freeze-up was not far off. Finally, after searching in many directions, I radioed the Royal Geographical Society of England and learned that the British exploring ship *Discovery II*, which had been cruising not far from us in the vicinity of the Devil's Graveyard, had meanwhile put into New Zealand to refit. Captain Nelson, who commanded her, offered to relay a doctor to the northern edge of the pack if we would meet him there with the *Bear*. My relief, to put it mildly, was tremendous. This generous act was typical of British sportsmanship. I owe all concerned an enduring debt of gratitude.

Because it would take the *Discovery II* a fortnight or so to reach the rendezvous, I seized the opportunity to take the *Bear* into the unexplored seas to the northeast of Little America. Although we were gone only ten days, we had a most exciting time of it; and, when I returned, it was to find Little America reëstablished as the capital city of the Antarctic.

It was a grand sight to travel down the Barrier rim and see the reborn city rising—the rectangles of the new tunnels reaching between the shacks, the mounds of gear steepening, and already in place the first of the diamond-shaped antennæ, which would make it possible for us to talk, as easily as one could cast a cry over one's shoulder, to Buenos Aires, Honolulu, San Francisco, New York, London.

One saw taking form in the glittering white vacuum one of the most remarkable cities on the face of the earth—a city which would boast, among other possessions, of electric light and power, a complete broadcasting and field communications plant, a well equipped aviation service enlisting four modern planes and skilled personnel, various machine shops, four tractors, nearly 150 dogs, a first-class meteorological station, a scientific staff and laboratory equipped to delve into twenty-two branches of science, a dairy plant with four head of cattle, adequate medical facilities, a well-stocked galley, library, a meteor observatory, even a motion picture theater wired for sound. None of these enterprises was quite finished. But Little America was taking root. It was rising. In the teeth of blizzards and cold it was growing like a boom town.

Not even the discovery of myriad cracks in the ice sheet on which Little America rested—the sudden fear that the whole place might drift out to sea on a borning iceberg—the quick necessity of establishing an emergency retreat camp on the high barrier to the south—not even these matters could inhibit the reincarnation of Little America.

While we were dealing none too happily with this situation, the *Bear* returned from her rendezvous with the *Discovery II*. She had had anything but an easy time. Gales had buffeted her both ways, and she had to punch her way through miles of pancake ice before she could gain the Bay of Whales. But she had the doctor aboard, and additional gasoline for the tractors, sound payment for her risks. The new medico—Dr. Potaka, solidly built, with a good-humored face, an English accent, and Maori blood in his veins—came up at once to Little America in a tractor. He was liked from the start.

Came now what was for many of the departing men (and no less for me) the bitterest hour of the expedition; the final weeding out of the Ice Party. Perhaps this phrase is objectionable; for the process wasn't so much a weeding out as of merely saying *no* to those we couldn't keep on the ice. It wasn't necessary to tell men they were assigned to the Ice Party and would therefore stay. They knew that already. The others had been told they would return with the *Bear*.

Now a great deal of nonsense has been written about the peculiar psychological dangers of the polar winter night, and the searching examination to which candidates for the wintering party are submitted prior to selection. Of course, these psychological hazards exist, and care must be taken in the selection of men.

But the business isn't half so mysterious as superstition would have you believe. In my delvings in this particular branch of human psychology, as in all my other interests, I always strove for simplicity, common sense and faith. Above everything else—faith. I've had wide enough experience in the choosing of men for hazardous jobs to know that human behavior is unpredictable for the reason that the sets of circumstances in which it operates are also unpredictable: and that no wise man is so poor a judge of himself as to dare to call himself a good judge of men. Of a few men you can be absolutely sure. They are born with stability and loyalty. Some men are doubtful, either because of the absence of these qualities or because of other qualities which are bent to mischief. Occupying the far-flung middle ground is the remarkable amorphous aggregation of the average. I have always had to deal with a few men, who from the first to last try to tear things down; that I always expect. But I have also learned to credit the great majority with at least a latent instinct toward honesty, honor and the other central Christian principles. These qualities, I have found, will generally triumph over the moral and emotional strain of a winter night or any other polar circumstance. Hence I make no pretentious claim to a unique power, such as the laying on of hands, by virtue of which obscure men are magically transformed into angels who will withstand, with unblemished record, the oppressions of the long winter night. I mostly hope for the best.

Altogether there were fifty-six men at Little America through the polar winter of 1934-35—the largest party ever to winter in the Antarctic. I credit myself with no generous motives for its size. It was the wisest mistake I ever made. Without the extra man-power we could never have done the things we did. For the expedition was never idle. It was in high gear all the time. So many activities were under way, so many parties were in the field that we had to make a wall map to keep track of their daily movements.

All this, however, was my problem. Down in the Bay of Whales, Lieutenant English was confronted by others equally grave. With the Ross Sea freezing behind him, and knowing that on the outward run the gales of oncoming winter would strike with redoubled force, he was anxious to be off as soon as he could.

"This new ice at the edge of the Ross Sea is tough enough," Lieutenant English said, "but the old ice 200 miles to the north is a damned sight worse. The same sort of heavy pack we got into on the northeastern cruise. Maybe it's the same ice. Maybe it has drifted over. No way of telling, of course. But we're going to need the breaks to get through."

Exactly eight hours after she touched the ice—at 8:30 A.M., February 26th—the *Bear* finished discharging her cargo, over 21 tons of it, including the gasoline.

"Let her go aft," Second Mate Davis shouted from the poop deck. The dog-drivers slipped the toggles. The *Bear* eased forward to take the strain off the bow line.

"Let her go forward," shouted Lieutenant English from the bridge. The bow line was slipped. Clear, now, the *Bear* backed out and stood off for the northern run.

The men on the ice lingered only long enough to see her go. Little by little the sea smoke claimed her. Higher and higher it rose along the ship till only the topmasts were visible, vaguely and indefinitely floating long after the ship had been enveloped. For once Lieutenant English had to forego tradition. There was no cheerful tootling on the whistle. The whistle had frozen solid. It couldn't even clear its throat.

Chapter *XIII*

∿∿∿∿∿∿∿∿∿∿∿∿∿∿∿∿∿∿∿∿∿∿∿∿∿

A LOUD AND STORMY MONTH

MARCH came in clear and cold, with a temperature of 15°. That evening Captain Innes-Taylor started south with his party—Ronne, Paine, Russell, Black and Moody, plus five teams. Their job was (1) to explore a safe route through crevassed areas for the fleet of tractors which would follow in their wake, and (2) to put down a series of food depots for the main southern journeys of the following spring.

I had a talk with Captain Innes-Taylor just before the start.

"You have a hard journey," I said. "Bitter temperatures in a fortnight. You'll be suffering. That's when you'll want to be on the homeward run—not trying to push still farther south."

Innes-Taylor's party made a grand sight moving off. The air was clear and still; the horizon flamed with color. The pick of 135 dogs went south, Innes-Taylor's team was made up of heavy-shouldered, big-boned Manitoba huskies, descendants of the dogs used by Shackleton. Sam was his leader, a buff-colored giant, one of the most intelligent leaders in Dog Town. Moody's team consisted of white-eyed Siberian malamutes, small and wiry and vicious. The leader of this pack of assassins was Caesar, docile and ingratiating as a setter; his only fault was an insatiable appetite for harnesses. In a month he chewed fifteen of them to ribbons. The other teams were combinations of the unfathomable cross-breeds that made up the canine roster.

Tuesday, March 13th, the wind mercifully stopped blowing, and the sun shone again. Thankful for these small blessings—even for the temperature of − 20°—we again dug out the

Fokker and Pilgrim, hopeful that the weather would hold good
long enough for the pilots to squeeze in two freighting hauls
toward the base which we were planning to establish to the
south, and toward which Captain Innes-Taylor was bound.
The boxes were stacked up for them; they had been ready for
days. The price of the respite was a crash.

Schlossbach had the Fokker ready first. Before loading up,
he decided to make a short test hop. Zuhn, Dustin and Young,
who had helped him dig out the plane, asked if they might
go along. None had ever flown before. "Ike" waved them in.

The plane got off very quickly—much too quickly, I
thought. I think the plane was bounded into the air by a ridge
of sastrugi before Schlossbach could get the right speed on
the ground. The surface was glossy-hard and roughened by
sastrugi.

Anyhow, it was apparent the instant the plane got off that
it was in difficulty. Drifting across the radio towers it seemed
unable to gain altitude. The nose sagged, then Schlossbach
edged into a long swinging curve, evidently trying to make for
smooth snow rather than risk crashing into the pressure in
the Bay of Whales.

His fight to save the ship was in full view of the camp, which
watched appalled and silent.

A tractor pulled up. "Get out with a load of chemical
bombs," I yelled at the driver. "Ike's going to crash."

About 500 yards east of the camp, still in the turn, the
Fokker hit in an explosion of snow, ground-looping as the left
ski tripped over sastrugi. The right ski smashed down with
great force; the steel-tubed landing struts collapsed; and the
plane twisted awkwardly, stabbing the right wing into the
snow.

The plane heaved as if about to flop over on its back, then
fell back, skidded thirty yards or so, and stopped wearily. The
right wing was practically torn off, the left wing pointed
clumsily at the sky.

That instant all of Little America, by dog team, tractor and on foot, broke for the wreck.

When we got there the four men were out of the wreckage. Schlossbach had yelled to the others to brace themselves just before the crash; they made fast to whatever fittings were handy. They were all suffering slightly from shock. Zuhn, still dazed, kept mumbling something about a pair of socks, no doubt the subconscious workings of his Iowan thrift. At Little America we measured a man's fortune by the number of clean socks in his sea chest.

The Fokker was a complete washout. The port ski and pedestal were torn off, the right wing (a monoplane cantilever wing of plywood construction) was splintered from tip to center. The longerons buckled, and the stabilizer and flippers were destroyed. Engine, propeller and instruments were the only salvage.

A severe loss, but there was adequate consolation in the fact that no one was hurt, that no one was at fault. Aviation took up as if nothing had happened. An hour later Bowlin and Bailey made a brief test in the Pilgrim and before sundown completed two flights south with nearly a ton of stores.

But these were minor distractions; the night watches of March 14th saw a situation evolve that drove everything else into the background.

I had repaired to my shack after supper. Sterrett rapped on the door. When he came in, his face was grave. Pelter, he said, was ill, quite ill.

"What do you think it is?" I asked.

"I'm not sure," Sterrett said, "but I think it's appendicitis. Anyhow, Dr. Potaka should examine him."

We got hold of Dr. Potaka, who immediately went over and examined Pelter. Sterrett's diagnosis was right. A bad appendix, Dr. Potaka said, which would eventually require an operation, but perhaps not immediately. About 10:30 o'clock, however, Pelter had another relapse, and Dr. Potaka resolved to operate at once. Pelter, very pale and very weak, was boosted up the shaft of the Old Mess Hall; with Sterrett supporting him, he walked to the radio shack, which was cleaner and more comfortable than the other buildings.

Since his arrival at Little America a fortnight before, Dr. Potaka had had no time to unpack his instruments; he had been trying to convert the former library in the Administration Building into a medical office. Much of his medical gear was buried under five feet of drift. His surgical instruments, still unboxed, lay under a small mountain of things in the vestibule. Among these things the Doctor was pawing, when suddenly his pressure lamp went out. He started to fill it from a gasoline drum perched on a box nearby. The flame could not have died in the mantle; for there was a puff of smoke, the stream of gasoline ignited in Dr. Potaka's face and, startled, he dropped the lamp. In a moment the narrow vestibule was choked with smoke, and a pool of burning oil eddied around the boxes, setting them on fire, the crate of surgical instruments among them.

Tinglof and Von der Wall, who had heard Potaka's cry, hurried to the door. Still in their underclothes (most of the men in the building had either turned in, or were undressing) they plunged into the vestibule, holding their breath as they scuttled up the hatch ladder. Tinglof dashed one way after fire extinguishers, Von der Wall made for the galley to get a gas mask. The others in the building, the Doctor and a dozen or more, were cut off. Drift and ice had wedged down the skylights: the men couldn't open them from below. Smoke filled the long room. Demas slammed shut the door, to close off the draught down the hatch which was fanning the fire.

Thanks to the quick action of the men in the "Ad" Building, there was no tragedy. The skylights were kicked in from above, and fire extinguishers passed to the men below. Von der Wall, a grotesque figure in flapping balbriggans and gas mask, dropped down the hatch to save the surgical instruments, the charred box of which was hoisted to the surface. The blaze was quickly extinguished. No great damage was done.

Even then Dr. Potaka was nearly at his wit's end. The sterile sutures were missing. He hurriedly broke open innumerable boxes which the men brought in from his smoking cache before he found them. *A table? What shall we do for an operating table?* Somebody remembered a table which Tinglof was building in the Science Building: It had no top, but stretchers could be laid across. *Where are the stretchers?* Some one found them in the medical cache, under six feet of snow. Quickly they were excavated and thawed out over the galley stove. *Lights! What are you going to do for lights?* In his quiet way Dyer remembered the thousand-watt lamp used to stabilize the camp load on the electrical circuit. He got it, then ran a line across the ceiling over the operating table. *But suppose the generators conk in the middle of the operation! How about light then!* Bailey said he would stand by in the Kohler shack, with three generators running simultaneously, ready to switch the instant one spluttered. *How are you going to keep the room warm during the operation? You can't have an open coal fire with all this ether. It's twenty below. This room's going to cool off fast the moment you douse the fire!* Plug the cracks, then: seal the ventilators: get a good hot fire burning until the room temperature is up around 80°; then rake the ashes and carry them out. And to hold heat in the room, Cox and Tinglof fitted a door into the unfinished partition dividing the shack, while Pelter watched uneasily from the bunk.

At last matters were in hand, and at five minutes past midnight the anaesthetic was administered. I shall not quickly forget the scene—the narrow room with its rude bunks, the drifted skylights overhead, and the first pale aurora dimly seen through them, and Potaka, Sterrett and Perkins crisp in sterile white caps, gloves and gowns. The gleaming scalpels, forceps, retractors, haemostats and scissors and the vials of sutures were racked on a small table which ordinarily served as a stand for the radio broadcasts. Wash basins, boiled and scoured till they shone, were spread out on the top of the small collapsible organ used in the broadcast.

At Dr. Potaka's signal Sterrett started pouring the ether into the gauze-covered cone. Pelter answered to the count: "one ... two ... three." At first instantly, then draggingly: "twenty-four ... twenty-five..." No answer at twenty-seven. Pelter stirred and in true Navy fashion he murmured quite clearly:

"Quit kiddin', Doc, I can count, too. I'll let you know when I can't...."

Then he went inert, and the operation proceeded, with Sterrett gently dripping the ether with one hand while he held the other under the ramus of the jaw, one finger pressed lightly under the carotid artery to register the pulse action while he heeded the eye reflex, the breathing and the color of the blood: with Dr. Perkins handing the instruments which Dr. Potaka in his crisp British way called for, and with the Doctor himself, short, dark and dynamic, cutting deftly and with sureness. The small room was terribly crowded: Dr. Potaka was backed against the stove, and once, when he turned swiftly, he just escaped falling over it.

The operation dragged; it seemed to last forever, because, in the end, Potaka had to do most of the important details that trained assistants usually perform for surgeons. Before it was over, we were all exhausted and shivering a little, too, because the temperature in the shack had steadily dropped. Then the fire was started, and Pelter was gently transferred to the bunk, still unconscious.

On Monday, March 19th, the tractor fleet, led by June and Demas, put out from Little America, in the wake of the dog teams, on the extraordinary mission of transporting materials for a complete weather station into the heart of the Ross Ice Barrier. The advance was unique in the history of polar travel. Theretofore the Eskimo husky had dominated land travel. But this advance was entirely mechanical. The four tractors alone (the three Citroëns and the Cletrac) represented thirteen tons of machinery. The crew numbered nine men—four drivers, Demas, Hill, Dustin and Skinner; two radio operators, Petersen and Waite; and Siple and Tinglof, whose particular job was to assemble Advance Base. The portable shack for the Base weighed close to two tons. The remaining loads were taken up with trail rations and equipment, lubricating oil, tools, clothing for the tractor crew, and the gear and stores assigned to the Base.

In order to understand the importance of this journey, an understanding of the purposes of Bolling Advance Weather Base is necessary: it seems to me that this is the right place to tell how the idea of this unusual base was born, what purpose it was expected to serve, and in what manner it was to be manned and equipped.

To the ordinary person, who can see little or no worth in polar expeditions, at least an investigation of weather seems to possess some practical merit. Recent years have witnessed a widening interest in polar meteorology, especially that of the South Polar regions; and as a consequence of the activities of various expeditions more people are beginning to realize that the great South Polar ice caps play a dominant—perhaps even a predominant rôle in maintaining the broad circulation and movements of air on which depend the climates of the world, and with them all human activities. Most of us have a dim schoolbookish understanding of the theory of simple circulation: an air current flowing over the earth from the Poles to the Equator, a return current moving poleward above it, and that this endlessly renewed interchange is the breathing of the planet on which we live. It is interesting to note that in the nineteenth century (when the shining bulk of Antarctica had only just been raised above the horizon) the attention of meteorologists centered rather on the tropical regions as the mainspring of universal meteorology. But little by little, as the scope of polar

exploration widened and the accruing meteorological data became more meaningful, the emphasis slowly drifted poleward
to such a degree that a theory has been advanced that the
key to southern hemisphere atmospheric circulation, may be
found on the lofty Antarctic plateau.

So far as theory and such go, I claim no better than a lay-
man's general knowledge of meteorology: but in discussing the
subject with Haines during the first expedition it was plain
to me that the most valuable source of Antarctic weather data
was still unprobed. What data existed had largely been collected at fixed bases on the coast (Little America itself
was on the coast) or on islands adjacent to the coast, on
ships exploring coastal waters, and by parties, meagerly
equipped for meteorological research, engaged in fast summer dashes into the interior. Meteorologically, the vast
interior was still a complete blank. No fixed meteorological
stations had ever been established in the interior; no winter
observations had ever been made beyond the coast; the frag-
mentary data collected by field parties extended only over
the comparatively mild summer months. Yet, inland, past the
moderating influence of the sea, was the greatest cold on the
face of the earth; it was there that one would expect to find
typical continental conditions.

From this reasoning it was but a step to the idea of Advance
Base; and I was determined that when—and if—I returned
with a second expedition I should bend every effort to establish a well-equipped meteorological station in the interior and
have it occupied during the winter night. Haines and I discussed the plan many times. In 1933, when the second expedition was being organized, the first practical step toward that
end was taken. In a loft in Boston, from a blue print worked
out by Czegka with a few suggestions from me, Tinglof built
the shack for the outpost. The necessary meterological equipment was loaned by the U. S. Weather Bureau.

But between the original plan of 1929 and the accomplished

fact of March 25th, 1934, there was considerable disparity. The Antarctic has a way of tripping up the best laid plans.

For one thing, the original plan called for three men to occupy the shack. But the terrific strain on our transport during the unloading, plus the final blow brought by the break-down of one of the tractors sixty-odd miles south of Little America, forced me into a new decision. In the brief time remaining before the onset of the winter night, it would be physically impossible for the surviving tractors to haul sufficient stores to maintain three men for seven months, and morally a mistake of leadership to ask them to attempt it. Therefore, the shack had to be occupied either by two men or (as it finally happened) by one. Meanwhile, the tractor party, flogged by blizzards, spent its bolt approximately 123 miles by trail south of Little America.

On the morning of March 22nd Siple and Tinglof broke ground for Advance Base about 100 yards east of the snow beacon marking the depot on the southern trail blazed by Captain Innes-Taylor and his party. And that morning, also, I flew from Little America to direct the setting up of the Base.

As I have said earlier, we were not able to advance sufficient supplies to staff this meteorological outpost with three men. The alternative was either two men or one man. After gravely considering the choice for a long time, it seemed to me that to man the Base with two men was impracticable. My own experience in the polar regions, together with what I knew about men who had been isolated in the Arctic, convinced me that the chances were small that two men by themselves could achieve temperamental harmony. Remember, this outpost was to be sunk in the crust of the Ross Ice Barrier; and, as we gauged the risks then, whoever went out there had to be reconciled to isolation for at least seven months, no matter what came to pass. Four of these months would be in complete darkness, under the most unfavorable conditions that life contrives anywhere on earth. Life in that spot would resemble life on a dark, dead,

and bitterly cold planet, and for some months would be almost
as inaccessible as on that planet. For the men would be jammed
together at arm's length in a tiny shack; they would live by
the dim light of a lantern in a state of perpetual congestion
and intrusion; they would hardly be able to take a step without coming into collision; they would hardly be able to express
a thought without running athwart each other's prejudices.

Under such a set of circumstances could a man predict the
reactions of his best friend? Could he be sure of his own reactions?

In all events, I was determined not to assume the responsibility for creating such a situation. Few things are really impossible, least of all in human psychology. But I personally preferred the risk of being alone at Advance Base to the hazard
of having to endure the humiliation that a second man might
involve.

In the woods it would be a different story. One would have
diversions and familiar things. Even in the Arctic there is
abundant life in places, as is so well described in Stefansson's
Friendly Arctic. It was necessary, as I said, that we should
occupy the Base. Even if it had been possible to staff it with
three men, I should still have had to be one of them; but, since
I felt it had to be one man, it seemed definitely up to me to go.
I could not—and would not—ask another man to go. There
was the advantage, too, of eliminating the need of having a
second man beyond the services of a doctor.

But the decision wasn't really hard to make. The truth of
the matter is, I really wanted to go and keenly looked forward
to the experience. When I left Little America, I said I was going because I wanted to go. I could not bring myself to say I
was going only in the interest of science because I sincerely
believe I was as much interested in the experience, for its own
sake, as I was in the meteorological work for which the Base
was designed. Therefore, I couldn't say, nor do I say now, that

I was making a sacrifice for science. That did not enter my head.

As for leaving the camp without a leader, well, I had confidence in the officers and men at Little America. No hazardous undertakings would be attempted during the winter night. Then there was a chance that I would have radio contact. Just before my departure, I wrote the following order:

The following new appointments are made, to be effective during the absence of the leader:

Second in Command.........Dr. Thomas C. Poulter
Third in Command................William Haines
Chief of Staff.......................Harold June
Executive Officer...................George Noville

These officers will be obeyed and respected accordingly....

The principal instructions the leader leaves behind are few and simple:

1. Work industriously on obtaining scientific data and in making plans and preparations for the spring and summer operations.
2. Make and abide by strict rules for safety as to fire, getting lost in storms, or down crevasses during the night or thick weather of any kind.
3. As with all undertakings of this nature conservation of food, fuel, clothing and shelter becomes of vital importance. Strict orders regarding the conservation of fuel will be issued and enforced.
4. Every man in this camp has an equal right to be treated fairly and squarely, and the officers are requested to hold this fact in mind.
5. More minute instructions will be given to the second in command.

It took only a few hours to arrange my affairs. Bowlin and Bailey waited impatiently in the Pilgrim. The engine was idling. Though hot oil had just been poured into the engine, it chilled rapidly. Blobs of black smoke were puffing out of the exhaust. The temperature was − 13°.

We took off for Advance Base at 10:35 A.M. Gaining altitude across Ver-sur-Mer Inlet, Bowlin made a banking turn around Little America, before squaring away for the south. I took in every detail, photographing the scene in my mind— the dark tracery of antennæ, the dog crates, dogs tethered outside, the drifted caches, the unfinished, uncovered trenches of the tunnels, the lumpish mounds in which the buildings were pocketed and the plumes of smoke lingering over the ventilators and chimney pipes—a snug harbor in a vast rolling plain of white. Perhaps I felt homesick at the thought of leaving it; I'm not sure. I know that I should hesitate to describe what the place means to me.

A sweeping glance to the north showed the Ross Sea was frozen, a still, dark immensity. The whitish shimmer of ice blink laced the horizon.

Like welts in the unspoiled flesh of the Barrier, the tractor tracks ran south. Bowlin sped over them at an altitude of fifty feet. A dark speck on the horizon resolved itself into a cluster of tents and tractors—Advance Base.

Where Advance Base lay, the Ross Shelf Ice was quite as flat as the Kansas plains. Snow rose to meet the blue sky in an unbroken round of horizon. How spacious and empty it seemed, and how huddled and puny the aggregation of tractors, dog teams and men! A pin-pricking effort in infinity.

The plane landed at 11:55. It was quickly unloaded. Bowlin and Bailey wasted not a moment: too great a chance that cold would stop the engine. Fifteen minutes later they were off for Little America. In the super-cooled air the vapor from the exhaust trailed for miles behind the plane. When I landed, the combined dog-team and tractor parties were already digging the pit which would accommodate the shack. It was bitter work, with the temperature at − 60°. June, Siple, Waite, Petersen, Black and Dustin lingered long enough to make the Base shipshape. Waite installed the radio equipment, strung the antennæ and satisfactorily tested the hook-up with Dyer at Little America. With Siple's help, I set up the meteorological equipment—

instrument shelter topside, triple register in the shack. On the recording drums the whirring anemometer cups were already spinning out a tale of winds, the thermometers a tale of temperatures, at the coldest spot ever occupied. This day, March 26th, a numbing wind buffeted the Base. But the job was finished; at 5 P.M. the following day, after having dug out their cars and heated the engines for hours, the tractor crew finally departed only to creep back a few hours later, having been stopped by mechanical breakdowns a few miles out. All that night, with the thermometers reading − 59°, the drivers tinkered with frozen radiators and capricious carburetors.

At 12:10 P.M., March 28th, the cars again set forth for Little America. My isolation had begun.

Wednesday, March 28, Midnight.

The tractors are off at last....For more than 200 days I shall see no living thing. But I'm in the midst of chaos with a very lame shoulder. I wrenched it when I fell while lifting a heavy box onto a tractor. It's very painful and an unfortunate handicap just now, because everything is in confusion, and days— even weeks—of hard work are needed to put things to rights.

Boxes, loose clothing, books, and odds and ends past counting are strewn about. I haven't the faintest idea where anything is. I've searched conscientiously for the alarm clock and the cook book, and the suspicion is growing that I left them at Little America. It would be an ironic joke if, in the pretentious planning for every contingency, we forget these most commonplace and vital necessities.

Another thing: the fuel line from the tank to the stove is leaking and is therefore something of a fire hazard. Hope my shoulder mends soon. It's difficult to do anything with it....

Bolling Advance Weather Base was situated at Lat. 80° 08' S., Long. 163° 57' W., within a hair's breadth of being due south of Little America. It lay near the heart of the Ross Shelf Ice, which itself is one of the grand natural wonders of the world, a vast sheet of ice rolling from the Ross Sea to the foot of the Queen Maud Range, 400 miles broad and upwards of 600 feet in thickness; its basement rests in many places (we know now) on submarine ridges and depressed mountain tops, and much of it floats buoyantly upon the sea. Where the Base was no life had moved, nothing had stirred for centuries; the Ice Age was in complete ascendancy. In whatever direction I looked, north, east, south, or west, the vista was the same, a spread of ice fanning to meet the horizon. But it was not flat, as I had at first thought. There were a great many long hills and valleys that so blended that at first glance the surface appeared flat. The shack itself faced west for no particular reason, now that I reflect on why this was so, since it lay locked within the Barrier crust. Anyhow, a hundred yards or so to the west were the eight-foot snow beacon and the orange-topped tent identifying 100-Mile Depot on the southern trail. But as the trail itself went, twisting and detouring to escape crevasses and profit by good surface, the Base was actually 123 statute miles from Little America. A thin line of orange flags, fitted to 24-inch bamboo sticks, fled northward to Little America. At first these flags were planted at intervals of a third of a mile, but June had later reduced the interval to one-sixth of a mile by doubling the number of flags.

The day my isolation commenced the shack itself was completely roofed by snow. It was set up underground for three reasons: first, to benefit from the warmer and more constant temperatures prevailing within the crust; secondly, to shelter it from the penetrating winds which search out every crevice; and, thirdly, to protect it from the drift which mounts, with the velocity of a tidal wave, around every exposed object. Only the 12-foot anemometer pole with its silver wind cups and weather vane, the beehive-shaped instrument shelter holding the thermometers and barographs, and the radio antennæ strung on 12-foot bamboo poles showed above ground. A double-action trapdoor set in the projecting roof of the shack, with a flat-runged ladder rising to it, communicated with the surface. This narrow projecting roof formed a small vestibule underground, from which emanated two narrow, parallel tunnels, forty feet long, running east and west. In the southern tunnel was cached the food, the boxes themselves partly forming the side walls: in the other, the fuel drums. In the southern tunnel the small gasoline generator which powered my main radio set was disposed in a box set in a niche in the snow wall, with an exhaust pipe discharging on the surface.

Altogether, it was a neat and not uncomfortable arrangement. Every likely source of risk that could be foreseen had been studied, and means made available for overcoming it. Against cold and blizzards the Base seemed staunch as a steel turret. But the small flaws which several months later were to make that place a living hell were present. For one thing, several stovepipe sections were lost in the transportation of stores from Little America; and to fit the unequal sections together rough joints were made from empty fuel tins, which couldn't be rendered air-tight; so noxious fumes seeped into the room. And the stove itself was a make-shift affair. The oil-burning stove which had been brought from the United States was rejected as being defective after many tests at Little America; and at the last moment Siple had had the machinist replace it with an ordinary coal-burning caboose stove into which a burner had been inserted. Coal would have been the ideal fuel; but the weight and bulk of coal prohibited its consideration. The fumes leaking from these sources, together with the fumes thrown off by the gasoline engine which powered my radio set, were the cause of my subsequent misfortunes.

Still, in March, 1934, the outcome was concealed. With confidence, even with keen anticipation, I turned to meet the oncoming winter night. There was much work to be done; the 40-foot escape tunnel to finish, and the stores to be sorted out. Meteorological and auroral observations occupied a substantial part of the day. The following meteorological records were made: a continuous mechanical registration of barometric pressure, temperature, wind direction and velocity; twice daily visual observations of cloudiness and the state of the weather; twice daily readings of maximum and minimum thermometers in the instrument shelter topside; and twice daily visual observations of the barometer. The four instruments themselves exacted constant attention. In addition, I stood four or five auroral watches daily whenever the sky was clear enough for such displays. The intensity, structural form and direction and altitude of the aurora were noted, for subsequent comparison with the observations of observers who watched simultaneously at Little America. So I never had reason to complain of nothing to do.

~~~~~~

Chapter XIV

THE WINTER NIGHT

DIRECTLY after Admiral Byrd was established at Advance Base the expedition's fall operations drew to a close. The tractor fleet, fighting off at the end of an epidemic of mechanical breakdowns, limped into Little America on March 29th, and two days later Innes-Taylor's Southern Party hove into sight. We were glad to see them all, and pleased that they had pulled off the operations as well as they had.

Now that the pressure of field operations was lifted, the fifty-five men at Little America turned to the still formidable task of holing in for the winter. It was a pretty grim prospect. Here was April upon us, the sun due to depart in a fortnight, and the three planes and all the tractors and dogs were still on the surface; a hundred tons of coal, gasoline, food and various general stores were still a mile distant at either Retreat Camp or East Barrier Cache; two hundred seals had to be hauled from the various caches scattered through the pressure ice; one radio antenna and four telephone poles were still to be raised; a whole system of tunnels had to be mined for hooking up the scattered buildings; these and various other problems required immediate attention. Lord, we thought, will it never end. The burden was all the heavier by reason of the fact that half a dozen men were still on the sick list, and many others were so occupied with fixed daily routine that they couldn't be spared, except for brief intervals, for the common burdens upon which the well-being of the camp depended.

Unloading ship and ramming the stuff through the pressure had been unreal enough. Then the sun made its unhurrying round of the sky; even with the temperature below freezing one could still work outside as late as February with nothing more on than a light shirt, breeches, underwear, shoes and a single pair of socks. But in April the sun was dying; the cold came in and settled like a dead weight; the blizzards became more venomous; and a crazy, lurid, Hollywood orange moon, swollen by refraction, shoved its bulk out of the Ross Sea. And it was strange still to be working then; an unfathomable uneasiness permeated the camp, as if by leaving so much to the last we should be roundly chastised for our impudence, like the cricket who stridulated the summer away, while the wise squirrel stored his winter supply of nuts. But neither impudence nor improvidence had anything to do with it; the prostrating levies made upon limited man-power and transportation by more pressing needs had driven these jobs into the background. Now, as the sun rolled along the horizon, rising each day a little later and setting a little earlier, they exerted their own vehement demands.

In April, too, the dog-drivers not engaged in hauling fell eagerly to the job of completing the building of Dog Town, which had been spasmodically under way while the drivers were in the field. Not very much progress had been made, and with the nights lengthening and the cold increasing the dogs were beginning to suffer. They were still on the surface, being locked up at night in the wooden kennel crates in which they made the voyage from Boston. Several had recently died of cold.

Fifty yards or so south of the new buildings, eight tunnels 100 feet long, in parallel and meeting at right angles a main tunnel running from the Seal Chopping House, were started. The side tunnels were about 6 feet deep and 3 feet wide. In these, at ten-foot intervals, the kennels were set in the walls, the kennels in one wall facing the center of the blank stretch between the kennels in the other. Thus each dog, within the orbit of his tethering chain, had a small ranging ground which he need not dispute with his neighbor. At any rate, that was the theory. In practice it worked out quite differently. One way

(© Paramount Pictures, Inc.)

LAYING THE FOUNDATIONS FOR
ADVANCE BASE

(© Paramount Pictures, Inc.)

ADMIRAL BYRD AND SIPLE (LEFT)
EXAMINE THE INSTRUMENTS

(© Paramount Pictures, Inc.)

FAREWELL—FOR THE WINTER NIGHT

(© Paramount Pictures, Inc.)

THE TRACTORS DEPART FOR LITTLE
AMERICA

SCENES AT ADVANCE BASE

THE FIRESIDE PHILOSOPHERS

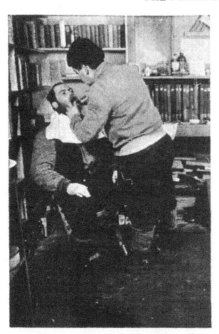

(Photographs by Joseph A. Pelter)

DOCTOR POTAKA USES "PAINLESS
DENTISTRY" ON COREY

GEORGE NOVILLE, EXECUTIVE OFFICER

LIFE DURING THE WINTER NIGHT

or another there was always the devil to pay in Dog Town: dogs slipping their chains, or bursting loose to run the gamut of slashing teeth en route to liberty, or else foolishly switching their rear ends around in such a manner that a vigilant neighbor, by leaping the full length of his chain, could get in a slashing stroke. Dog Town was one long uproar; and yet for all the turmoil, and the blood-spilling, and the wild free-for-alls that broke out every time a couple of dogs got loose, it wasn't, as dog-lovers will instantly suspect, a terribly cruel place. Dark, yes; dark as the other side of the moon; wherever you looked, glittering eyes hung in an uncanny suspension. Cold, yes; but the air was always steaming with the heat from their bodies and breath. And smell! Oh Lord, all the perfumes in France couldn't have rid Dog Town of its gamy aroma. It was appalling enough in its own primitive essences, but when Messrs. Paine and Russell stoked up the Blubber stove in the Seal Cutting cave at the head of Dog Town, the combination was richer than the lee side of a gas house. The air in the tunnels was thick enough not only to be cut with a knife; spiced with a dash of garlic from the bulbs that hung over Noville's door, it could have been served as pemmican.

Yet, I dare say that if it were possible for the dogs to render their own account, they would say that as such places go, Dog Town wasn't too bad. Anyhow, they were always friendly, always eager to see you; the first glimmer of a light at the head of the tunnel was a signal for an ecstasy of sound; and you could hardly get through for the dogs leaping and twisting within the orbits of their chains for the passing caress. "Stu" Paine used to say that when he grew bored with the interminable controversies and the microscopic issues of humans he could always find something amusing, something lovable and fine in the simple society of Dog Town.

On April 19th the sun set for the last time; it departed without ceremony; in point of accuracy it must be said that it took French leave the day before, because the 19th was cast out of the same gray mold of fog as so many days were before it. The going of the sun isn't the sudden, spectacular event that so many people seem to imagine; there's no abrupt walling off between night and day. It's just a gradual, lingering passing of one, and a slow washing in of the other, like the ebb and flow of an infinite tide. Days after the sun set for the last time a gray twilight expanded at noon, diminishing a little bit each day, until, by the middle of May, there was just a watery crimson smear at noon on the northern horizon. But even at midwinter day, when the sun was at its greatest northern declination, that stain, overlaid with a faint yellowish glow, still persisted on the frozen margin of the Ross Sea.

If the last day of the sun was drab and colorless, not so the several days preceding it. Day gave way to night not in the golden eruption of a New England fall, but in a lingering ecstasy of meeting. Lower and lower the bright wheel of the sun rolled along the northwestern horizon; more delicate and exquisite became the colors. The high cirrus clouds took on the extravagant opulence of tropical plants. Yellows, golds, greens, pinks, blues of a delicacy and novelty past describing; they are never the same and even as you watch they are in subtle distillation. The bold, solid Antarctic blue of the upper dome of sky; the rose-mist of the northern and southern horizons; the cliffs and the headlands of the Bay and the pinnacled pressure digging long furrows of shadows; and the soft swales of the Barrier luminous with a creeping sheen that seems alive. So the day dies, with colors waving and waning, then the night pours in, profound and vast, wheeling its lavish constellations and spreading the fluttering ballet of the aurora. It is an exciting thing to watch, this transition, if you don't mind the cold too much. On such clear days, especially when the sun is very low, no hour—no minute, for that matter—is ever the same. The colors of an infinite prism are in a state of flux, flowing, melting, merging, dividing in a lovely and intricate rhythm, as if the day were loath to leave. You notice

your shadow—a monstrous, inhuman thing, and the great
shadows in the pressure, solid cones of blue seeming to have
neither beginning nor ending. The spell of those hours never
leaves you. I suppose that's why, in the writings of explorers,
you come so often upon passionate descriptions of colors. How
rare these days are you are inclined to forget until you look
at your diary or riffle the daily meteorological reports: "overcast—light gray fog—poor visibility—horizon three miles. . . ."

Of course, by that time the animal life which in summer
months flourishes in the Bay of Whales had long since taken
leave. It seemed suddenly to melt before the cold of mid-March.
In February the skies were raucous with skua gulls; they
quarreled among the garbage heaps and over bloody seal
carcasses. Lindsey, the biologist, counted as many as 160 dis-
puting over a single dead seal. But they all vanished during
the first week of March. With them went the snowy petrels.
The first week in March a flight of one hundred of them fluttered moth-like in the haze above the camp. During the second
week we saw one or two; after that, none at all. Early in March
Lindsey saw a lone Emperor penguin and a couple of Adélies
footing it northward along Barrier's edge, as if looking for an
easy way down to the Bay. They were the last tourists of the
season. After March 15th even the seals disappeared from
their snoozing places in the pressure. But the day before the
sun went down the biologists, Siple, Lindsey and Dr. Perkins,
found three breathing holes in the new ice near the foot of
the pressure, and a groove furrowed in drift which indicated
that a seal had within twenty-four hours come to the surface.
But otherwise Nature had packed up and abdicated. Only
man was audacious (or vain) enough to remain.

Or perhaps it would be more correct to say that we were
too busy to be conscious of audacity. For snow hangars had
to be built for the airplanes, a garage for the tractors, and
tons of stuff moved back to Little America from Retreat
Camp. All these things took time, partly because we were

exhausted, partly because the blizzards would drive us below ground before we could finish a task. The consequence was that we were weeks doing jobs that, under better conditions, might have been finished in days; and all through the last of it we were working by the light of torches, with the temperature often in the subfifties and sixties. Yet done it was, at last; the planes and tractors were berthed underground, the dogs were safe in Dog Town, the food and coal were safely stored in the tunnels, Little America was a well-knit and well-fortified community, and we could look with some satisfaction to the quietness of the long winter night, the movies in the Mess Hall, the chess games in the radio shack, the free-for-all discussions in the Science Hall, and the amusing conversations in Dog Heim, where Innes-Taylor and Noville held open house.

No doubt the strain of the winter night was more intense in the past, when exploring parties were smaller, comforts were scarcer, and there wasn't the opportunity to take up the slack by overhauling tractors and airplanes and preparing for half a dozen major journeys. All winter long there was a buzz of power saws in the galley, a whine of drills in the machine shops, the click of Bailey's radio telegraph key, the smell of blubber from the Seal Cutting House where Russell, Paine and Stancliff were manufacturing dog pemmican, a litter of rations being stacked on the Mess Hall tables, the busy hum of Miller's sewing machine, the pulse-like beat of the Kohlers and calls for volunteers for this job or that—secure the tarpaulin over the big plane, haul gas in for the Kohlers, clean out the snow melter, shore up a caving tunnel or, as not infrequently happened, help Cox get the bull under control. The darn thing was growing like a weed, and it took three men to chivy him into the stall whenever he got loose. After one exhausting bout, Noville said to Cox, "Listen, the next time that animal gets loose, don't call on me because I've got too many things to worry about, all of them having to do with getting home alive."

I suppose each man will take the content of the winter night with a different measure; but for me, and I know for others, it was one of the most pleasurable periods of the whole polar experience. The dark months were quiet months; there was not so much of the impatience, the hurry and push, that came with the sun. One had time again to breathe.

The night has a queer replenishment and dignity of its own. Nowhere on earth will you see anything lovelier, with more quiet strength and authority, than the Ross Ice Barrier, by moonlight—foaming waves of pressure ice, the planed cliffs emerging from the darkness with classic purity of line, the sea ice spreading into the shoreless night, and a pale strand of green-yellow light on the horizon, the longest lance the deep sunken sun can throw.

Whether you stood on the surface of the Bay of Whales or among the slender upperworks of Little America, you felt the beauty and the repose of the night, its immensity and movement, whole armies of stars and wheeling constellations, and the tidal movements of the aurora, now lying like a pale ocean river of light through the zenith, now bursting into insane displays, becoming searchlights, puckering and flying curtains, groping rays. And you could glance up from the wastes of the Barrier and see taking shape in misty showers of ice crystals, the magical refraction phenomena of the moon —haloes, paraselenae (moon dogs) and, rarest of all, the corona, with the moon a polished ancient silver coin framed between concentric rings of color, pale blues, greens and smoking reds.

When you look upon such things, there comes surging through the confusion of the mind an awareness of the dignity of the earth, of the unaccountable importance of being alive, and the thought comes out of nowhere that unhappiness rises not so much from lacking as from having too much. Like Peter in *War and Peace*, something exclaims, though the words may not form: "All that is mine, all that is in me, is me." And you guess the end of the world will probably look like that, and the last men retreating from the cliffs will look out upon some such horizon, with all things at last in equilibrium, the winds quiet, the sea frozen, the sky composed, and the earth in glacial quietude.

Or so you fancy. Then along comes a walloping blizzard and knocks such night dreaming into a cocked hat. The peace is shattered as by a vast concussion; the world becomes a vindictive, brooding extravagance of plunging wind, foaming breakers of drift, furious shadows, as if the Barrier were disintegrating and flying to leeward. The blizzard has a queer taut sound, full and resonant, like the drumming of a mountain river in spring. And above and through it come rhythmic overtones, the creak and rattle of stovepipes, the hiss of snow melting against hot metal, the clack of the wind-driven generator atop the radio towers, and the violin-like notes of the meteor reticles and the antennæ wires.

The sound fills and dulls the ears until it ceases to hear them. But in the night, sometimes, a subtle altering in the texture of the atmosphere, something indefinable, like the lifting of a pressure, will awaken you out of a shallow sleep. Then you recognize it for what it is: the quiet, the creeping, rustling quiet of great cold—ah, the wind has stopped.

As for the cold, it was more tolerable than one might think. However brutal cold may be on the trail, it was no great hardship in the life of the camp. Some men were out every day of the winter, except when drift was too severe; we had some grand skiing parties down on the Bay of Whales even on the coldest and darkest days. On the three occasions the temperature crossed − 71° (June 21st, August 30th and 31st) at least half a dozen men were out skiing several hours.

As a matter of fact, there was real joy in being out in such air, if only to rid the lungs of the stale, smoky fumes of the shacks. The air had an exciting taste to it; when you drew a breath it seemed to hit the back of the head, and the nose and throat tingled with the feel of it.

The tolerable quality of great cold, I mean in the low sixties, is that it almost invariably occurs in still air. The air is utterly quiet, and the anemometer cups over the "Ad" Building lie stopped for hours. Sometimes, when there is the barest breath of wind you can hear the breath freezing as it floats to leeward, a strange, rather uncanny sound, like the explosion of tiny Chinese firecrackers.

Of course, in moving about or running on skis, you get nipped often enough. Most of the men who made a habit of skiing had scabrous, frost-bite sores on the cheek, hands and under the chin where the helmet strap chafed, which in the dim light of the shacks looked like leprosy in an incipient stage. But you accepted frost-bite in the natural order of things; it was as inevitable as sunburn at home in the summer, if considerably more annoying, since a good frost-bite leaves the skin sensitive, and for a long time afterwards a new bite is sore as blazes. So every little while you stop, slip a bare hand out of the warmth of the mitten and mold the flesh until the blood goes shooting through the veins.

Yet, the beauty of the coldest days was the clarity of the night and the great joy of skiing. Never were the stars brighter than when the temperature was sagging through the fifties and sixties. We could see and hear for miles. Sounds carried with tinkling clarity. Way down on the Bay we could hear the Kohlers puffing at Little America. The clang of a hammer, even a loud shout seemed to carry forever. The swish of skis on hard snow was startlingly loud. And often out of the darkness would float the round sounds of the pressure working—mysterious creakings and groanings, distant muffled sounds like those of a train running away off in the night, and sudden crashings and tumbling noises as unseen blocks let go. But the strangest noises of all were those of the seals under fifteen feet of ice—the thud of heads blundering against obstructions in the depths, the scrape of bodies, half-strangled gurglings, chipperings, pipings and a trill that was almost bird-like. On first hearing these sounds you could scarcely credit your ears.

C. J. V. M.

Chapter XV

THE WINTER JOURNEY

ABOVE everything else the winter night was a period of preparation for spring enterprises. The big push was ordered for October, and for four months the order regulated routine. Little America talked, lived and, I dare say dreamt field operations. They were the principal topic at meals; the subject of untiring conferences. Dr. Poulter, Innes-Taylor, Rawson and June worked closely with party leaders; and from time to time, over the thrice weekly radio schedules with Advance Base, various problems were taken up with Admiral Byrd.

Not counting the flights of geographical exploration, which will be discussed later by Admiral Byrd, three major sledging journeys, each requiring long-range support, were on the program. Although aimed into previously unexplored regions, the objectives of the several surface parties were scientific rather than geographical exploration. The purpose of the operations was to transport scientists to certain crucial areas for special studies.

So there really was no stopping even after we retired underground. The sledging parties immediately fell to work overhauling their gear and packing rations for the main journeys in the spring; Dyer and Hutcheson of the radio staff were building more powerful radio sets for these parties; Bowlin and his aviation crew slaved over the planes; and Demas and his tractor crew labored all winter long in the drafty, ramshackle garage overhauling their cars, building wooden cabins which were intended to convert the cars into rolling camps; Ronne and Eilefsen rerigged the lashings on the sledges and renewed broken runners and cross-members; and Innes-Taylor and Rawson conducted for the field parties a sort of university course in field practice and navigation, which met every other day in the Mess Hall to take up the finer points of sledging. Thus we always had something to do, above and beyond even the routine business of caring for ourselves; and, now that I look back upon it, I sometimes think that part of our subsequent difficulties came from the fact that we were too much preoccupied with our own leisurely existence to realize what might be happening in the south.

Nature has a curious way of working seemingly aimlessly and to no apparent purpose; then at the right moment something happens and all the disconnected and remote things fly together, forming a significant design.

Toward the end of June, in the middle of winter darkness, such an obscure motivation was to turn our minds with heightening misgivings and anxiety toward Advance Base.

Poulter's unexpectedly good results with the meteor observations—the remarkable things Demas was doing with the tractors—the general progress made in spring preparations, all had their rôle in the hidden purpose.

From the day Admiral Byrd commenced his isolation on March 28th we were in frequent radio communication with him. Three times a week, Tuesdays, Thursdays and Sundays, Dyer contacted him at KFY, Advance Base, speaking to him on the telephone and the Admiral responding in code.

Everything seemed to be going nicely. Admiral Byrd was unfailingly cheerful. As a rule, the contacts were quite short, and would have been even shorter if he were a better operator. His sending speed was about ten words a minute. For the most part the time was given to an exchange of personal messages. Occasionally, however, the officers of the camp took up with him various aspects of the field operations.

Occasionally, too, Admiral Byrd made passing reference to the sort of life he was living—the steady demands of his meteorological records, the little things he was doing to avert monotony, the pleasure and peace of the place, the weather. On the whole his temperatures seemed to be running from 8° to 10° colder than Little America. For example, on May 20th, when our own thermometers stood at − 62°, he reported a temperature of − 72°.

Toward the end of June Demas was getting along with the tractors. No. 1 was about ready for a trial run on the surface. Dr. Poulter followed these preparations with keen interest.

On June 21st, he took up with Admiral Byrd, over the radio, a scheme he had long been weighing: a trip to Advance Base to observe meteors. He was anxious to undertake this trip in order to secure a second observatory for simultaneous observations with the first station at Little America. As vigorously as he could, the senior scientist outlined the accruing benefits to the scientific program, especially now that the deep darkness heightened the opportunities for such observations. He explained what was being done to the tractors, the increased safety factors, the probability that in a day or so No. 1 would be ready for a trial trip.

Dyer copied down Admiral Byrd's brief comments. If Poulter thought the project feasible and essential to his program, he was perfectly willing to approve the trip—in fact, he might himself take advantage of the tractor's arrival to return earlier to Little America to assist spring preparations. However, he recommended withholding final decision until the test run gave a line not only on the tractor's performance but also on how readily the trail flags planted in March could be followed.

At that time, we know now, he was at the end of his tether—dying from the effects of the poisonous fumes cast off by the stove and gasoline generator, scarcely able to walk, existing on half-frozen foods he was too ill and too weak to prepare properly, not daring to use the fire more than a few hours a day on account of the poisonous fumes from the stove, which he could not control. All this in the presence of cold which, at times, dropped toward − 80°.

Admiral Byrd was then approaching the fifth month of isolation and in the third month of darkness.

But in June we had no such insight. The design was still concealed. Code is impersonal and, unlike a voice, does not give one away.

In a day or so No. 1 was ready, but cloudiness and high drift held it underground until the 26th. In the morning the wind dropped, and Noville promptly mustered all available hands for digging out the ramp. A mean job in darkness, working by the blinding light of pressure lamps. As the picks, shovels and saws dug deeper, scores of boxes cached there in the hurry of securing the shack in May came to light. The moon was obscured by a dry, cold fog, and there was a vague smear of a moon dog to either side. The temperature was — 15°.

Presently No. 1, with Skinner at the wheel, backed up the steep grade, complaining and balking as the treads spun for traction. That evening, about supper time, Poulter, Demas, Skinner and Waite took the car on a trial run, following the flag-marked southern trail past Retreat Camp toward Amundsen Arm. The darkness and mist quickly swallowed up the car, but long after it vanished we could see the reflection of its lights above the ridge.

They were back about midnight, enthusiastic over the car's performance. Between Retreat Camp and the northern shore of Amundsen Arm, Poulter said, a good many flags were either drifted over or blown away. They had to reconnoiter on foot to locate the big depot flag marking the transit through the crevasses across the Arm. The few miles across Amundsen Arm were very good; the flags stood out prominently, and such upheavals as had occurred did not hinder the passage. In the pressure at the foot of high barrier sloping down to the southern shore of the Arm they stopped to fill a small crevasse. Gaining the crest of the Barrier about eleven miles south, they found the flags still visible though many were drifted up to the cloth.

On the schedule of June 28th Poulter reported to Admiral Byrd the results of the test run. He said the trail appeared to be good and that he foresaw no great difficulty in following it to Advance Base. On the strength of this report, Admiral Byrd tentatively approved the journey. He insisted, however, that the departure from Little America be regulated by weather, that no undue risks be taken with personnel, that above everything else the tractor should hold to the flags put down in March, rather than risk stumbling upon new crevasses in the dark.

These safety precautions virtually doomed the success of the first attempt, and with it his own relief.

Departure was set for the full moon period of July 18th-23rd, at which time the party, if the air was clear, would have the benefit of moonlight and the enlarging twilight of the south-swinging sun as it boosted itself a little bit nearer the northern horizon at noon each day.

July must have been an unspeakable ordeal for Admiral Byrd. Fighting off an infinite weakness, though despairing of ever recovering, he was ever so meagerly gaining strength;—enough, anyhow, to keep up his observations, to defend his line of communications, lest the slowly evolving meteor venture be converted into a reckless, unenlightened relief effort. The mild weather of June crumpled under a fresh onslaught of cold. At Advance Base July rounded the corner frostily. Twenty-five times that month the thermometer level crossed — 50°; four times it passed — 70°; once it stood at — 80°. And this man at Advance Base, too helpless to do anything about it, watched the drift wash up over the roof of the shack, assailing his only exit.

In the wisdom that comes after the event, a blinding light falls upon things that once were meaningless and removed from purposeful design. Weeks later we at Little America were to feel cold shivers running up and down our spines when we saw how everything added up, and how unthinking, how undiscerning we were.

It was decided that the party should number five—Dr. Poulter, leader; Skinner, driver; Waite, radio operator; and Fleming and Peterson, the last two being assigned to Advance Base as observers. They would occupy the Base until spring, carrying on the meterological observations and making meteor observations as long as the darkness lasted.

On July 5th (the radio schedule having meanwhile been moved up to 2 o'clock in the afternoon) Admiral Byrd for the first time failed to come in. The following afternoon Dyer reestablished contact over the emergency schedule. As he spelled out the code on the typewriter, Dyer remarked the Admiral was using his hand-cranked generator.

"How do you know?"

"I can tell by the sound. It's unmistakable."

Admiral Byrd said that his main set was "shot." A coupling on the gasoline-driven generator powering his main transmitter had sheared off, disabling it. He was obliged to fall back upon the emergency set, a trail set, the transmitter of which was dependent for power upon hand-cranking.

It must have been a frightful blow. In his weakened condition cranking called for strength it was almost impossible to muster. Admiral Byrd collapsed after signing off that day, his diary shows.

Again, though we called twice a day over the emergency morning and afternoon schedules, we failed to contact him until July 15th. On this day, after having patiently given his always courteous and soft spoken call—"KFZ calling KFY Advance Base. Good afternoon. We shall stand by for you, Admiral Byrd. Please come in"—Dyer switched hopefully to the receiver. He turned to the typewriter just in time to catch Advance Base in the middle of a message:

... above all tractors must be absolutely certain not to lose trail or give out of fuel ... and [take] no chances with lives of men....

Poulter, who was standing at Dyer's elbow, didn't bother to ask the cause of the week's silence. (We learned later that something was wrong with the transmitter, that Admiral Byrd had struggled desperately to fix it, that at the cost of strength he should have saved for his own needs he broadcast reassuring messages in order to conceal from the men at Little America any hint of his desperate situation, and forestall any ill-considered attempts to reach him. Various small details in respect to the journey were cleared up.) Poulter said he expected to start in four days, if weather allowed. Admiral Byrd said that from the 20th on he would keep a beacon light burning on the anemometer pole. In the dark the tractor party might pass fifty yards to either side of the tiny upperworks of the buried shack and never see them.

Foreboding as was the week's silence, it failed to impress most of us very deeply. We talked about it and speculated; some thought it meant one thing; some another. But restoration of communication brushed away some of the uncertainty. The night was a lethargy that dulls perception. Besides, Admiral Byrd was unfailingly cheerful. There was utterly no hint of his distress. Invariably he signed off with an "OK cheerio."

The next month was a long nightmare, intensifying as shadowing meanings came out of the darkness.

The 20th came on fair and cold. On the verge of noon the slow-swinging sun washed up a pale rosy smear on the northern horizon.

At 2:20 o'clock in the afternoon, No. 1 started south, a grotesque, misshapen monstrosity drooling great plumes of vapor from the exhaust. By then the pale hint of oncoming day had drained from the north, and the darkness had closed in. The headlights dug deep furrows into the night. Skinner was at the wheel, and Poulter, looking like a Mongol in a yellow face mask with a contorted mouth, sat astride the hood, playing a searchlight over the trail. The others were sprawled out in the heaping mounds of gear in the cabin.

Through radio's sorcery Little America followed the car southward into polar night. Waite was reporting every hour to Dyer. Haines, who had moved up to command, left the engineer's elbow only to scan weather. On the blackboard in the galley Innes-Taylor rubbed out the rations formula and drew in a rough map of the southern trail. Every hour he checked off the car's progress. A crawling line, a painfully inching line. Only men who had slogged over that trail by daylight knew the punishment that went with every yard won.

At 6:45 P.M. the car reached the end of the tracks of the trial run. On high barrier they squared away for Advance Base. The first set-back came almost instantly. They circled an hour before they found the tall snow beacon just beyond. At 7 P.M. Haines took a balloon run—12 miles of northeasterly wind on the surface, switching into a 36-mile westerly at 4,000 feet. "A mite suspicious," said Haines. The moon was barely visible, obscured by a shower of ice crystals. At 9 P.M., unable to pick up the flags beyond, Poulter retreated to the beacon. Fleming and Waite got off with a lantern; taking a bearing from the light, Skinner and Poulter groped south in the tractor until they came upon a flag barely awash nearly half a mile beyond. A few inches of cloth on a dark ocean. To make good 11.8 miles they had cruised nearly 24 by the speedometer, searching for flags.

Midnight, and the bottom dropping out of the thermometer: — 58° below at Little America and still dropping. The tractor was 17 miles out—"snowing, viz. zero, flags sticking out two inches, but finding them all right." Poulter was sitting astride the hood, fanning the trail with a searchlight. A brief contact with Admiral Byrd at Advance Base. All well. The line moved forward on the galley blackboard. But on the trail the interminable groping for flags continued, right to left, back and forth, with the men skiing ahead of the car to widen the search.

The second day wore on. At Little America the temperature sagged to $-71.6°$; out where the tractor was, to $-75°$, the coldest day of the year. That afternoon a gain in hope— "arrived 50-Mile Depot. Cold." (Unable to find any more flags, they had pressed on; the searchlight picked up a burgee about 400 yards west of the depot, just at the edge of an enormous crevasse. Wheeling east they ran smack into the depot, eroded by wind from a square block to a drooping cone from which stuck out a gas drum and several bags of rations.)

No pause for rest. The critical stage of the journey lay dead ahead, the detour around a badly crevassed area. Little America had a sober discussion at mess. As the last sitting got up from the table, Innes-Taylor printed on the blackboard:

6:30 P.M. Tractor returning from 54 Miles to 50-Mile Depot to make fresh attempt pick up trail.

"What's the dope, Alan?"

"Evidently the flags are drifted over or blown away," he said. "Looks tough now."

The outcome was inevitable. The tractor had already traveled 173 miles to make good 62 miles.

At 12:30 A.M. on the third day, Dyer intercepted a message that Waite was broadcasting "blind" to Admiral Byrd:

We are at 50-Mile Depot unable to locate trail around crevassed area in six hours. Apparently snowed under.... Many flags completely covered. Think it inadvisable to proceed through crevassed area without more light since present trail can't be followed. POULTER.

Admiral Byrd didn't hear it. Too weak to crank his generator, he was harboring his strength to keep the beacon light blazing on the roof of his shack.

No word then for hours. A pitiless cold. The wind was steepening. Perkins froze his face badly just walking overland from the "Ad" Building to the galley. Haines mistrusted the weather.

"Take my word for it," he said, "it's going to blow like hell."

About two hours later, when the tractor was running at full speed for home, the blizzard struck—a gentle rustling in the ventilators, then a rattling of the stovepipe. Half a dozen skiers tumbled into the tunnel entrances, exclaiming that they had barely made it. The first warning was a wavering white cloud, moving with incredible speed across the Barrier.

For a while Skinner tried to push into the storm, but the engine was stalling as drift penetrated to the carburetor. The temperature was still in the minus fifties, and the air was molten metal. When Dyer reëstablished contact with the car, it was hove to 28 miles south in a wind close to hurricane force. Even in the sheltered valley of Little America the wind hit 60 miles an hour, the severest of the year. In the shacks the draughts backed down the stovepipes, filling the rooms with smoke, and the pipes themselves were rattled from the stoves.

Thus ended the first attempt to reach Admiral Byrd at Advance Base—an attempt the failure of which was in a large measure made inevitable by the precautions that Admiral Byrd imposed for the safety of the crew. Had these men known or guessed the suffering and illness that lay south of them that night east of the 50-Mile Depot, when they sat in the freezing cabin over bowls of hoosh and debated whether to hold to the letter of instructions or make a run for it, taking a chance on the darkness and crevasses, the car would never have been pointed north.

The blizzard blew out on the 23rd. Digging out the car, and the sledges, the latter from under four feet of snow, the tractor crew resumed the retreat that afternoon, arriving home about 8:15, having been guided all the way by the big beacon light Dyer and Hutcheson had installed on one of the radio towers.

Dr. Poulter's first question was, "Has Admiral Byrd been informed we had to turn back?"

He was told Dyer had been unable to contact him since midnight on the 20th.

"That's a pity," Poulter said. "I can imagine nothing unhappier than to be in that isolated place. expecting some one to arrive, and then waiting hours and hours, wondering what happened."

The truth of the matter is that the fear was creeping through Little America that the leader was in distress. There was utterly nothing to base it on. It had root in nothing tangible. Nobody had a name for it, intuition or logic; but there it was, a crawling uncertainty. Things were beginning to add up. The silence itself was suspect, and the simple explanation that Admiral Byrd was having trouble with his radio set didn't entirely account for it. After he became dependent upon the hand-cranked generator, Dyer remarked how slow and ragged his sending was. The messages filtered through in groups of three and four words. In between he would spell out "wait." Minutes would elapse before he resumed. The same hesitation occurred in the dim, reassuring messages he broadcast "blind" after the tractor turned back.

Were these pauses meaningful? One couldn't tell. When asked about it Admiral Byrd explained he had a "bad arm" which made it difficult to crank, but insisted that it did not otherwise inconvenience him.

But it was a ghastly feeling to look southward into the depths of the night and think that a man, a close and beloved friend, was isolated out there, perhaps too proud to call for help or unwilling to place another man in jeopardy.

In all events, Poulter now determined to make a run of it to Advance Base, ignoring instructions to hold to the trail. He reduced his crew to three—Demas, Waite and himself. It was Demas's turn to drive. He and Skinner had tossed for the right to make the first trip.

The weather, however, was uncertain, squally at times,

cloudy. On Haines' recommendation Poulter deferred the start until conditions stabilized.

On August 2nd Dyer heard Advance Base—"Where is tractor? I have heard nothing for days."—repeated over and over again.

Dyer broke in and miraculously restored contact.

Hutcheson hurried out and got Poulter. In the calmest sort of way the scientist reviewed the journey. He planned, he said, to leave on the first break in the weather, being hopeful of getting through in time for satisfactory meteor observations. He said nothing that might give Admiral Byrd an inkling of the rising concern at Little America.

But, now for the first time there was something to go on besides meteors.

Over one of the schedules, Admiral Byrd made a suggestion as to navigation. The message being garbled, he asked to repeat. He had always been most courteous about that. He commenced again. Then abruptly the code call thinned out and faded.

Dyer waited for him to come in. The seconds passed. Dyer fidgeted nervously at the dials, but nothing came through.

"Are you ill? Are you hurt?"

The tired answer drifted out of the south, spelled out with infinite slowness: "Please don't ask me crank any more. I'm okay."

At that instant the fears and intuitions, the speculations and apprehensions of July were confirmed.

Tractor No. 3 squared away on the morning of the 8th. Dyer, looking terribly thin and haggard with great dark circles under his eyes, stayed up again for the radio watch. Hutcheson would relieve him in the morning. An hour later the car was back—a balky oil pump. Von der Wall, Skinner and Hill, who were still working over No. 1, rushing it for standby duty, gave them a hand. Maybe they stayed half an hour. Nobody kept a stopwatch at such things. Anyhow the car, with the engine wide open, struck again into the mist. The temperature was — 44°, and the sky utterly dark.

At 7:45 o'clock Waite advised they had picked up the sledges, which they had dropped when the pump trouble had forced them to return, at 23 miles.

For three days Little America didn't draw a happy breath.

In spite of poor visibility Poulter made 30 miles before he camped. In the early evening of the 9th, having fetched up with 50-Mile Depot, they headed around the crevassed area. Poulter was lining the car up on the course with flashlight bulbs and lighted candles stuck in perforated tin cans planted on snow beacons.

At 7:45 on the morning of the 10th a bewildering impact of good and bad news. They had picked up the flags of the old trail, had come upon the drifted hulk of the abandoned tractor, but . . . "generators going haywire, ignition failing every few minutes. Been going since 8 A.M. yesterday. Save daylight."

The last meant they intended to remain under way rather than lose the gray twilight hours of the forenoon. Though they were headed into the darkness of the south, there were a few hours now before noon when the lower northern horizon was suffused by a rosy light.

At 3:45 that afternoon they were at 81 miles. The generator burned out, the brushes on the spare were badly worn; they were whittling tiny blocks of wood to hold them in place. Waite told Dyer they were freezing hands and faces every few minutes. Fagged out, too. "Eating and going right through," Poulter reported.

Then we lost contact with them. Advance Base was also silent.

Shortly after they pushed on from 81 miles south, Poulter, sitting atop the cab, had seen the blue light of a magnesium flare, well up in the south, linger, then die away.

Two hours of what seemed to be creeping progress, though they were making five knots, then a winking light on the port bow. Just before midnight, a livid burst of flame split the darkness as they topped the last rise.

The searchlight picked up a man in furs walking slowly toward the tractor. "Come on down, fellows. I have a bowl of hot soup for you."

Slumped over the key, Dyer was calling, calling, calling. Flashes of liquid light welled up in the tubes, and on the racks various needles sprang to attention like startled grenadiers.

"Nothing yet?"

Dyer's tired eyes framed a negative. From time to time he would swing around in his chair, cut off his own transmitter and listen gravely. As he turned the dial the whole world piped up—London, New York, Frisco, ships at sea, aircraft reporting to ground stations—you could hear them all bustling with cheerful confidences.

But from the south—nothing.

Midnight came, went by; the flame went out under the primus stove and the coffee froze in the pot.

"Try Advance Base, John," somebody suggested. "They must have gotten there."

Not hopefully, Dyer went to the new frequency. Out of the background murmuring of the atmosphere there boiled up, like a trout smashing at a fly, a vibrant note, deep, surging, welcome: "KFZ de W1OXCD ... KFZ de W1OXCD ... "

"Here's the tractor," Dyer said, wheeling to the typewriter. Words hurried across the message blank. "Heard you calling me on REB's receiver. Will go back to shack to finish schedule. Confidential. Found him weak from fumes. WAITE."

First-class news was never broken in a more oblique way. Exasperated, confused, wondering what tale the next few minutes would bring, we waited and counted the minutes it took Waite, more than a hundred miles away, to descend the shaft at Advance Base, speak to Poulter, and fall to with the hand-cranked generator.

Ten minutes by the clock. Up came the familar mounting

whine of the hand-cranked set and the code calls ripping cleanly across it.

....The fumes from the stove got REB down about June first.... Please don't publish as it would be hard on his wife. POULTER.

"For God's sake," somebody snapped at Dyer, "tell Poulter we want to know how Byrd is."

The answer floated back: "Pretty weak now, but think he will pull through."

And with that we shut down for the night.

Later on we learned what had happened—the gradual poisoning from the fumes of the stove; the almost fatal blow on May 31st, when the gas from the gasoline-driven generator running in the tunnel felled him; the ghastly struggle to live through the cold and darkness of June and July and finally into August; the obvious reason he declined to call for help and yet steadily tried to hold communication, and, finally, the things the tractor crew found, the litter of cans under the bunk, the instructions hanging from a nail.

The pattern at last had come together. The coalescing clue was a man's sense of dignity, honor and responsibility. Through the chilling realization of what might have happened during the two and a half months Admiral Byrd lay ill at Advance Base welled up happiness that it had finally worked out all right.

"The meteorological records are complete," Poulter advised. From him, a scientist, it was the highest compliment he could frame. They would remain, he said, until Admiral Byrd was well enough to travel.

How long would that be? He didn't know. At least a month, anyhow. For Byrd had been about as close to death as a man might expect to get and still not die, and he was terribly weak when they found him, so weak that it was actually two months before he had the strength to undertake the return to Little America.

Slowly the oncoming day was rising phantom-like out of the night, unreal and soundlessly; and in the eastern sky a carpet of cold, lustrous sheen was being spread for the sun. On August 21st we glanced up from the wash basins to the enthralling discovery that a perfect light was growing in the ventilators and the skylights, a light you couldn't call mauve, or pink, or rose, or any other color—just the loveliest, most significant color you can imagine.

As the daylight came flooding in, the tempo at Little America quickened. All the field parties, poised for a start scheduled for mid-November, hastened to finish their preparations. The snow hangars which had housed the planes were broken apart, and the planes hauled out. It took several days of the hardest kind of digging and very nearly the entire man-power of the camp to bring the big Condor to the surface from its submerged rookery. Every fair day McCormick flew the autogiro on what we called meteorological hops—sounding the upper air with instruments to measure the temperature and barometric pressure at various altitudes. These hops came to an end late in September when the gyro crashed. McCormick luckily escaped with nothing worse than a broken arm. Meanwhile the Eastern Tractor Party, commanded by June and made up of Rawson (navigator), Von der Wall (driver), and Petersen (radio operator), had set out for Mount Grace McKinley in the Edsel Ford Range, with the double mission of laying down food depots for Siple's Marie Byrd Land Sledging Party and locating possible emergency landing fields for the flights of exploration which would soon be launched over that sector.

So the big push was coming, and the knowledge that we were at last coming face to face with the problems which had engrossed our interest and energies throughout the winter night brought a fresh tension into the affairs at Little America. Yet daylight did not necessarily mean the end of winter. During the first three weeks of September the daily minimum temperatures almost always reached the minus fifties or sixties; and there was a good deal of wind, too, which made the cold that much more punishing. Even so, the sun had a warmth to it that the thermometers did not show; and finally, toward the end of the month, Innes-Taylor decided that the dogs should be brought to the surface for good.

Out they came, one by one, with a driver's hand firmly holding the collars—Russell's white-eyed, slinky Siberians, black and wiry; Coal, the furtive pint-size assassin who slew four dogs half again as big as he in the dark ambushes of Dog Town; Paine's great leader, Jack, with a windproof bandage around a stump of a tail; Navy, alas, hopelessly crippled; Nero, the bouncing MacKenzie River husky, who rocked back and forth on his feet when he pleaded for chow; Rattle, who traveled the pitch-black length of Dog Town, running a gantlet of slashing teeth all the way, to kill slow Olav; Tobey, the monstrous Shamboul who roamed the Barrier for ten days in the middle of winter and lived to find his way back to Little America; Taku's seven pups, now grown to great size, rich golden coats and fine strong paws. One after another, 121 of them. Many were missing—Marve, Cæsar, Don, Weedy. The "wolves" had come off badly. Of Corey's team of nine wolves, only five survived. Good-humored Pony, driven to distraction by their slashing attacks, went berserk and knocked off two in succession.

The instant a dog topped the hatch, he blinked at the unaccustomed brightness of the day, looked frantically about as if searching for something dimly remembered, while the drivers roared; "Yes, sir, old boy, it's still there!" Of course, the telephone pole hard by the hatch.

"Well, I saw the first bird today," said Young at the evening meal.

The uproar of talk stopped.

"Oh, yeah?"

"Where? What sort of bird?"

"Over the camp," said the British sailorman. "A sort of brownish bird, very fast of flight."

Lindsey remarked that would be an Antarctic petrel.

C. J. V. M.

Chapter *XVI*

~~~~~~

MYSTERY OF THE STRAIT

It is hardly necessary to add to what has already been written in the foregoing chapter about my experiences at Advance Base. What happened out there was substantially reported. From June on, till the tractor arrived in August, it was tough sledding. The chances of my survival seemed very slim. But March, April and May were more than all right. I had a great time. The trying months that followed have never succeeded in taking away the joyful memory of the earlier period. However, that's neither here nor there. When I went out to Advance Base, I expected it to be hard—not quite so hard, I'll admit, as it turned out to be—but in all events, I had no reason to be surprised or rueful, whatever the turn in affairs. My auroral data are being studied by scientists. The meteorological records are now in the possession of Government meteorologists. If they add only a little to present knowledge of Antarctic meteorology, I shall consider myself rewarded. With the exception of a few blank pages and a few observations missed, the data were complete and continuous from the day the Station was occupied (March 25th) until it was abandoned (October 12th).

I was in a frightful condition. It was to be months, years, before I was to get my strength back again and to feel once more the glow of real health.

As for Dr. Poulter, Demas and Waite, I cannot say too much for them. Theirs was a hard, dangerous journey. It was one of those indescribable moments when, looking north over the black ocean of the Ross Ice Barrier, I suddenly saw far off (I tried to tell myself, as I had so often done before, that it was just a star) the wavering pin point of a tractor searchlight.

I was still an ill man when I returned to Little America. In fact, it was to be another year before I was to get my strength back again; but I did my best to keep my real condition from my men. There were few indeed who realized my real condition. Nevertheless, it was imperative that I take up the reins of leadership. And it was truly good to join afresh the life of the expedition, and to feel under my hand the lively stir of a variety of enterprises. With the main parties whipping their gear together, the camp was pretty much in an uproar. Fortunately, I had time enough to look over their equipment and discuss matters with each of the parties. The gear was in excellent shape (for which Captain Innes-Taylor and his dog department and Demas deserve the highest praise); the men knew exactly what was expected of them, and a sound system of rations, depots, weights and support schedules had been worked out. All they needed was the word go.

On the 14th, one day ahead of schedule, the Marie Byrd Land Party (Siple, leader, biologist and navigator; Wade, radio operator, geologist and driver; Corey, supplies and driver, and Stancliff, driver) started eastward with four teams.

Two days later, the Geological Party (Blackburn, leader and geologist; Russell, in charge of base laying, and driver; Paine, navigator, radio operator and driver) with two nine-dog teams, and the Plateau Party (Morgan and Dr. Bramhall, co-leader; Ronne and Eilefsen) started south on parallel missions to the Queen Maud Range.

Notwithstanding the dullness of the air, the six teams made a grand spectacle as they moved off, one behind the other, well-spaced, with a nice spread to the dogs and a clean run to the sledges. I noticed with quick understanding how soon, after the emotional impetus of the start was spent, the teams slowed down to a walk.

Scarcely had we thus dispatched two parties when the first

field party—the eastern tractor expedition—returned from Marie Byrd Land, jubilant over a first-rate discovery. After steering past the Rockefellers they had found a huge plateau rolling unbrokenly to the south and east past the Edsel Ford Range. Beside this, they had the satisfaction of being the first surface party ever to penetrate a land discovered by aviation. It was a brilliant piece of work. When the tractor halted on the outskirts of Dog Town, there remained but a pint of oil in the engine and 25 gallons of gas in the tanks. The men looked quite tired; their faces were yellowed from frost-bite, but they were all in high spirits.

Now aviation, which would carry the burden of long-range geographical discovery, made ready for its opportunities. The plans for the aerial attack had long since crystallized.

First off, a thrust into the 517-mile gap of unknown between the Edsel Ford Range to the north and the Queen Maud Range to the south.

This white gap, running north and south along the 147th meridian, between the mountains of the coast and the mountains rimming the south polar plateau, held one of the most crucial secrets in Antarctic geography—the secret of the great Ice Strait. Of the unsolved geographical riddles of the modern world, this was one of the most challenging, perhaps the most important. For this theoretical Strait, if proof of its existence could be found in the undiscovered interior, held out the promise of a great potential waterway connecting the Atlantic and Pacific oceans across the bottom of the globe.

Associated with this problem of the Ice Strait, was the equally important problem of the Andean fold chain. A glance at a map of the South Polar regions will show why this is so. South of Cape Horn the diminishing backbone of the South American Andes, after vanishing under the South Atlantic Ocean, seemingly rises afresh in the mountainous islands of the Antarctic Archipelago (sometimes called Graham Land

and Graham Land Peninsula) and impinges on the Antarctic Continent at Hearst Land, recently discovered by my friend, Sir Hubert Wilkins. That this ridge, referred to by some authorities as the Antarctandes, is a continuation of the Andean fold chain, many geologists believe. The crucial question was: Is this chain continued across Antarctica; and, if so, in what direction? Does it march into the heart of the continent, as some authorities believe? Or does it, after recurring on the coast of the Antarctic continent, make a broad sweep to the west, skirting the South Pacific Ocean, finally to join the mountains of Marie Byrd and King Edward VII Land? And finally, in either case did "an arm of the sea," the so-called Strait, separate these mountain chains?

Thus the double problem, as fascinating to me as a modern search for a short-cut to Cathay, a new Northwest Passage.

The discoveries of June, Rawson, Petersen and Von der Wall in the tractor trip across the previously untraveled ice of Scott Land to Marie Byrd Land forged two new links in the chain of evidence. First, the Edsel Ford Range, instead of bearing south, appeared rather to stream off to the northeast. Mount Grace McKinley, they reported, was the southwestern anchor of the western front range. Secondly, the new elevated plateau appeared to roll to the south and southeast. From the peak the tractor party's range of vision was possibly fifty miles. Hence, new questions were excited. How far south then, does this plateau extend? Does it roll to the foot of the Queen Maud Range? Does it destroy the concept of the Ice Strait?

So, the issue, now, was sharply drawn. If the Great Ice Strait existed, it must of necessity debouch somewhere through that 517 mile gap of unknown along the 147th meridian between Mount Grace McKinley, anchor peak of the Edsel Ford Range, and the loftier masses of the Queen Maud Range.

So, after careful consideration, we laid a flight course which would strike in the heart of this gap, and enable us, for all practical purposes, by running north to the Edsel Ford Range, to close the gap from the coast halfway to the Queen Maud Range.

The flight track, as it was planned, roughly described a scalene triangle, with a base line running from Little America to Mount Grace McKinley, and the apex resting at Lat. 81° S., Long. 147° W., the latter serving as the halfway point.

But you will protest: Here you have a land smothered in ice. Suppose a passage does exist. It would be frozen to the bottom under a heaping mass of ice riveted to the ice cap doming the whole continent. How, then, from an airplane could you expect to isolate and define an Ice Strait from an immense and anonymous sheet of ice?

The answer is: We purposed to sound all doubtful areas with the plane's altimeter, and delicate barograph, brushing low over the ice to get the elevation as registered by barometric pressure.

Which must instantly excite the second protest: Even so! Granted you find a significant area of low elevation, what more will it be than ice elevation? The thickness of the continental ice cap is absolutely unknown; estimates run from a few hundred to several thousand feet. How then could you possibly tell whether or not you merely have, at low elevations, just a thin veneering of ice overland above sea-level, or a deep heaping of ice over land well below sea level?

The answer to the second question is: From the seismic soundings which Morgan would take on his journey, together with those Poulter would take roundabout Little America, we hoped to be able to determine something about the thickness of the Antarctic ice cap and of shelf ice (that is, ice over water). This data would be a pretty good check against altimeter determinations. Let's put it this way: If, for example, the altimeter showed the ice elevation of a region to be 1,200 feet above sea level, and Morgan's soundings showed an ice thickness of 400 feet generally prevailing at such an elevation, it would indicate that the land underneath was about 800 feet

above sea level. The altimeter soundings would also show
where the steep gradients were, thus indicating the junction
points of shelf ice and upthrusting shoals.

Anyhow, there was the problem, and we were eager to try
our hand at solving it. My deepest interest has always lain
in exploring from the air. A successful flight would polarize
the problem of the strait, but I was counting on the data of
the other field parties. Remember, at this period as aviation
made ready, we had three parties running toward strategic
areas—the Marie Byrd Land Party headed eastward for a
geological reconnaissance of the Edsel Ford Range, the Geological Party headed on a similar mission toward the Queen
Mauds, and the Plateau Party, on the verge of making a shift
to the new plateau and combining forces with a supporting
party of tractors under Demas. This gave us three main
units engaged in a flanking attack on the same broad sector.
On the evidence accumulated by these three units, together
with the discoveries by flight, we would rest our case for or
against the Ice Strait.

Shortly after midnight, November 15th, the break came.
The clouds vanished as if erased. Fleming, night watchman,
who every half hour was supposed to look at the sky, roused
Haines and Grimminger, the weathermen. At 4 A.M they took
a balloon run, the most encouraging in a fortnight, a light
southwesterly wind at the surface which gradually shifted
through south into southeast at 3,000 feet with a velocity of
5 to 10 miles per hour, then above that at 7,000 feet a layer
of southeasterly wind increasing in velocity to 35 m.p.h.—
headwinds on the outward track, but drying winds, the winds
we had been waiting for.

The aviation gang was awakened at once. Bowlin, Swan and
Dustin fell to on the *William Horlick*. The heater tents were
rigged over the engines, and the blow torches started.

At 6:30 o'clock all hands came piling out of the bunks to
stand by for work details in connection with the main flight.

Planning a Flight—Admiral Byrd, Rawson, Petersen, June, Pelter, Bowlin, and Smith

(Photograph by Joseph A. Pelter)

The *William Horlick* Comes Out of Its Winter Cocoon

HEATING THE MOTORS

(Photographs by Joseph A. Pelter)

THE RADIO STAFF—BAILEY, WAITE, DYER, HUTCHESON

Though the temperature was − 9°, the air had such a bland warmth to it that the men working were presently stripped to their underwear.

An hour later, the Marie Byrd Land Party, camped thirty miles northeast of Mount Grace McKinley, reported: "Clouds —none, wind—none, viz.—excellent."

As Wade went off the air, Waite with the tractor party broke in from the south: "Tractor Party WX—temp. − 12°, wind S 15, increasing rapidly. Clear, viz unlimited, no clouds, looks good for flight if that wind doesn't bother you."

It wouldn't. Orders were given for a departure as soon as June finished gassing the plane. We had to have clear weather to make the flight productive from a scientific standpoint.

This brings up the matter of a decision which I have deferred mentioning here, as I staved it off in my own mind at Little America, until the hour of choice arrived—the decision of whether or not I should fly.

Though I had come up a long way since Poulter reached me at Advance Base, I was still in bad shape. My whole system was torn to pieces from having been subjected to the poisonous fumes thrown off by the stove for more than half a year; and even in November my muscles seemed to have little tone and no recuperation. The muscles of the heart, which had become unspeakably tired, still had little reserve. Dr. Potaka urged me strongly not to attempt a long flight.

On these counts the hazard was entirely mine. But what made the decision doubly difficult was the knowledge that in the event of a forced landing, especially under conditions that might make it necessary for the flight crew to foot it back to Little America, my weakness would render me a burden upon my companions.

Nevertheless I decided to go. I shall not try to justify the decision. My reason for going would take more space than I am warranted in giving to a problem which, however painful

it may have been at Little America, ceased to be a problem the
instant the flight was completed without mishap.

The flight crew consisted of June and Bowlin, pilots; Bailey,
radio operator; Pelter, aerial cameraman; Rawson, navigator;
and myself.

At 11:54 A.M. June raced the big plane across the Barrier
surface into a light southerly wind. The skis slammed and
jolted over hard, glazed ridges of sastrugi, but the engines had
a rich, full sound. Easily, at the end of a short run, they
cleanly lifted a gross load of 17,000 pounds. The foaming
pressure ridges of the Bay of Whales swirled under the great
wings as June banked.

A beautiful day, a perfect day for flying. A fleckless sky,
visibility that seemed to run on forever, and the plane's shadow
running ahead of it across the wind-riffled Barrier. All that
broad white plain running to the horizon, whiter than any
white on earth, and all untrodden, unexplored.

Making eighty knots we ran down the southeastern leg of the
triangle. Like a ship lifting and sending on a long, easy swell,
the plane swayed in the surge of the high, cold currents pouring off the polar plateau. The side benches over the long, flat
tanks on either side of the cabin were stowed high with emergency gear—rations neatly sacked, trail gear, cookers. Overhead two very light, very shrewdly made manhauling sledges,
skis, and tents were lashed in place. Bailey had his radio apparatus aft, behind the main bulkhead. He was working with
Dyer at Little America; but Siple's party in the Edsel Ford
Range, and the tractor party 165 statute miles south southeast
of Little America, a fair distance west of our course, were both
stopped and listening, watching the weather. Rawson had the
charts spread on a folding table dropped from the port side.

At 1:26 o'clock, ninety-three miles out of Little America, I
caught sight of an interesting formation of crevasses, an irregular pattern of them, lying directly across our course. We
dropped low to study them. At 400 feet by the altimeter the

surface was still well under us, a hundred feet at least. All low Barrier. Far, far away in that crystal clear air the ice lifted and met the horizon in a shining golden encirclement.

Practically at the end of the first leg of the triangle, we had just risen again when, over June's shoulder, I sighted dead ahead another grossly disturbed area, a great swirling whirlpool of pits and fractures, coming in from the west and folding back through north to west in the shape of an enormous horseshoe. As a matter of fact, that was the name we gave the area, the Horseshoe. We made for it. Near this area we again dropped low for an altimetric sounding—again little over 400 feet. The crevasses lay in a band from half a mile to several miles wide. Many had caved in; and the regular furrows and the dark colors in the depths put you in mind of earth turned over by spring plowing.

East, west and south, to the limit of vision, the Barrier seemed to roll at the same low level, so low the ice must surely be resting, if not on water itself, at least on land below sea level. And here, it seemed to me, beneath this glittering carapace of ice must be, if it existed at all, the trough of the Great Ice Strait. Did these crevasses mark the southern reaches of the new plateau? We were nearly 4,000 feet below the highest altitude calculated by June and Rawson when they crossed the plateau on the way to Mount Grace McKinley.

At 2:16 o'clock we turned north, to run down the second leg of the triangle to the Edsel Fords. The turn was made at Lat. 81° 05' S., Long. 146° 30' W., 275 miles southeast of Little America.

The second leg would carry us abeam and east of Mount Grace McKinley, just within the western margin of Marie Byrd Land.

Odd how difficult it is, under certain conditions of light, to judge relationships, depths and distances. The snow becomes an intricate and deceptive arrangement of flashing planes. Though the surface seemed to be rising underneath I should have hesitated to swear to it. So, between the 78th and 79th parallels, we dropped down again for a sounding by altimeter. The elevation had risen to 1,975 feet—the dome of the new plateau.

Drawing within range of the Edsel Fords we commenced to climb, steeply, with the engines lustily digging in. At 10,000 feet Bowlin leveled off. Now the pyramidal peak of Mount Grace McKinley, a glistening cone on an ivory plain, swept up on the port bow; the sugar loaf of Haines came up on the starboard bow. Five years before we had first seen these mountains from 100 miles to the northwest. Now we were striking at them from the south. I trained my glasses on the horizon, waiting with a keenness I should hesitate to describe the momentary rising of the other mountains.

Now they appeared—one, two, three, four ... faster than I could tick them off mentally, a swift and violent eruption of black peaks, popping up like heads behind a fence in a ballpark. Dozens of them, streaming off behind the western front range.

Making 100 knots with a quartering wind, and again climbing a little, we approached the heart of the second problem.

At 11,000 feet we passed by Mount Grace McKinley. A bow and beam bearing put us 28 miles east of it and exactly on our course.

From this lofty perch we had a full view of this refrigerated world, a view which, once seen, can never vanish from the mind, but lingers with the unrelaxing clarity of something at once so terrible and still so beautiful that it impoverishes all other spectacles. Gray masses of rock that a giant hand might have strewn about like so many pebbles filled the northeastern horizon. Battered, eroded, carved and splintered by an ice sheet which still drowned all but their highest shoulders and ridges, they looked what they were, the shattered derelicts of an ice age, the remnants of the land which had stood off the warring assault of the ice. Somewhere down there (though we failed to see him, and he failed to see or even hear the plane) Siple was grubbing above the ice line for traces of life—mosses and lichens, bird rookeries and microscopic things. It was hard to believe that any life could find nourishment on that bleak landscape.

What we had seen as we approached from the south was confirmed. At 11,000 feet we had vision of 130 miles. The trend of the new mountains was definitely east and northeast. Moreover, the plateau, passing Mount Grace McKinley, seemed to roll endlessly to the east along the axis of the range. Forty miles on our beam I raised an enormous mountain, a block of steel-gray rock, apparently granite.

At 4:30 o'clock we turned west, on the homing leg to Little America, a run of 255 statute miles. The turn was at Lat. 77° 30' S., Long. 146° 30' W.

A straight run, now, for home. The sky continued flawless.

As we drew near the Rockefellers something tumbled out of the recesses of memory. On the southern slope of Mount Helen Washington, in the Rockefellers, the Fokker, which Dr. Gould, June and Balchen had flown there in 1929 on a geological survey, had been destroyed in a hurricane. There was the barest chance the wreckage might still be visible; I mentioned it to June.

So we altered course a few degrees to pass the mountain, and presently banked sharply around a bare shoulder of rock.

June was gesticulating and shouting, "There she is, right where she hit!"

Twisted and crumpled into a ball of metal, the wreckage lay imprisoned in a lake of green ice at the foot of the mountain. It was remarkable to find it awash after four and a half years of blizzards. There was practically no drift around it, no doubt because of the steady down-drafts of wind.

At 6:43 P.M. we landed at Little America. Altogether we had been in the air 6 hours and 43 minutes. We had flown 777 statute miles and surveyed, within our range of vision, approximately 50,000 square miles of unknown Antarctica—a very satisfactory beginning of the flight program.

But because the sky still remained miraculously clear and because Haines thought it might last, there was no resting on the oars.

After conferring with Dr. Poulter and Rawson (Rawson was always most helpful in the discussion of geographical problems) we decided to aim the next flight due east of Little America into Marie Byrd Land. Within the limits of the plane's range, we wanted to confirm the easterly trend of the new mountains of the Edsel Fords and observe the easterly reaches of the new plateau.

A peremptory reason recommended a temporary shift of attention to this quarter. This sector was the weather breeder, the home of the dirtiest fogs and storms. Being near the coast, it was earlier affected than the interior by the inpouring of clouds and fog that marked the advent of summer. If we ever expected to get into the east at all, we had better seize the first break to ram a flight in that direction, leaving the southeasterly sector to the last.

The opportunity broke almost before we were ready for it. During the early watch of the 18th the wind veered into the south and dropped to a gentle breeze; the clouds drained, leaving a sky as clear as my lady's looking glass.

Aviation had been up most of the night, slaving to finish the overhaul before weather improved. Nowadays the entire unit— June, Bowlin, Smith, Swan, Dustin, Skinner, even Boyd, the machinist—was bivouacked in a tent colony near the planes.

At 7:30 A.M. Siple, in the Edsel Ford Range, advised a gusty southeast wind, clear skies and excellent visibility. The tractors reported a mere breath of northwesterly wind and cavu—ceiling and visibility unlimited. At noon Siple said no wind, no clouds, excellent visibility; and the tractors said again cavu.

Aviation, sweating from hurry, at last fitted on the cowlings.

Dog teams arriving with gas from Retreat Camp—900 gallons pumped in by hand, strained by chamois, two hours' work; oil bubbling and seething in a cauldron in the aviation shack— heated over blow torches to a temperature of 120°, to be called for just before the pilots were ready to start the engines; the square heater tents drawn over the engines and the blow torches started—an hour's heating at a temperature of 110°. A quick inspection of control wires and landing gear. Drift brushed and pounded from the fabric, wings, fuselage and tail structure (as much as 200 pounds of snow were taken off the plane after a severe blizzard).

All ready, now. Tents whipped away from the engines. Men hurrying from the shack with steaming buckets of hot oil. From June in the cockpit, "Clear?" From Swan on the ground, "All clear. Let her go." The lugubrious whine of the engine starter, then, gratefully, the explosive retort of the engines, first one, then the other.

Leaning against the blast from the propeller, the flight crew scrambled into the cabin—Bowlin, Rawson, Petersen, Pelter. A raffish looking crew. June bulking in the port bow, stripped down to his shirt-sleeves, with a beard that made him look more like General Grant than Grant ever looked himself. Petersen tall and lean, uncombed reddish hair falling past his helmet, looking like one of those strange, undernourished ascetics of the fifteenth century. And Rawson, with a thin silken beard, like a Manchu gone to seed.

For the time being, I felt, I had better stay behind. Though it was disappointing to give up the satisfaction of discovery, there was compensating satisfaction in being able to pass on the honor to able and conscientious men who had shared my burdens. June was a reliable flight commander, cool and practical. As for Rawson, he had, on the earlier flight, demonstrated his mastery of air navigation. For a man of 24 years, he was competent in many directions. Not only in the field, but in the organization and demobilization of the expedition, he, as much as any man, contributed to its success.

For the first time in the unaccustomed rôle of a listener seeing remote discoveries through another man's eyes, I followed by radio this flight through a region which I looked upon as peculiarly my own. Dyer had hooked up a loud speaker in my shack. For an hour or more, till the plane moved too far away for the words to remain intelligible, I could hear Petersen reporting on progress on the telephone set. Afterwards, he and Dyer turned to code; bulletins came to me every fifteen minutes. It was the first flight of exploration launched by any of my expeditions in which I had not participated. It was not easy to turn away from it. I was acutely conscious of my own invalidism. Years ago, I used to play football, and I had learned how hard it was to sit on the bench after you have gotten used to carrying the ball.

Petersen's voice, blurting through the static, and the hum of the generator, filled the room: "We're five miles north of Amundsen Arm, flying at 90 knots and climbing to 10,000 feet.... Okay.... Yes, werry clear. Some clouds, that all.... Ross Sea is still frozen.... There's a lot of sea smoke, though, on the noddern horizon.... Boy, wouldn't it be great to see the ole Yacob Ruppert steaming into the Bay...." Petersen, though an American citizen, was Norwegian born; his j's and the w's were the delight of the radio engineers.

Across Scott Land into Marie Byrd Land to Mount Grace McKinley they kept to a great circle course. By the time they had the Rockefellers abeam they had attained their altitude objective of 10,000 feet. Here, over the position where Rawson on the eastern tractor journey had gotten an astronomical fix, they flew a complete circle, so that Pelter, with his mapping camera, could compass the horizon.

Over Mount McKinley at 4:56, still at 10,000 feet, they circled for another round of photographs. At 5:01 they struck east, breaking past the limits of the flight track of the 15th.

All ahead of them now was new, undiscovered and uncharted.

On their port hand the new peaks of the Edsel Fords were marching past, massed in a wedge streaming to the northeast. The exposed peaks, weathered to a yellowish-gray, bitten and raked by ice, were only the starved and eroded remnants of the mightier blocks that had stood on that land before the ice came. Even now, though the ice is in retreat, only the tallest peaks have struggled through the frosted capping. Their ridges and shoulders lie mantled by glacial ice, and the bulging in the snow that marks them is like the swelling of muscles under flesh.

The big mountain mass I had raised through binoculars on the 15th was rising to the north and east. At 6:40 o'clock they drew abeam of it and circled again for another round of photographs, to tie this peak in with the mountains astern.

Very definitely now, in the altering perspective, the bulk of the mountain masses were seen to be gathered in a tight jumble of peaks to the northeast, which dissolved presently into a single, thinning chain of smaller peaks, bending little by little through east to southeast.

Somewhere behind that rim of rock lay the undiscovered coast—the coast we had struggled so often to attain. Perhaps it was quite near. The whole northern horizon, the flight crew said, was laced with a dark ribbon of water sky.

Now they slanted south a little, to resume their easting on the 78th parallel. The scattered panels of cirrus clouds on the southern horizon were giving way to gross storm clouds. The air was getting rougher, and the fuzziness on the horizon was indicative of cloud.

North of their line of flight, about 100 miles away, a magnificent peak appeared, dwarfing the thinning line of peaks flowing about it. They were then about 150 miles east of the previous limits of discovery. The straggling chain of peaks far down on the northern horizon appeared now to be trending southeast. Mere dots on the horizon of the great white plain, they were too far away—-too indistinct—to be photographed, but they were visible through 7-power glasses.

Ahead of them, about 30° on the port bow, a monstrous mountain mass was shouldering through the white roofing of the plateau. They thought it must be close to 10,000 feet, to bulk so prominently over the plateau. June was impressed, too, by the curious structure of the mass. It seemed to him to be an extinct volcano, the southern side of which had been blown out. A not improbable surmise, since Siple was presently to come upon the ice-eroded remnants of a volcano in the eastern reaches of the Raymond Fosdick Mountains.

They were holding a course to pass close by this mountain and were about 69 miles off, when June, observing that the clouds had closed in to the northeast and were thickening ahead, decided to turn.

At 7 o'clock, at Lat. 70° 00′ S., Long. 135° W., approximately 448 miles east of Little America, they wheeled for home.

Shortly after turning they dropped to sound the plateau elevation, skimming the crust for a mile to let the altimeter settle—4,486 feet by the corrected atmospheric pressure. Then they rose sharply, running for Little America at 9,000 feet, with the clouds threatening to cut them off.

In a little while the sound of the engines was heard in the ventilators. At 10:32 o'clock the *William Horlick* landed on the south side of Ver-sur-Mer Inlet, having been gone 7 hours and 36 minutes.

June and Rawson came below to make a report. George Noville had a fresh pot of coffee for them steaming on the stove. Still deafened by the engines, they were shouting at us at the top of their voices. We got the charts out from behind the stove and started roughly to fill in the new discoveries.

"Any sign of the coast?"

"Couldn't see it," June said. "The mountains blocked it off, for one thing. But for 100 miles across the plateau on the way out there was a decided water sky on the northern horizon.

Rawson confirmed this. "It may have been a cloud formation," he said, "but in color and character it was the same sort of horizon we saw over the Ross Sea, all the way from the Bay of Whales."

"How did it bear?"

"Well, it seemed to curve in behind the mountains," June said.

Of course, this was the purest speculation, but it was the first tangible hint of the trend of the unknown coast.

There rose now the question how these facts, and especially the implications of the plateau, would affect the problem of the Strait.

"Did the plateau appear to continue indefinitely when you turned?"

"So far as we could tell, yes," June said. "It was definitely rising. The altimeter sounding, which was nearly 900 feet higher than any we got on the tractor trip between the Rockefellers and the Edsel Fords, proves that."

"How about to the south?"

"Same thing," said Rawson. "The clouds were getting heavier, but as far as we could see the plateau rolled unbrokenly in that direction."

Odd that we should have found that apparently sea-level trough 215 miles south of Mount Grace McKinley. Could it be that on the 15th we had stumbled upon a mere indentation— an embayment—in the western shore of the plateau? On the basis of the fresh evidence, it seemed unlikely that between this massive plateau flowing south from the coast and the great mountain structures of the Queen Maud Mountains, damming back the 10,000-foot Polar Plateau there could exist a sea-level strait.

June and Rawson thought it unlikely. I wasn't sure. But my

belief in the significance of the low elevations we had found in the Horseshoe crevasses at Lat. 81° 05′ S., was shaken.

The next step toward the solution had already suggested itself—a deep thrust southeast to attempt to define the great sweep of unknown south of Latitude 81°, and to verify the trend of the Queen Maud Range. If we could raise these factors into the realm of discovery, we should know more clearly where we stood. The flight would also have the effect of closing the southern half of the corridor.

For three days unsteady easterly winds and clouds at Little America, together with the unfavorable reports of the field parties, grounded the plane. But on the 19th, in the routine progress report of the Geological Party which was bearing toward the Queen Maud Range far east of any previously traveled track, there occurred an illuminating sentence:

Held in camp Saturday by high SE Wind. . . . Continuing south to 375 Depot, 8 miles yet to go. Appears to be high land east of 350. Very large crevasses running NW to SE commence there and continue for 7 miles. Had some difficulty. Dick's trailer went down nose first. . . .

It was the mention of high land 100 miles north of the Queen Mauds that riveted my interest. This was of commanding importance to the problem of the Strait. The crevasses were a definite suggestion of land. I got into the radio shack as soon as I could, but Dyer informed me that Paine had just signed off. I had to wait for their next schedule on the 21st.

On the 21st, in reply to my query, Blackburn advised:

Apropos crevassed area between 350 and 375 Miles. Crevasses with NW to SE trend. Fragile bridges, rows of haycocks. Pressure must be active here because of insubstantial bridging. Along trend of this pressure area to east of 350 appeared definite rise in shelf ice commencing within a mile of that point. From 350 southerly our course has crossed roll after roll with crests from 2 to 10 miles apart and up to 100 feet in elevation above troughs. . . .

It was as exciting as building up the causational chain in a problem of induction—sleuthing for a continental mystery concealed in an ocean of ice.

In the later afternoon of the 21st the air commenced to clear and aviation took the drift covers off the engine. About 6 o'clock the tractors reported excellent weather 161 miles out, a little east of the plane's course. Bill Haines deferred judgment till the evening balloon run. The air aloft yielded its signs and portents. "Good enough, now," said Bill, with his characteristic caution, "but I don't know how long it will last. It's a mite skittish. If you don't waste any time," he said to June, "you ought to be able to get this one in quite nicely."

Bill has rarely called a closer one.

June was again in command, Rawson was navigator, and Pelter again manned the cameras. But Smith sat in Bowlin's seat as co-pilot, and Bailey replaced Petersen as radio operator. There was, of course, no question of competence in the shift: merely a sharing of the honor of making important flights.

At 12:10 o'clock on the morning of November 22nd they took off with a load of 19,400 pounds—the heaviest load, to my knowledge, ever flown on skis.

Now for the flight log as it grew on Dyer's typewriter. Dyer maintained almost continuous watch on the plane, breaking off at scheduled periods to snatch weather reports from the Marie Byrd Land and tractor parties which were hove to.

1:15. "Everything OK. WX looks fair. There is a bank of cumulus clouds about 50 miles SW. Nothing but high cirrus [elsewhere]. PX [position] 75 miles course 141° at 1:15 A.M. June.

2:15. OK. at 2:05 passed tractor trail.

(But June passed the tractors unseeing and unseen, about 40 miles to the west, though Bailey was in contact with Waite.)

2:40. OK. Motor spitting [a pause, then a reassuring] OK. QSK [meaning will see you in 10 minutes.]

3:00. PX at 2:55—[Lat.] 81° 10′ S., Long. 152° 30′. Changed course to 126°. Tested altitude—1600 feet. Tractor weather same.

(They were on the threshold of the critical area, and this abrupt rise in elevation meant high land—land well above sea level—land that held the fate of the Strait. A quick calculation placed them about 267 miles southeast of Little America and about twenty-eight miles southwest of the trough in the Horseshoe crevasse we had marked on the 15th.)

3:40. PX [Lat.] 81° 42′ S. [Long.] 146° 15′ W.... Elevation 2000 feet. Surface steadily going up. No topographical features.

(So this blank white surface rising ahead of them, unmarred and unbroken by exposed rock, must be plateau—high land entirely capped by ice. Part of the same high land, certainly, that Blackburn, Russell and Paine had raised near Lat. 84°, between 350 and 375 Mile Depots. The southwestern margin of the Ross Ice Barrier.)

4:20. PX at 4:15 [Lat.] 82° 02′ S., [Long.] 142° 30′ W. Nothing in sight but great smooth level plain as far as can see, About 2,000 feet high and exactly like area to east and south of Haines. All well. JUNE.

(At 4:15 they were 356.5 statute miles out—more than 184 miles beyond the crevassed area—and with vision of more than 50 miles over the snow surface in all directions beyond that point. The identical nature of this "great smooth level plain" they were exploring to the broad plateau swirling around the Edsel Ford Mountains, was already inclining the flight crew to the belief that these plateaus were one. Well, we'd withhold decision till the next elevations. And there was still that trough, now narrowed to a slit, near the Horseshoe at Lat. 81°.)

4:45. DR PX at 4:45 [Lat.] 82° 19′ S., [Long.] 138° 20′ W. "Averaging 75 knots. Tested elevation at 4:35. 2,000 feet." RAWSON.

5:10. Plane says: OK.

5:35. OK.—reeling in again. BAILEY.

("Reeling in" meant that Bailey was cranking in the plane's antennæ. June must be dropping for another sounding—brushing low over the ice to test elevation by altimeter. Really a new technique in exploration, a shrewd tactical method in the search for the Strait.)

6:00. Geological Party WX: "Viz. excellent. Stratus clouds in east." Tractor Party WX: "perfect."

6:25. Turned around at 6:05 in [Lat.] 83° 05′ and [Long.] 119° W. Sighted high mountains in S. Judge to be Queen Mauds. Tested elevation at 6:15—3,350 feet.... Yes, turned at 6:05. Then had 500 gals. gas. WX perfect. Many thanks for message. All well. JUNE.

(I had flashed them a message congratulating them on discovery. Discovery of the plateau and with it the further definition of the eastern shore of the Ross Ice Barrier was by itself a superb achievement: but discovery of a new mountain group approximately 170 miles east of the last known extension of the Queen Mauds was a capping triumph. Yet, as it turned out, this last hung by the proverbial eyelash. They had decided to turn a few minutes before 6:00 o'clock. But with weather so excellent and head winds diminishing, they were tempted to prolong the flight a few minutes more. Smith had spelled June at the controls. About 6 o'clock, just when they were about to wheel, Smith made the landfall—a cluster of snow-clad peaks 45° on the starboard bow, barely awash on the horizon. Smith excitedly called June's attention to them: Rawson hurried up forward with the field glasses. The peaks must have been well over 100 miles away, Rawson said, when Smith first saw them—too far away for Pelter's mapping camera. But the flight crew held their course long enough to be absolutely sure of what they saw. Then, at Lat. 83° 05′ S., Long. 119° W., 552 statute miles southeast of Little America, they turned for Little America.)

7:00. OK.

7:15. Plane PX: [Lat.] 82° 23′ S., [Long.] 136° W. WX perfect. Viz and ceiling unlimited. Marie Byrd Land Party WX: "7:30 A.M. Bar. 27.20 Falling clouds—50 per cent overcast. Wind E—35 m.p.h. viz fair. We are camped on blue ice and antennæ won't stay up...."

(Siple's party thus breaks in with a warning—clouds and a blizzard over the Edsel Fords. Haines, who throughout the night has sat at Dyer's elbow, appraises the report anxiously, then hurries topside for a glance at the sky over Little America. It remains fair, but low down on the southeastern horizon, between the plane and the Base, a smudge of cloud is broadening. Haines decides to take an immediate balloon run.)

9:20. We have not passed tractors yet. Still have 300 gals.... JUNE.

9:40. KHNGHT [the plane] calls Waite and sez cannot find tractors because of low ceiling.

(Curious. The plane must be over ground fog too heavy for June to risk breaking through it. Yet only twenty minutes before the tractor party reported perfect weather. That's how quickly weather can close in on you on a flight.)

9:40 (cont.) We sighted tractor trail thru hole in clouds but surface instantly obscured again so have headed for LA. MSG [for] Haines: "Please give surface barometer at L.A." JUNE.

(They wanted the barometric pressure in order to set the altimeter at proper pressure in case they had to make a blind landing at Little America with ceiling zero.)

10:00. Engines wide open. Still over clouds.

10:30. Clearing up. Can see surface now. Very thin clouds. Guess we can beat it in. BAILEY.

11:05. LA in sight. Now.

Thus, racing the fog, they brought to conclusion an 1,100-mile flight of discovery which carried to Lat. 83° 05′ S., Long. 119° 00′· S., 552 miles southeast of Little America.

In the whole eastern coastline of the Ross Shelf Ice there remained, now, for all practical purposes, only a 40 or 50 mile slit, between the 81st and 82nd parallels and a similar gap between the limit of surface vision of the plane crew on the southeastern flight and the new mountains. In the first gap we had found low-level ice; north and south of it were steadily rising plateau elevations. The problem was reduced to one of elimination—to wipe out these slits as rapidly as possible. They held the rapidly expiring destiny of the theoretical Antarctic Strait.

Therefore we resolved, as soon as weather lifted, to ram home another flight.

Next morning—November 23rd—the fog commenced to lift, and aviation hurried preparations for departure in the afternoon.

On the flight to close the gap I was again in the plane. My strength was slowly coming back, and I felt up to another effort. At 5:16 P.M. we were off for the southeast.

The flight crew consisted of June, Bowlin, Rawson and Petersen.

The beauty of the evening was past describing. The Barrier was an enchantment of pure gold.

Making close to 90 knots, we struck directly for the Horseshoe crevasses which had yielded the only sea-level elevation we had found in the whole broad stretch between the Edsel Fords and the Queen Mauds.

Close to the crevasses we coasted down for an elevation sounding, skimming the ice for a mile or so to allow the altimeter to settle—771 feet above sea level.

The ice was rising—rising toward the 2,000-foot plateau elevation the others had discovered, the day before, just a few miles south. We steadily bore east for 60 miles on the parallel of 81° 10′ S. Three times we stooped for soundings—1,105 feet, 1,204 feet, 1,338 feet. East of the Horseshoe the crevasses were petering out: there were fewer black holes. And past the point where we turned, approximately on the 140th meridian, the land was still rising, a golden bulwark in all directions.

Nevertheless, to satisfy the last lingering doubt, we ran north about 16 miles. A sounding here of 1,591. Then west again, paralleling the outward course and completely squaring the line of inquiry about the crucial gap. Three more soundings—1,138 feet, 1,085 feet, 669 feet, this last just a little north and east of the Horseshoe.

I think that when we took our eyes off the flickering needle of the altimeter we all drew a sigh of relief.

"That's it," somebody shouted above the sound of the engines.

The trough—the sea-level depression we had blundered into on the 15th—was nothing more than a bight in the eastern shore of the Barrier. The eastern coast of the Ross Shelf Ice was now filled in. Rimming it was a massive and unbroken plateau, 4,500 feet high behind the Edsel Fords, drooping to a moderate elevation near the center, then rising again to 3,000 feet near the foot of the Queen Maud Range. A solid barrier to the Strait. It was land, all land: land over-ridden by ice, to be sure: but land which, were the ice to melt, would stand as solidly interposed to the questing keel of a ship as the Atlantic coast stood before the sixteenth century navigators seeking a strait to Cathay.

Antarctica, almost beyond a shadow of doubt, is one continent. There is almost certainly no strait between the Ross and Weddell Seas.

On these data we rested our case.

Chapter *XVII*

~~~~~~

DEATH OF A CITY

AFTER the flight to close the gap, aviation moved for a while into the background of expedition affairs. There remained unliquidated only one important flight of geographical exploration on the program—a long thrust to the northeast to attempt to fill in the coast behind the Edsel Ford Range. Whether we should ever be able to execute it, I could not say. Weather in that sector was too treacherous, too uncertain. Haines was anything but sanguine. The stagnant conditions of summer, the fogs, the overcast and the light summer snows, were already upon us. The day after the flight the fogs again clamped down: for thirteen days the skies were overcast, snow fell on every day but two.

Monday, Dec. 17, 11 P.M.
   The hottest day of the year: the barometer soared to +38°. Really uncomfortably warm. The paths between the buildings are shin-deep in slush. Shacks are all leaking like second hand umbrellas. A heavy snow storm came up in the afternoon, the wettest snow with the largest flakes I've ever seen in the south polar regions. They stick to everything they touch; the dogs curled up near the hatch were transformed into huge snowballs.

Thus December wore through its clammy cycle. A towering cloud of water sky was climbing over the Ross Sea, like smoke from a great forest fire. Toward the end of the month the aviators discovered that the ice was slowly breaking out between East and West Capes. The bay ice was cracked and broken and the biologist found it more difficult to sledge across the Bay. The mild manifestation of a polar summer! In December snow fell 16 days; 8 days were foggy; 20 days were cloudy or partly overcast. The lowest temperature was −1°, and the highest +38°; the mean was +16°. To be comfortable outside one needed only the lightest of clothing—light shirts, underwear, trousers, a single pair of woolen socks, ski boots. Indeed, when the sun was out, one would usually see the skiers traveling with backs bare and the tops of their underwear tied around the waist.

Now, in quick succession, the field parties raced home: Siple came in from Marie Byrd Land, excited by the discovery of a skua gull rookery in the heart of the Edsel Ford Range, by the finding of microscopic life on the frontiers of Marie Byrd Land. Then the combined Plateau and Tractor Party staggered home, with a tale of miraculous adventures among crevasses and of a succession of mechanical difficulties which had forced them to abandon one of their machines; but Dr. Bramhall had his valuable magnetic observations and Morgan the seismic sounding data which were indispensable in estimating the depth of the continental ice sheet. And, finally, the Geological Party, which had stood on the rim of the Polar Plateau, returned, after three months in the field. Less than 200 miles from the South Pole, at an altitude of some 7,000 feet, they had discovered huge deposits of coal, and fragments of fossilized trees, all valuable data for the paleontological record of Antarctica. More than that, from where their exploratory track had carried them, they had seen enough, in the high land rising to the east of them, to help clinch the case against the Ice Strait by closing the last of the slits left open by the flight crews.

By this time the *Bear of Oakland* had already started south, the *Ruppert* was making ready to leave, and with only the Geological Party in the field, the active life of the Second Byrd Antarctic Expedition was rapidly drawing to a close.

Now Little America came up by the roots. Noville and Corey, with their gangs, were tearing the tunnels apart to bring the unused stores to the surface. A clattering and hammering of boxes rose in every shack, and a wild confusion, made buoyant with the almost incredible intelligence that a ship would presently steam into the Bay of Whales, rose in the town. On the Bulletin Board in the Mess Hall the noon and midnight positions of the *Bear* were enthusiastically printed in huge letters; and Carbone each day crossed off one day, one day less to go on the longest sentence, he said, he ever had to serve.

Then one morning of the 19th a distant explosion shook the air—the *Bear* was in! Dane and Herrmann had fired the dynamite signal which meant she was rounding West Cape.

Out of the hatches, out of caved tunnels, out of the ventilators, out of recesses I hadn't known existed issued a spontaneous eruption of humanity as might have risen to greet the millennium. The ridge to the north was fairly crawling with explorers, hot-footing it for the ship, on skis, afoot, by dog team and tractor. If they had moved in such lively fashion toward the unknown, there wouldn't be an unsolved problem in Antarctica today. The cook was in the van, a Moses leading the Israelites across the Red Sea. In fact, in the cool of the evening we had to dispatch a dog team and a master at arms to bring him back, lest we meanwhile starve to death at Little America. He returned to the galley singing, once again contemplating the world through rose-colored glasses, and from time to time permitting himself the luxury of a hiccough which was the envy of all who heard it.

Practically everything stopped the instant the sacks of mail were carried into the galley. Noville took over the distribution of the mail. "Abele ... Blackburn ... Bramhall ... Corey...." In twenty minutes the throng in the low building had melted away; and for the next few hours there was scarcely a sound except for the tearing of envelopes, the riffling of pages, and ocasional sudden bursts of confidences.

And so it ran, life bursting into a long-stagnant pool, small

joys and disasters, the hopes and fears of a year and a half
of ignorance and uncertainty all crammed into a few minutes
of reading. Radio communication is marvelous; but mail is a
miracle.

From the *Bear* the dog-drivers returned singing the praises
of Tony the cook, and of the rare viands in his galley: pork
chops that tasted finer than terrapin, lettuce of an incredible
greenness, and potatoes that met the palate in lingering
ecstasy. I found Dr. Perkins in the galley exclaiming over the
green, earthly delicacy of raw onions; and oranges and apples
were being passed around as the rarest of gifts.

Hurry-hurry-hurry was again the order of the day. Get out
and shove off as rapidly as possible, while the Ross Sea was still
open, before the incalculable movements of the pack interposed
fresh obstacles.

It was the repetition of the white nightmare of unloading,
except that now our steps were turned in the opposite direction.
There were the same flogging imperatives, the same exhausting
tasks, the same conspiracies of pack and wind and swell, the
inconstancy of the ice, and the icebergs loping down from
Marie Byrd Land to harry the ships in the Bay.

The wind blew most of the time; days when it would be
almost calm at Little America the *Bear* would be plunging in
a gale tearing across the Bay of Whales, fighting for her skin
among the pack bursting out of the Bay or heaving down from
the northeast. Our old friends, the east and northeast winds,
hummed steadily, repeatedly driving the ship from her berth.
The temperature was almost stagnant in the plus twenties.
The surface grew fearfully soft, and the dogs were sinking to
their bellies. On the 26th, with the temperature at $+32$, a
snowstorm for a little while became the finest of rains—a wet,
steamy sort of misting which almost instantly froze and covered the antennæ wires and stays, even boxes and upended skis,
with a thin veneering of clear ice. From January 9th to Febru-

ary 2nd we never saw the sun except for a few minutes at a time.

The *Ruppert* entered the Bay of Whales late in the afternoon of January 26th, groping through a driving snowstorm on radio direction finder bearings from the *Bear*. Cheerily the ships exchanged greetings; whereupon the steel ship, having no choice, joined the barkentine in her prowl up and down the Bay, steaming up to the Barrier for lee, then lying and drifting, then up to the Barrier again, two elusive phantoms weaving in and out of the confusion of fog and sea smoke. You can perhaps imagine what a gay parade this was for the men watching from the Barrier cliffs.

In the whole stay at Little America this was probably the most wretched week. It was like having a reprieve handed on an elastic band. Again we were in the familiar situation of being confronted by one of those sullen, glacial moods of Nature against which human ingenuity and engines are powerless. All you can do is sit and wait and let the winds and the pack fight it out. The men who came back from the Barrier said the ice was going out fast—had broken past Eleanor Bolling Bight. We were in almost hourly communication with the ships. The masters reported high seas, pea soup fog and heavy out-rushes of ice. The wind-driven generator above the camp clacked night and day.

In the end we solved the situation by using the *Bear* as a relay ship between the shore and the *Ruppert*, which we did not dare to lay alongside the barrier. It meant that every item of stores had to be handled innumerable times, but we had no choice. To bring the *Ruppert* in meant risking her thin sides against an onslaught of ice which might easily have sent her to the bottom. So for six days the tractors out of Little America discharged on to the dog teams which waited halfway, and the dog sledges discharged into the *Bear* lying in the Bight, and the *Bear* discharged into the *Ruppert* hove to beyond the pack near the middle of the Bay. Along the eight-mile endless chain of transport—tractors, dogs, auxiliary ship and steamer —Little America, bit by bit, was vanishing into the *Ruppert's* capacious holds.

On the night of February 3rd all that remained on the beach were the four airplanes, the tractors, three aircraft engines, two machine lathes, the sections of two houses, the cows and about 15 tons of miscellaneous gear, most of it too heavy or too big to be handled by the *Bear's* hoists.

Shortly before midnight the *Ruppert* moved into the *Bear's* berth, the first time she had touched shore, the first time we had seen her crew, since she put into the Bay eight days before. The sea for once was quiet as a millpond but a light snow was falling.

With the *Bear* moored on the opposite side of the Bight to act as a buffer and tug if she were thrown out by a calving of the Barrier against the opposite side of the Bight, the *Ruppert* started to clean up the job. One by one the planes were hoisted aboard—the Condor and Ford aft, the Pilgrim and Fairchild forward. And after these the cows, jerked up one by one inside a crate into which they were peremptorily jimmied by the impatient shore crew, were deposited on the forward well deck. They trooped into their stalls on the shelter deck, with not even a lightening of the melancholy with which they had contemplated the whole expedition. "Cheer up, old girl," said Cox, thwacking Deerfoot heartily on the stern sheets, "you'll soon be in clover."

Little America had meanwhile closed its second phase. In the afternoon I returned with Demas in a tractor to collect the last of my things. The shacks, for once, were utterly silent. I can't say that the place looked beautiful or even attractive. The tunnels were broken up and smeared with dirt, broken boxes, cartons of bunion plasters, tooth paste, bottles of mouth wash, frozen cans of food. The shacks, with one or two exceptions, were little better—littered with the debris that only a polar expedition seems able to accumulate.

Noville and Rawson, who had remained at Little America to direct the loading of the last tractors, said everything was all set. Sisson notified Bailey on the flagship that he was shutting down KFZ. Boyd came out of the machine shop with a handful of tools. With Demas we traveled for the last time the road to the ship, and Little America receded except for the shining radio towers.

On the Barrier remained only a number of gasoline drums, a bit of hay and a small mound of nondescript things.

Five minutes later the *Ruppert* headed westward along the Barrier, bound for Discovery Inlet to make a catch of live penguins. The *Bear* was on our quarter, under sail and steam. Though the sky was partly overcast, still it was a lovely afternoon, with a creamy green and gold paneling at the horizon; and so bright and cleanly shining were the Barrier cliffs above the wine-colored sea that they seemed to have the buoyancy of a mirage.

Elsewhere on board men too exhausted to sleep were absorbing the new smells and new sounds of the *Ruppert*, the conversations of men from the outer world, a sensing of expanding existence which was already causing Little America to sink into the miasma of memory—and some, not quite so expansively and certainly without the same enrichment of the senses —were absorbing the motion of the ship and foundering with dreadful laments. It was *so long!* again to Antarctica, and no one left behind.

THE END